# THE STUDY OF ACQUAINTANCE

# The Study of Acquaintance

Steve Duck, M.A., Ph.D., A.B.Ps.S.
Department of Psychology,
University of Lancaster, England

SAXON  HOUSE

© Steve Duck 1977

All rights reserved. No part of this publication may be reproduced, stored in a retrieval system, or transmitted in any form or by an means, electronic, mechanical, photocopying, recording, or otherwise without the prior permission of Teakfield Limited.

HM
132
.D83

Published by

Saxon House, Teakfield Limited,
Westmead, Farnborough, Hants., England.

ISBN 0 566 00160 8

Manufactured in England by Short Run Publishing Services
Printed and bound by Ilfadrove Limited, Barry, Glamorgan, S. Wales.

# CONTENTS

PREFACE

EVERYDAY EXPLANATION OF EVERYDAY    1
PHENOMENA: AN INFORMAL INTRODUCTION
TO THE STUDY OF ACQUAINTANCE

    Acquaintance and common sense    2
    When common sense fails    12

1    SYSTEMATIC STUDY OF ACQUAINTANCE    14

    What is acquaintance?    14
    The problem of measurement    25
    Experimenting on acquaintance    36

2    SOME THEORIES OF INTERPERSONAL    43
    ATTRACTION

    Explaining affiliation: Why does association    45
      occur at all?
    Explaining specific selective choice and liking    47
    Explaining development in relationships    63
    Some observations and a plan of this book    72
      henceforward

3    THE BACKGROUND TO ACQUAINTANCE    75

    What the observer takes into interaction    76
    The stimulus person's properties    96

4    LIKING BEHAVIOUR DURING INTERACTIONS    105

    Behaviour in interaction    107
    Assessing the interactant    122

5    ATTITUDES AND ACQUAINTANCE    136

    Influences of attitudes    136
    The attraction paradigm    142
    The information-affect debate    160

| | | |
|---|---|---|
| 6 | PERSONALITY AND ACQUAINTANCE | 164 |
| | Disclosure of self | 166 |
| | Pairs of personalities in acquaintance | 171 |
| | Relationships between personalities | 174 |
| | Conclusions | 181 |
| 7 | DEVELOPMENT AND BREAKDOWN OF RELATIONSHIPS | 185 |
| | The growth of love | 185 |
| | Learning to like: Friendship in childhood and adolescence | 189 |
| | Relationship failure and breakdown | 194 |
| | Epilogue | 198 |

| | |
|---|---|
| REFERENCES | 200 |
| NAME AND FIRST AUTHOR INDEX | 230 |
| SUBJECT INDEX | 233 |

# PREFACE

To most people there is little that is more important than friendship, liking and acquaintance - and to most people there is little whose basis is still so great a mystery. What does cause friendship, attraction and love? Why do we like some people and not others? Why do some acquaintanceships succeed and some fail amidst misery and despair? Although such issues have exercised the poet, novelist and common man during all recorded time the questions still remain. Research psychologists are the people that modern man now expects to offer systematic scientific answers - and the recent growth in research into the nature and causal basis of interpersonal attraction testifies to their willingness to accept this challenge.

One thing that such research reveals is the sheer extent of the problem and its ramifications; the diversity of its forms and applications; the urgency of its solution. During the last 20 years or so, scientific work on interpersonal attraction has burgeoned and its implications for human social interaction have been systematically researched in a large number of areas including: the formation of first impressions; jury decision making (how far and in what ways is the attractiveness of the defendant an influence on juries' verdicts?); family relationships; loneliness; child development (and how individuals learn to relate to one another); formation of relationship; mental disorder precipitated by relationship failure; marriage (causes of courtship, success and failure); job satisfaction (or rather, satisfaction about the people with whom one works); dating; psychiatric and marriage counselling (insofar as they deal with collapsed relationships as precipitators of abnormality) and love - to name but a few!

I hope that this text will serve the purpose of showing aspirant social scientists the humanitarian significance of the understanding of acquaintance and the wide applications of the research into it. I hope it does this in the course of offering a structure through which to interpret some of the massive literature that has been accumulated.

## The structure of this book

This book considers work that has been done to date in the area of interpersonal attraction and acquaintance and it suggests a theoretical perspective through which to interpret it. It does this by being overtly biassed: that is, it does this by attempting to offer a particular structure for the enormous range of material that has been published on the topics related to attraction and acquaintance. My own inclinations are towards seeing the development of acquaintance as a process of gathering information (from many different sources) about the other person's personality so that one can assess the degree to which it supports one's own. The arrangement of topics in this book reflects this view. Early chapters deal with the kinds of information that are available to interacting strangers: subsequent chapters deal with the sorts of information that apply when two people know each other better. In this way several threads of the attraction literature are drawn together and a fabric of interpretation can be created. Thus some readers may find several traditional groupings of material recast into other contexts than their familiar ones. However, one of the most significant problems for other individuals (i.e. those who are newly acquainted with the acquaintance literature) is precisely that which is represented by the above view of how acquaintance proceeds: that is, initial lack of knowledge that develops in characteristic ways. When we meet strangers we have a context of past experience in which to interpret them not as individuals but as stereotypes; when we meet the acquaintance literature we have a context of past experience (usually called 'common sense') with which to interpret the problems we expect to encounter. An informal introduction to this book thus begins with an analysis of some of the notions that seem to underlie a common sense view of acquaintance. Subsequent chapters examine the ways in which common sense views have helped or hindered rigorous study of acquaintance phenomena, as well as examining the specific contributions which have been made by this scientific study of that most personal experience: acquaintance.

## Acknowledgements

Many people supported me in direct and indirect ways during the final preparation of this book, either by engaging in discussion, helping to shape ideas, pointing out new possibilities or reading drafts of chapters. Their help and encouragement, challenging criticism and sheer diligence were much appreciated. Foremost among these were Donn Byrne, Gordon Craig, Heather Gaebler, Barry McCarthy and David Miell. I am particularly grateful to Barry for the sheer extent and helpfulness of his efforts undertaken in such a willing and constructive spirit.

Others helped in other friendly ways. Phil Levy gave support and encouragement, allowed a good research atmosphere to emerge, and was always available for consultation and advice; Neil Johnson, as usual, gave helpful advice and broadened my horizons by calling on his extensive publishing experience; Julia Brinnand, Mary Howard and Wendy Hopfl cheerfully tolerated intolerable handwriting to do an admirably efficient job of typing the manuscript.

Sandra, of course, although primarily concerned with her own little production during the gestation of the book, was a constant source of affectionate support. But most of all I am grateful to Christina Louise who thoughtfully postponed her birth (with all its attendant disruptions to a new father's working schedule) until the final manuscript was nearly completed.

Steve Duck
Halton-on-Lune, Lancaster
March 1977

# EVERYDAY EXPLANATION OF EVERYDAY PHENOMENA:

## AN INFORMAL INTRODUCTION TO THE STUDY OF ACQUAINTANCE

To most people friendship is such an integral part of everyday behaviour that they do not always grasp how significant relationships are or question why they are necessary. To be sure, most people realise that loss of friends can be deeply disturbing, but few would realise that those who are deprived of sociable company often hallucinate about people in the same way that the starving hallucinate about food (Schachter, 1959). Both the mild and the more serious forms of distress strongly suggest that friendship serves some <u>psychological</u> function for people and if psychologists want to help to alleviate such distress they must find out what this function is. Why do people have friends? How do friendships develop? Why are some individuals unable to form relationships? For all the importance of these questions, the basis of friendship and acquaintance remains elusive and the poets, novelists and scientists have not yet given up the quest for a satisfactory theory.

Nobody would claim to have a common sense theory of <u>spina bifida</u> but pretty well everyone would claim to have one about friendship or acquaintance. Since research psychologists and students are also human social beings they are actually involved in the social phenomena that they study and thus have both friends of their own and, most probably, some common sense theory of why they have them. It is indeed a characteristic of many social psychological theories that they grow out of 'common sense' propositions that had been made about the topic before the social scientists came to it (Heider, 1958). He cannot ignore these notions without good grounds but they will not always be helpful. Unless he can tease apart their useful and useless components the social scientist cannot properly prepare the ground for an adequate application of his special methods of enquiry, his skills and his theoretical work. An introduction to the Study of Acquaintance most sensibly begins, therefore, not with a lengthy historical review of what previous researchers have thought, but with a discussion of the adequacy of the common sense views about acquaintance that a reader or a student or an aspirant researcher may bring to the topic.

**Acquaintance and Common Sense**

There is no Book of Common Sense, but magazines in dentists' waiting rooms seem to have a reasonable claim to embody the everyday view of life. They usually concern fictional embellishment of attraction and acquaintance and they are especially prone to offer particular views of acquaintance, as it seems to me. There seem to be ten components but they are not mutually consistent (see Table 1). However if common sense were not only consistent and unequivocal but also manifestly correct, then there would not be the present need for a psychology of acquaintance. Yet, as Table 1 shows, we do need to appraise it in order to see which parts are worth pursuing in the psychological study of acquaintance.

1. The first principle of this everday approach is that acquaintance is taken for granted as an everyday part of life. This amounts to saying that, even when it is regarded as a special kind of behaviour (see below), it is taken for granted as a process without special psychological significance. However we are entitled to ask why human social relationships occur at all, yet there is no easy answer to this question. And once the question is asked it is clear that some systematic effort is going to be needed to answer it. For obvious reasons the same kinds of experimental studies cannot be done on humans

## TABLE ONE

### Intuitive components of a 'common sense' view of acquaintance

1. Acquaintance is taken for granted as an everyday part of life and has no unique or special <u>psychological</u> function.

2. However, people are not involved in 'acquainting' in <u>all</u> everyday interactions with others.

3. Acquainting is special behaviour, often different from other behaviour in characteristic ways.

4. People set out consciously to make friends.

5. People possess qualities which make them attractive to others.

6. Different types of relationship exist, each with its separate function.

7. Acquaintance, friendship and attraction are based on 'gut' emotional reactions rather than upon dispassionate intellectual assessments of various cues.

8. Reactions to others are rapid and instant rather than mediate and slow.

9. The breakdown and disruption of relationships happens for different kinds of reasons from those which led to the establishment of the relationships.

10. Individuals bear responsibility for their choice of friends.

as they can on animals, but the origins of the general human 'need to affiliate' (or to have others' company) and the origins of satisfactory human interpersonal relationships may well parallel the processes observed in some animals. For example, Chapman (1928) has shown that the Tribolium beetle (which lives on flour) regulates its population size according to the amount of food available: fertility increases when the food supply is large; the death rate increases and fertility decreases when food is scarce. On a related issue in the context of human relationships, Griffitt and Veitch (1971) found that discomfort induced by 'hot and crowded' conditions tends to decrease subjects' likelihood of being attracted to other subjects in the situation. Other work on animals by Latané and his associates has examined both intraspecies attraction (rat-rat) and interspecies 'affection' (rat-human). Thus, Werner and Latané (1974) have shown that rats are gregarious even when there is no specific survival or reproductive advantage inherent in the gathering. Rats were as 'sociable' with human hands as they were with other rats and Werner and Latané concluded that the opportunity for interaction itself seemed to be the source and satisfaction of social attraction in the rat. Perhaps the same applies to humans and only a systematic study of acquaintance could tell us (cf Chapters 2 and 3, for example).

However, this work concerns the general need to affiliate or be in company with others or form into social groups. It does not explain the specific choices that individuals make. Whilst increased anxiety levels may make people more gregarious or more likely to seek to be with groups of other people (Schachter, 1959 and Chapter 3), this does not necessarily explain why a given person prefers individual A to individual B. Yet it does raise one interesting issue which could be studied and tested. Do people have different levels of tolerance for interaction with other people and do they need to achieve a certain number of friends - replacing those that they lose in order to keep this number 'topped up'? If, as is a principal theme of this book, acquaintance serves the psychological function of 'supporting' an individual's personality then various experimental hypotheses follow. For example, people with measurably complex personality (Crockett, 1965) should require more friends to support the complex structure than are needed by someone with a simple structure. Equally, once an individual has achieved a stable number of friends, his resistance to further acquaintances should be raised - just as when someone who has just become engaged is more likely to eschew further deep relations with opposite sex partners.

2. A related point can be made in connection with the second component of this common sense view (Table 1): that people are not involved in 'acquainting' in ALL of their everyday interactions with others. Obviously there are various formal and informal means and levels of everyday interaction (e.g. fleeting encounters; being bored by fellow passengers in a railway carriage; dealing with shop assistants; talking to colleagues at work; carousing with friends). These all form a part of every-day experience and one may at first sight expect different psychological processes and rules to operate in the several cases. For example, the list of permissible topics for discussion on the train is likely to differ from those covered in conversations with friends; the beha-viour is likely to be more ritualised or 'spurious' (Lemmert, 1962). But a psychologist must ask the question whether all of these examples truly have the same function and if so, which processes shall be selected for study. Alternatively if they have different functions one is faced with two issues: (a) How shall psychologists examine the differences and the different functions? (b) Are some everyday interactions 'about' acquaintance and others not; or are all everyday inter-actions somehow to do with acquaintance? People rarely think of themselves as actually involved in dynamic acquaintance processes when they are talking to shop assistants, for example, or even to their close friends. In the one case the relationship can stop at 'friendly' rather than 'friendship' and in another case the relationship is already established and fixed. People tend, therefore, to regard them as defined and fixed rather than dynamic, continually unfolding and changing. Thus it feels, commonsensically, as if people are not involved in 'acquainting' in all their everyday interactions with others.

Viewed in the context of work in social psychology, however, this feeling becomes implausible - indeed it makes more sense to assume exactly the opposite. Acquaintance involves finding out more about other people; attraction is based on or embodies liking; liking is a judgement made about people on the basis of what is known or felt about them. Why should we assume, as common sense asks us to do, that normal human judgemental processes and responses are suspended or held in abeyance in certain sorts of encounter? Do we only make judgements about people in some circumstances (those we happen to define as acquaintance)? Do we find out things about people - and evaluate them on that basis - only in special circumstances? There is no reason at all to assume that individuals adopt a thoroughly different style of thinking when they start acquainting nor is there any likelihood that they suspend these normal processes of humanity. If acquaintance involves these processes (collection of information; judgement; assessment; evaluation; attribution of characteristics) - and it does - then acquaintance is potentially occurring during any social interaction. It may be that there are other processes which stop this potential development where the person wishes to let them do so - and such processes may relate to social conventions about whom one should become friends with (Kerckhoff, 1974, and Chapter 3). For example, only certain types of others are usually admitted as potential friends; e.g. those with similar levels of intelligence or economic background (see Chapter 3). The acceptance of this point makes a fundamental difference to the study of acquaintance, since it makes it as important to explain why individuals are not attracted as why they are. Common sense says 'Look for the triggers that switch on acquaintance'; the present view says 'Find out the basis on which individuals filter out people that they do not want to be friends with'. The latter suggestion has infinitely more potential for explaining a key problem in acquaintance (viz. why established relationships collapse and break down) whereas common sense approaches looking for stimulus 'triggers' are faced with the problem of saying why something can be an attraction trigger one day and suddenly changes its attractive properties (affective valence) the next (see points 9 and 10 here and in

Table 1).

3. A third component of the common sense notion is that <u>acquainting is special behaviour</u>. It is set apart from other behaviour, different, peculiar, something characteristically different from many other forms of everyday activity. This feeling of specialty is heightened by the frequent and notable differences in the behaviour which accompanies some acquaintance, especially intersexual acquaintance. Special clothes are worn (suits, party gear) and the ritual overtones of the process are sanctified by incense (in this case, spray-on deodorant)! Whether the same feelings of specialty can be justified in other forms of acquaintance is arguable, but it is obvious that there are several activities which are 'acquainting' as opposed to other everyday activities like 'conforming' or 'helping'. The question is whether this means that it has an identifiable and equally special or peculiar psychological function, or whether it can simply be subsumed under some general explanation for behaviour.

4. Following from these common sense principles, is the notion that <u>people set out to make friends</u>; that is, that the process is largely conscious and intentional - even if people sometimes do not know why they like someone (i.e. even if they cannot verbalise the relevant cue which they find attractive, they are still conscious that it is there - as yet unnamed). People like to feel that there exists some control over the selections which they make and that it does not happen too often without their realising! On this basis it is frequently assumed (especially in the sources mentioned earlier) that people seek ideals (Mr. Right) and carry around models of people they will be friends with.

The problem with this Identikit Theory of Attraction is that it concentrates most on initial reactions and surface characteristics, leaving little room for the development of attraction during progressive interactions. It thus allows little room for <u>mutual</u> influence or for change, but regards the initial stimuli as the ones which fix the attraction response. Furthermore this idea suggests that people always form social relationships whilst having these Ideals and their properties to the forefront of their minds, so that they should be able to answer questions about what properties their prospective acquaintances must have. Systematic study of acquaintance can pick up this idea and find out not only whether they can do this but also whether they are accurate.

5. This entails the further notion that <u>people possess qualities which make them attractive to others</u> (i.e. that they have these properties fixed, immutable and objectively). So there should be some degree of cultural agreement about the properties and their attractiveness: people would recognise that a certain person has a given quality (e.g. blondeness) and would respond appropriately (e.g. by preferring that person). Whilst widespread in its belief, this view manifestly fails to account for the fact that the same people are not in fact attractive to everyone and the blanket statement that certain types of people will be attracted to certain types of others ('Gentlemen prefer blondes') cannot survive any analysis.

Obviously there are some cultural agreements about what is attractive (see Chapters 3 and 4), probably (but not exclusively) most applicable in the case of physical characteristics. However the fact that such norms exist does not necessarily mean they are powerful in determining given acquaintances. For example, common sense itself offers the untested proposition that beauty is only skin deep. Whilst psychological studies have shown that inferences based on physical characteristics are often extensive and <u>do</u> go deep (Dion, Berscheid and Walster, 1972, showed that physically attractive others were judged to have more interesting personalities and to lead more exciting lives), to assume that acquaintance or attraction is rooted solely on physical characteristics does Man (and Woman) a disservice. Physical characteristics are important pieces of evidence (see Chapter 4) but not exclusively the cause of attraction. Equally, the 'normative' common sense approach can also be rejected in application to other characteristics. Whilst cultures may have norms about whether 'modesty' is preferable to 'conceit', one man's 'arrogance' is another's 'justified self-confidence' and we can expect considerable lack of agreement about the classification of certain acts and motives at this level. Thus, the common sense view that people possess qualities which invariably and inevitably make them attractive is, at best, shaky pending further systematic examination (Chapter 4).

6. The acknowledgement that <u>different types of relationship</u> exist may be forced by <u>everyday experience</u>, which thus makes it a component of the common sense view. However, this just raises some questions for study. Do different types of relationship all come about for the same overall reason (e.g. does each different type satisfy a given psychological need in a different way or to a different extent)? Or do they all satisfy entirely different and unrelated needs? Or do some of them satisfy needs and some not (see Chapter 6)?

There is another side to this coin: there are different levels of acquaintance - individuals know some people well and some not so well. Do the different levels amount to different <u>kinds</u> of acquaintance (and, if so, what distinguishes them)? Or are they different stages of one general process (and, if so, what functions do they represent and why are they staged, ordered or arranged in the sequence they are arranged in)?

7. One further important feature of the common sense view is this: <u>acquaintance or friendship is a 'gut' reaction, specifically in contrast to an intellectual one.</u> This point relates to the previous one, since, as it stands, it offers no explanation in terms of the psychological function of such intestinal responses. Reactions to others, this view claims, are made on the basis of presented cues which have certain values and people do not cogitate over them and assess the relative strengths of their various components, nor do they evaluate others relative to some psychological requirements. This approach leads to no very exact line of progress in the study of acquaintance, no precise or testable predictions. On the other hand, Chapter 5 is devoted to a psychological theory which argues that the 'gut' responses are learned and which relates such learning to the satisfaction of a psychological need to operate competently on the world (i.e. for individuals to learn to be effective in dealing with the outside environment - see pages 144-6). This position generates several very specific predictions and so adds

something to the basic suggestion provided by the common sense view.

8. As a corollary of this, it follows that <u>reactions to others are rapid and instant rather than mediate and slow or developing</u>. When someone claims that 'it was love at first sight' we take this at face value, as it were. This entails the view that acquaintance is not necessarily a <u>process</u> and there is correspondingly no theory of how it develops and unfolds. Clearly this view is consistent with several of the other common sense principles (cues are fixed; people have Ideals and respond to them quickly; people recognise the Ideals when they see them; the 'top' level of acquaintance is sometimes an instantaneous gut response). This raises all sorts of difficulties, however, and a few interesting possibilities. It cannot explain how people can come to realise that someone to whom they took an 'instant dislike' can sometimes turn out to be quite personable; or how their reflections and ponderations on their relationships can lead them to growing to like someone more. However, it does raise the interesting question of whether some cues are more closely related to the ultimate function of friendship than are others and whether, when they notice these, people react faster to them. But this question presupposes an answer to the thematic issue here: whether friendship and acquaintance do have some psychological function and whether all levels serve the same functions. This is a question that can be answered most satisfactorily by experiment rather than speculation.

Rather more important for a psychologist are the two next components of the common sense outlook. Both relate closely to the other aspects - especially to the view that we set out consciously to make friends. These two important components are: 9. that <u>the breakdown of relationships happens for different reasons from those which led to their establishment</u> (e.g. gentlemen prefer someone because she is blonde - they break the relationship off because they find her impossible to get on with); and 10. that <u>individuals bear the responsibility for their choices of friends, or their failure to maintain relationships</u>.

If acquainting is special behaviour and if people engage in it consciously, then it follows that their choices are some indicator of their own qualities or inner selves ('A man is known by the company he keeps'). It is assumed that choices reflect purposive and deliberate acts. This belief also rests on two assumptions: that people carry round notions of acceptable friends which represent their structure of priorities, and that they are able to exercise their choices freely and as intended. For this reason, people are often held responsible for the success or failure of their relationships. However, it is clear from much research reported here (e.g. Argyle, 1969; Cook, 1977) that many people lack the skills which enable them to initiate friendly encounters, and, to the extent that this restricts the range of those they meet, will have a restricted range of choices open to them. Those with more extrovert or easy manners are likely to have a wider range of choices for more developed relationships. It is thus more helpful if research identifies ways in which to assist people who find relationships difficult - much more helpful than simply stigmatising their failures as 'common sense' so often does (see Chapter 4).

Common sense explains the breakdown of relationships in a way similar to its explanation of the failure to set them up in the first place. This argument goes as follows: if people react quickly to others and do so on the basis of 'pre-arranged' cues, then attraction and the acquaintance process are initiated according to predetermined and inexorable patterns and the breakdown of relationships must be attributed to some other cause than that automatic process which accounts for its establishment. One standard objection to such an explanation is that it is unparsimonious; that is, it specifically adopts one set of explanatory rules for one part of a process (formation of relationships) and another set for its opposite (breakdown of them). It does not explain the processes economically by means of one set of tenets - and this is a luxury that psychological theorists are not allowed. In sharpening the common sense approach, therefore, a consistent theoretical structure which accounts for set-up and breakdown would be an advantage (see Chapters 2 and 7).

## When Common Sense Fails

The above facets of an everyday approach to acquaintance are often supported by intuition and anecdote but do not amount to a systematic theory about acquaintance and certainly do not often help to identify ways in which it should be studied. They are outlined above in order to show that whilst the psychological study of acquaintance might choose to <u>start</u> from a common sense base, it needs to modify it, test it and reject some of it right from the start.

One reason for rejecting common sense as the theoretical indicator for studies of acquaintance is its imprecision about the subject matter being studied. The terms 'acquaintance', 'attraction' and 'friendship' have been used loosely and interchangeably without any indication of their specific referents. The first task of an investigator would be to tie them down more carefully. The second reason for rejecting a common sense approach is the fact that it is not <u>an</u> approach but several different conflicting approaches. <u>It</u> offers us the notion that 'Opposites attract' at the same time as the proposal that 'Birds of a feather flock together' (i.e. similarities attract!). One task of a scientific worker would be to choose between hypotheses by defining the areas where each may apply ('oppositeness' of what? similarity in what respect?). He would then draw up a suitable test of the relative effectiveness of each - but this requires agreement about the terms of reference. A third task of the scientist would, therefore, be the measurement of and experiment about the phenomena to be studied.

In short, the purpose of this informal introduction has been to awaken the recognition that the mechanisms of acquaintance are significant problems to which common sense has no apparently consistent answer but which the psychologist may unravel by use of his special methods of enquiry. This is a deliberate attempt to lead the reader to think about the problems in a new way and to demand more satisfying proofs of ideas (whether they be commonsensical or not) before they can be accepted as grounds for confident statements about the bases of acquaintance. These, as we can deduce from the Preface, would be a basis of alleviating much human suffering and improving human personal relationships.

This informal introduction has also shown that generation of hypotheses about acquaintance, attraction and liking is misleadingly easy - especially given that these terms are used loosely and we all _feel_ that we have an intuitive grasp of what they refer to. Anyone can generate hypotheses in such circumstances: the difficulty lies in _testing_ the hypotheses in order _to explain and account for agreed specific phenomena_, assessing the value of the hypotheses and building them into an established framework of knowledge. These aims necessitate systematic study of acquaintance in agreed ways - which immediately raises certain issues about the practicality of doing this. Can one really study something so personal as acquaintance under scientifically acceptable conditions? How can one hope to study it systematically without destroying it? What methods can be used to achieve this? A great deal of ingenuity has gone in to answering these issues, and so has a lot of detailed study. For otherwise dispassionate scientists, there is, however, (indeed there must be) more joy over one rigorously-tested idea confirmed at the 0.05 level than over ninety-and-nine apparently brilliant intuitions that fail to yield conventional levels of significance. Only then can the study of acquaintance stop being a dull and ill-directed ramble through vague and ill-defined territory and start to become an exciting and challenging treasure hunt after specific ideas.

# CHAPTER ONE

# SYSTEMATIC STUDY OF ACQUAINTANCE

The systematic study of acquaintance has one single goal: a full grasp of the lawful relationships existing between the variables that are relevant to acquaintance; i.e. the discovery of what makes people grow to like or dislike one another. The achievement of this goal does, however, have three prerequisites in relation to the context provided by the Informal Introduction: <u>first</u>, definition of the nature of the topic, based on a greater precision about the phenomena of acquaintance, attraction and liking (i.e. what is acquaintance and what aspects of it is the researcher particularly concerned to explain?); <u>second</u>, a decision about how to measure it; <u>third</u>, discussion of how to experiment on it. This entails agreement about the ways in which to test out relationships between variables (i.e. agreement about the methodology appropriate to studying acquaintance).

## What Is Acquaintance?

Given the discussion of common sense in the Introduction, the reader could predict for himself that researchers' ingenuity in defining acquaintance will likewise be extensive. 'Acquaintance', 'attraction' and 'liking' are used by the common man on the one hand as convenient constructs to help him explain and understand how others behave: as such they are generic terms which cover lots of different types of behaviour from intense sexual desire to mere co-operation. Although he may apply such terms to a variety of events, the researcher on the other hand cannot afford the luxury of too much generality and straightaway limits his interest, therefore, to those human relationships where the individuals come together for their own sake and not simply in instrumental pursuit of other goals. For example, although people who like playing tennis have to find other people to join in with them because it cannot be played on one's own, the researcher would be more interested in those people who joined a tennis club because they liked the other people (and also happened to want to play tennis) rather than those who simply wanted to play tennis. In more formal terms, the 'conceptual variable' (i.e. the hypothetical construct that he wishes to examine: that is, attraction or acquaintance, is a variable that causes people to choose to associate with one another for their own sake <u>as people</u>.

Defining the terms

This general focus of interest in personal relationships simply identifies a common theme rather than narrowing down the areas for study. Several different behaviours are performed because the people like the other people involved (see Introduction) and the real question is whether the differences matter to the psychologist. One clear difference between liking relationships is that some are long term (with a past history of complex interdependency, shared experience and so forth) and some are short term (spontaneously evoked liking towards a perfect stranger). The central question in the study of acquaintance is precisely the psychological relationship between these two types of liking and the particular concern of this book is with the way in which short term liking is converted into long term liking. Our major concern is therefore with <u>Acquaintance</u>, a term that covers the process of getting to know someone in depth from first encounter to established relationships - whether this provokes an increase in liking or not. As such this term covers and embodies most of the other terms below - and some others (e.g. hating, 'enemyship' and Feindschaft - Harré, 1977) - and it concerns the long term processes by which affective relationships are constructed rather than with short term influences on desire to affiliate, first impressions, liking and sexual desire. <u>Affiliation</u> is seeking out other people as company or a willingness to become involved in social situations. <u>Liking</u> (or 'positive affect', 'sociometric positivity") refers to positive regard for someone in either the long or the short term, often indicated by or inferred from choices actually made or from expressed intentions. It is a component of 'acquaintance' but conceptually distinct from it: Liking refers to a feeling about someone whilst acquaintance refers to the process whereby increasing knowledge about someone is associated with increased liking (or disliking). <u>Attraction</u> would seem, on the face of it, to be co-terminous with Liking, but has actually acquired a special sense in this area of research. It usually refers to stated liking and actual choices but is usually restricted to apply to initial responses to strangers, first reactions, short term rather than longer lasting positivity (for which the term 'Liking' is preferred). Confusingly, the term <u>Interpersonal Attraction</u> is the blanket term usually applied to the whole area of research on acquaintance, liking, attraction and positive regard. It is reserved for use in this sense henceforth. It therefore includes special cases of liking such as <u>friendship</u> (usually assessed in terms of reciprocated choices made by individuals independently, or mutual selections from a whole range of possible choices), <u>dating</u>, <u>courtship</u> and <u>marital selection</u>. The difference between these latter terms may be summarised as follows: 'marital selection' is best used when the researcher is in a position to know who marries (or lives with) whom; 'courting' is best used when choices have not yet been cemented in any legal or recognised form; and 'dating' is used when the respective parties have shown less commitment to the relationship than a courtship pair, before they are institutionalised or 'going steady'.

**Which topics should be studied, then?** Should all these phenomena be thought of as essentially different or essentially the same? What is the conceptual link between them? For example, it is presumably the case that all Liking starts with Attraction and hence that Attraction should be the starting point for any study of Acquaintance but we cannot conclude that the antecedents of Attraction need be the same as the antecedents of Liking - nor that a rigorous understanding of Attraction phenomena would allow us to predict the course of Acquaintance or the likely 'success' of a new relationship. This may become clearer if we look at the different ways in which these phenomena are suited to systematic experimental study.

Some of the phenomena of acquaintance can be studied in the laboratory more readily than others, and some of them can be studied informatively without recourse to the laboratory at all. For example, in the study of marital choice one might use sociological techniques to assess the extent to which choices were determined by partners' respective class or social origins, economic group and so forth. But these kinds of study do not identify the psychological mechanisms beneath the choices: they may indicate relevant limiting features, necessary conditions or correlates of choice but not causes. Equally, in such studies an assumption has to be made that causes of choice are the same as causes of subsequent satisfaction with and continuance of the relationship; and furthermore they presume that those relationships that last longest are the best examples of the mechanisms we wish to study. However, there are many factors which keep marital couples together besides liking: the costs of leaving the relationship increase as the relationship lengthens; opportunities for further choices diminish with passing time; other cultural, social and ritual pressures serve to maintain the relationship in various ways (Harré, 1977). Thus the study of marital choices needs to be supplemented with studies concerning other facets of choice such as are amenable to experimental scrutiny. One clearly related case of acquaintance is dating and one advantage of the study of dating is that it allows experimenters to <u>arrange</u> partners for their subjects discreetly yet in ways which suit their experimental purposes. It thus permits strong manipulation of relevant experimental variables. Thus Byrne, Ervin and Lamberth (1970) arranged subjects into 'blind date' pairs on the basis of similarity of attitudes; Stroebe et al. (1971) fixed subjects up with dating partners on the basis of level of physical attractiveness.

The study of dating is useful because it is a particular case of acquaintance where the rituals are clear; the intents are well understood; the methods are well known (even, in some cases, culturally defined and strictly predetermined); the outcomes are to some extent more readily identifiable. But the question is: can dating be taken as representative of other acquaintance processes or do these very characteristics make it different from other sorts? For one thing, people chosen as dating partners are often not chosen with any intention of forming a permanent relationship and so certain features of the relationship may be different from other kinds of acquaintance. Again, certain features of the partner may assume a prominence that is lacking in other relationships. Further, since many initial dating decisions appear to be taken on the basis of physical appearance, one might expect to be able to demonstrate a greater relationship between physical characteristics and, say, dating frequency than between it and other types of relationship. One should also therefore be able to demonstrate some kind of relationship between physical characteristics and marital choice (since one presumes that marital choices are made from amongst the selection of available dates). But what <u>kind</u> of causal relationship is predictable between the variable of physical appearance and the variable of <u>attraction</u> (or even the variables associated with dating and marital choice)? We shall see in Chapter 3.

This is not to say that some contribution to the study of the general process of acquaintance could not be made by close scrutiny of the special processes involved in dating and marital choice. Useful pointers can be identified which could provide food for thought in connection with other kinds of acquaintance (Chapter 7); but equally the problems raised by the study of these cues are and remain quite large. It is not adequate simply to show that physical appearance relates to choice, for one needs an explanation of why this should be so. It is not good enough to say that some physical cues are attractive and others are not, since this simply restates the problem for the psychological researcher and one needs to know <u>why</u> particular cues or particular deployments of physical characteristics are attractive to individuals and what part they play in the development of acquaintance.

If dating should prove an unsatisfactory object of study on its own, then other examples of acquaintance are provided by the close friendships with which most people are familiar. But by the time the psychologist knows that they are worth studying then they have become stabilised and choice patterns have become clear or less volatile. So one could study only the features which <u>now</u> characterise the friendship; only those things which <u>currently</u> relate to the choice pattern. It may or may not be the case that these factors relate to the original basis for choice. One resolution of this problem has been found and used in psychological studies of acquaintance (Newcomb, 1961; Duck and Spencer, 1972). This answer is to find a group of individuals who have not met before, to bring them together, take various measures and sit back in the reasonable hope that some of the people will form friendships. The subsequent choices (and of course the rejections also) can then be measured much later and related to various characteristics displayed in the _original_ measures. Student halls of residence (and the first year students entering them) often provide such sources of psychological supply. Yet students are not typical of the rest of the population; the student halls of residence (and particularly the experience of joining one on first entering a university) are not typical of everyday friendship sources. However, it is likely that some contributions to our overall levels of understanding of acquaintance can be achieved by studies of that type - even if we must later recognise the need to be cautious in generalising beyond the specifics of the particular situation and population sample. Such studies have the advantage that their design gets round a conceptual problem that otherwise exists (Wright, 1968). Wright argues that if researchers seek an existing group of friends and then take various measurements in the search for the causes of the friendship, then they are making a fundamental confusion. They are treating friendship conceptually as the dependent variable (the thing caused by something else) but operationally as the independent variable (the variable that causes something else). For example, if they used this method and found that friends were similar, they would _want_ to say 'Similarity causes friendship' but would actually _be_ entitled to say at the very most only 'Friendship causes similarity' because of the conceptual confusion of independent and dependent variables.

One kind of acquaintance which is most well documented in the literature is that which occurs on first encounter. Study of this kind of relationship can be expected to reveal the kind of factor which sets an acquaintance in motion. Additionally, it is free from any contamination which previous knowledge of each other can import into other studies. For example it is hard to make firm friends believe some kinds of things about each other in an experimental manipulation (e.g. it is hard to manipulate beliefs about the friend's competence, intelligence or personality) since the friends already have some baseline of information about such things; but it is relatively easy to manipulate such beliefs experimentally when studying new acquaintances, simply because no baseline of experience pre-exists the study (see Chapter 5). However, it will clearly remain an empirical question whether the factors identified as influences on initial acquaintance processes will continue to carry weight as the relationship proceeds - and indeed whether these early factors predict subsequent outcomes at all.

Given the variety of the phenomena, the reader will not be surprised to find the rest of this book describing a variety of research into a variety of component processes that make up 'Acquaintance'. Indeed, since no single experiment and no single researcher can ever expect to answer all the questions associated with a particular topic, the nature of the research process practically dictates that different workers are most efficiently employed in studying different aspects of relevant phenomena. It will thus be true that systematic study of acquaintance will require a systematic study of several aspects of acquaintance, of both short term and long term relationships, of the antecedents and consequences of liking, of links between attraction and acquaintance. It is not a cause for dismay that there are different researchers looking at different topics (though it would be if no two workers ever looked at the same topics). What is important is that one should recognise both the fact that there are differences and the importance of the different topics as contributors to an overall picture of acquaintance phenomena. This book is about to report these different topics in a way that gives a conceptual superstructure for describing acquaintance and tries to fit them into a theory about the development of acquaintance. It thus intends to illustrate the fundamental similarities that underlie different workers' differences in approach and examines the extent to which a single psychological function may account for several diverse manifestations of behaviour.

Is Attraction an Attitude?

Whilst research on antecedents and consequences of the different forms of acquaintance is extensive, work on the precise nature of the attraction response is relatively sparse (McCarthy, 1976) - but before something can be measured its nature must be conceptualised theoretically and the present section considers this.

One similarity underlying different workers' conceptualisation of acquaintance is that attraction towards someone is an attitude about him and that this is true whatever the context where liking occurs (Berscheid and Walster, 1969). This assumption provides a theoretical basis for the belief that it could be measured like other attitudes: on a paper-and-pencil rating scale, or by behavioural indicators (e.g. whether someone chooses to sit next to or distant from a given person - Byrne, Baskett and Hodges, 1971). It <u>should</u>, however, mean that what is true of other attitudes is also true of attraction (thus it should relate meaningfully to constellations of other attitudes, should have the same susceptibility to influence, should be formed and caused similarly, should link similarly the attitude and behaviour, etc.). This is an alluring notion in many ways - but it can also be confusing. For example, attitudes are believed by some psychologists (e.g. Kelvin, 1970) to be composed of three distinct parts (cognitive, evaluative and behavioural): thus an individual's attitude to an object (or person) is composed of what he knows about that object, how he feels about it and what he does about it. If this principle is adopted in the context of interpersonal attraction then one would expect attraction to be composed of what the individual knows about someone, what he feels about him and what he does about it. Note, however, that the usual way of conceptualising liking is by means of the second of these components alone and the other two components would commonly be thought to be an antecedent of liking and an indicator or consequence of liking, respectively. Indeed the three components of liking are clearly more complexly interconnected than appears at first sight and this makes this particular attitude somewhat different from attitudes studied in other contexts (for example, where the focus is primarily on the relationship between a given attitude and other attitudes, or on how the given attitude is responsive to change pressures). In the acquaintance literature, the emphasis falls much more heavily on the things which lead to the formation of the attitude and on the behavioural consequences stemming from it. It could be deduced that, even if it does make sense to see attraction as an attitude, it makes equal sense to explore the <u>ways</u> in which this is true. Clearly attitudes to persons in this context are prima facie more complex than attitudes to objects or ideas: when you have to actually interact with the object of your attitude (as is the case in attraction) then the linkage between behaviour and attitude also has many more facets than in the context of other attitudes.

Therefore, whether or not it is sensible from other points of view to see liking as an attitude just like other attitudes, there are cognate problems in establishing the relationship between verbally expressed liking and actual behaviour just as there are with verbal expressions and actual behaviour in respect of other attitudes. Schwartz and Tessler (1972) have analysed this general problem of attitude-behaviour discrepancy and have identified four sources for it:

1. Overt behaviour is influenced by a multitude of factors in addition to those that are of interest to the experimenter (e.g. subjects may be motivated by fear of looking foolish or by desire to ingratiate).

2. An inadequate conceptualisation and measurement of the attitudes under study;

3. The fact that attitude and behaviour are seldom assessed together;

4. The fact that situational cues may change in salience between the times of measurement.

These points, although made in the general context of literature on attitude research, do have something useful to say in the context of acquaintance research also. However, the latter two problems identified by Schwartz and Tessler are less significant for attraction research. This is simply because measures of 'behaviour' and 'attitude' are usually taken together since the emphasis of interpersonal attraction research is upon the formation of liking where none existed before rather than (as is usual in attitude research) upon the changes exerted on attitudes by various intervening events. The problems for attraction research are thus rather the first two of Schwartz and Tessler's identified difficulties.

<u>Overt behaviour</u> in acquaintance is governed by many things. For example, there are situational constraints (i.e. constraints or influence not derived from the conceptual variable of liking) which influence expressions of liking. A restrained or understated expression of liking for a stranger is as likely to reflect the cultural taboos surrounding overt expression of

strong personal affect as it is to reflect the true level of liking or disliking. Equally, expressions of choice or desire to associate with someone are not good predictors of overt associative behaviour or of liking: people can be attracted to others that they cannot associate with (for, among other things, the extraneous - in this context - bodily olfactory variables emphasised by toilet soap manufacturers) just as they may sometimes choose people that they do not find 'attractive' (e.g. 'I hate his guts but he is a good worker') - Simons, Berkowitz and Moyer (1970). Similarly, the causes of choice may not be the same as the causes of satisfaction with a subsequent relationship. For these and other reasons, therefore, one can be reasonably confident that expressions of choice or liking and overt attraction behaviour may well, in certain circumstances, be orthogonal to one another. Indeed, some workers (e.g. Byrne, 1971) have chosen to advocate the view that explanation of the antecedents of verbal choice itself (rather than its relationship to other behaviour) is a proper concern for workers in acquaintance.

Recently Latta (1976) has argued that verbal measures of attraction and behavioural or nonverbal indices are essentially two 'nondependent dimensions; not necessarily independent but uncorrelated in many instances' (p.81) and he concludes that verbal indicators of attraction are not directly related to behavioural indicators. His proposal is that investigators use both methods of assessing attraction rather than one alone. Whilst this is a useful suggestion that would help researchers build up a picture of how 'attitude' relates to 'behaviour' in some degree, the solution is a solution to an issue that some researchers would not be prepared to regard as the only one to be investigated. It is only part of the task of the study of acquaintance to relate verbal and nonverbal measures of attraction - as indeed it is only part of the task to find out what are the antecedents of given levels of verbally expressed attraction or given levels of behavioural indication of attraction. Whilst Latta's point is a timely reminder of an important issue in the area, it cannot constitute grounds for giving up study of the other issues involved. Since acquaintance has so many variables associated with it, it does indeed seem fair to allow that the solution of the problem identified by Byrne (i.e. the problem of explaining why people express the verbal choices that they do, or make the paper-and-pencil responses that they do) is a central part of the study of acquaintance, and one which, when taken with other work will bear also on related aspects of the problems of acquaintance behaviour.

This consideration is linked to the second issue identified by Schwartz and Tessler (1972). The <u>inadequate conceptualisation</u> of the relevant variables of acquaintance is precisely the result of inadequate understanding of the mechanisms accounting for even such limited parts of the acquaintance process as verbal expressions of choice. Partly this lack of clarity is due to the acknowledged facts that interpersonal attraction is multi-determined (i.e. each of the phenomena of interpersonal attraction has a range of antecedents) and that it is multi-dimensional (i.e. its manifestations take shape in many forms of behaviour, its antecedents have a variety of origins and forms). Both of these problems increase the difficulty of linking 'the attitude' and 'the behaviour'. Partly, the confusion is enhanced by the fact that many readers (and even workers themselves) do not always note the multidimensional nature of the problems surrounding interpersonal attraction: thus there are problems concerning the relationship between other variables and those of interpersonal attraction (e.g. the relationship between physical attractiveness and liking); problems concerning the relationship between various aspects of liking behaviour (e.g. the relationship between liking and willingness to work with a person); and problems concerning the relationship between interpersonal attraction behaviour and other behaviour (e.g. the effects of liking on co-operation or competition between two people). A similar distinction has been made between antecedents of interpersonal attraction, indicators of interpersonal attraction and consequences of interpersonal attraction (Byrne and Griffitt, 1973). For example, some studies (e.g. Byrne, 1961b) have studied proximity or closeness of physical seating in the classroom, as a <u>cause</u> of attraction; some (e.g. Byrne, Baskett and Hodges, 1971) have used degree of physical proximity as an <u>indicator</u> of the degree of attraction felt for the other person; whilst yet others (e.g. Allgeier and Byrne, 1973) have studied physical proximity as a <u>consequence</u> of attraction. When such differences are clearly stated (as by the workers quoted above) progress can be made toward understanding the nature of the different relationships between variables in different circumstances. This is particularly important in view of the multidimensional nature of interpersonal attraction, which is as often disregarded as it is asserted. In such circumstances it is quite likely that different workers will be looking at different determinants of different aspects of the concept and it is therefore equally likely that many apparently significant conflicts between different workers are imagined rather than real (or, more accurately, are based on the mistaken view that since interpersonal attraction is a single concept it has only one form). On the contrary, it is only when the term is used in the same sense by all workers that we can be sure that all workers are attempting to study the same relationships between variables. This sureness can be enhanced by similar agreements about methods of measuring liking, and about frameworks within which to make decisions between competing explanations for the same relationships. Adequate conceptualisation of phenomena of interpersonal attraction thus extends to conceptualisations of methods of <u>measuring</u> liking.

## The Problem of Measurement

On the face of it the operationalisation and measurement of acquaintance seem easy. After all, we either are or are not friends with someone; we either do or do not like a new acquaintance (or we may feel neutral about him). When experimenting on acquaintance perhaps it is possible to get away with a bare statement to this effect and simply allow subjects to endorse it appropriately. But as well as the fact that this answer does not solve the original problem, for reasons given below, it has the additional disadvantage that it creates other problems, some relatively trivial and some rather more important. It fails to solve the original question because it provides no advice on how to measure attraction in a precise and scientific way; nor does it suggest the kind of measure to be used (verbal report? behavioural?). In addition it does not indicate which components of attraction (liking; preparedness to work with someone; propensity to socialise with someone, etc.) are relevant in the study of acquaintance.

Measurement Issues

But the objections put the cart before the horse. The more basic issue concerns the <u>kinds</u> of relationship which interest us here and from this follows the question of whether all methods of measurement are appropriate to all kinds of relationship and acquaintance. Not only can one distinguish between working acquaintances (colleagues), social acquaintances (bridge partners, for example), 'ritual' acquaintances (e.g. neighbours), nodding acquaintances (e.g. people who habitually take the same bus to work and recognise each other but do not interact) but one can also distinguish several levels and kinds of friendship (close friends; marital partnerships; dates; and so on). Within a given category there can be several types of relationship also. So what measures are appropriate to different relationships?

Lindzey and Byrne (1968) have reported the work of Procter and Loomis (1951) who distinguished the following six kinds of relationship:

1. A chooses B; B chooses A

2. A chooses B; B ignores A

3. A chooses B; B rejects A

4. A ignores B; B ignores A

5. A ignores B; B rejects A

6. A rejects B; B rejects A

This analysis however (which was completed in the context of discussion of racial prejudice) is too simple for our purposes. Choice and rejection have many forms; ignoring someone can be an active intentional act or a passive one due to unawareness. Furthermore, there can also be different levels of choice within each kind: for example, A may regard B <u>as a friend</u> while B (neither rejecting A nor ignoring him) regards A only <u>as an acquaintance</u> at some other level of intimacy or in some other category. These distinctions - perhaps irrelevant in discussion of prejudice about racial groups - are highly salient in discussions of more intimate personal relationships between individuals.

Furthermore, it does not make a great deal of sense to ask very close friends whether they are attracted to each other or not - especially if you originally chose to study them because you know that they _are_ close friends. It might be more useful to find out who lik_es_ whom within a given population. Nor does it make much sense to ask close friends how much they like each other on a scale running from 0 to 10 as may be appropriate for pairs of strangers. Even if you did this, the chances are that a high rating in those circumstances is either not very meaningful or is tinged with elements which differ from a high rating on the same questionnaire in other circumstances (e.g. first encounter with a stranger). One score might indicate 'I already like this person a great deal'; another may mean 'I would quite like to get to know this person a lot better' and these two statements are psychologically, qualitatively and functionally different. In some circumstances therefore it might make more sense to ask whether A likes B more than C and C more than D and so on. Or else one could use several operational measures. All of these points simply emphasise the fact that the question asked and the measurement taken will depend on various known factors concerning the relationship under study. The appropriate measures of acquaintance can be expected to vary as a function of the type and the temporal point of a relationship which is being tapped. Psychologically the same measure need not be appropriate for both long and short term acquaintances, or if used for both examples it may need to be taken at different face values. Of course this is ultimately an empirical issue, and one that will determine why researchers choose particular measures for their studies. However, a simple temporal dimension (i.e. just how long two people have known one another) may not be the only acceptable or even the best dimension for defining level of intimacy or differentiating kinds of social relationships and sorts of social choice (Levinger, 1974; McCarthy and Duck, 1976). For example, as a relationship becomes more intimate, the more the partners tend to disclose about themselves and their feelings (see Chapter 6), so that level of Self-Disclosure may be a useful index of the depth of intimacy in a relationship (Morton, Alexander and Altman, 1976).

Sociometric measures (i.e. those measuring relationships within a group, or choices by various parties) can as often identify features such as leadership status, popularity or numbers of acquaintances as they can cast light on the particular choices of an individual, or on the levels of attraction which he feels towards specific other people.

Clearly these differ functionally: to say that someone is popular is to talk of the numbers of people who choose him (how many people like him) rather than to say he is rated extremely highly by those who know him (how much people like him). Again, to say that two people are close friends may mean more, psychologically, than simply saying that they like each other or are attracted to one another. The measures chosen to operationalise acquaintance, therefore, will depend on the type of social relationship under study and the theoretical questions that one has in mind. It will not always be adequate to ask someone simply to state his choices.

Other issues are raised by the initial response to the question of measurement that began this section. The first is an extension of the above points. The bare question 'How attracted are you to this person?' may evoke a response based on many separate features even if the respondent correctly restricts himself to identifying the kind of social relationship you had in mind (i.e. if he realises that you are assessing his personal liking for someone rather than your evaluation of someone's leadership status or popularity). There are several functionally distinct components of a response to such a question and the attraction measure may obscure these different facets if it asks as broad a question as that above. For example, the respondent may in effect be rating the physical attractiveness of the Other; or something which amounts to a statement of how much he would like to work with him; or how exciting a companion he finds him and so on. So a first step in measuring attraction must be to differentiate such measurement scales operationally and measure each component separately (Byrne, 1961a). The psychological problem is even more variegated if one asks such a question of people in an established, rather than a new, ralationship since, as argued earlier, the psychological components of the response may in that case be very diverse and may even amount to a sum of several 'mini-responses' - another empirical question.

On the other hand, asking the question at all may sensitise an individual to some aspect of the Other which he had not considered. Suppose you are introduced to a new acquaintance and you find him very amusing and entertaining and are quite attracted to that person. If the experimenter then comes along and asks how physically attractive the person is, or how much you would like to work with him on a task, you may have to stop and think, not having used those dimensions to assess his attractiveness. Of course you could answer those questions now you are sensitised to them, but they may not have been the real basis for your original judgement. A second point is that your responses are likely to be influenced and enhanced by your previous assessment of his affability. Those who would argue that 'attractiveness' is the sum of such parts of mini-responses may not be unduly disturbed by such a 'halo' effect: but it may be found that when several measurement scales are simultaneously presented then responses to a scale measuring physical attractiveness are functionally separable from those measured on other scales. This would be all to the good and would probably mean that the investigator had successfully separated out those factors which exerted more and less influence on liking levels - whether or not the subject himself is conscious of the fact that he is responding to the factors in the way that he does.

**What should be measured?** For all of these reasons the measurement of attraction is a complex problem which runs a very great risk of superficiality unless backed up in other ways. For this reason it may be a good idea to use not only paper-and-pencil measures of liking but also some measures of actual behaviour which can be used to discover relationships between different types of attraction response. As discussed above, it is well-known that (even in experiments!) people's intentions and actions do not always match up one for one and someone's claim that he finds another person attractive as a potential workmate may not be worth the duplicated scale on which it is written. However, there are other ways of operationalising such expressed attraction. For example subjects can be asked to choose a work·partner who could assist them in a second part of the experiment; they could thus be made to add a bit of behavioural reality to their verbal statements of admiration. Aronson and Carlsmith (1968) have argued that one need not go this far but can settle for allowing subjects to express their choices in the belief that they will subsequently work with their chosen partner, even though the experiment is in fact terminated before this actually occurs. Such measures they term 'behaviouroid' measures.

The psychologist is, as we have seen, closely but not

exclusively concerned with this very issue of how far expressed liking is actually related to behaviour and vice versa. Indeed, several measures of liking are taken in a form that taps them behaviourally rather than on a self-report form, whether the behaviour is verbal or nonverbal (Byrne and Griffitt, 1973). For instance, one could count the number of times that two people are seen in one another's company, although this method is tedious, time consuming and not, in the long run, very informative about the kind of relationship or the depth of feeling they have for one another. One could refine this bald approach by taking measures of the kind of things they do together or the kind of things they expect each other to do (La Gaipa, 1977b). Physical or physiological measures of behaviour accompanying attraction are also possible; for instance, it is established that when individuals are attracted to one another their pupils dilate (Hess, 1965). More recently Clore and Gormly (1975) have measured amongst other things the changes in electrical skin resistance (GSR) and cardiac activity that accompany various components of attraction behaviour, particularly responses to attitudinal agreement or disagreement of the type that usually influence attraction. Much can be done using these techniques, as the Clore and Gormly experiment shows, but physiological measures simply cannot be taken in some circumstances whilst in others they are assailed by the disadvantage that, by their nature, most of them involve the subjects being fitted into complex or obtrusive apparatus with all the attendant effects on anxiety levels, attention, suspicion about experimenter's intentions and so on.

Intimacy and attraction for someone are also fairly reliably indicated by certain physical cues such as distance (since personal intimacy is often accompanied by physical closeness, Argyle, 1975) or by the amounts of time spent looking at one another (Gaze; Eye Contact - Argyle and Kendon, 1967; Cook, 1977). However the two have also been shown to relate (Argyle and Dean, 1965) so that the level of intimacy between two people is defined by the interaction of Distance x Eye Contact (as physical distance between two people increases, they will compensate for it by increasing the amount of eye contact so that the signal for a less intimate interaction - distance - is cancelled by the signal for increased intimacy - eye contact - and thus the overall intimacy of the interaction stays at the same level).

Altman (1974) has argued the conceptually distinct case that paraverbal, preverbal and nonverbal behavioural cues do not merely indicate the level of attraction between two people but also fit into a coherent system so that understanding of their function and purpose is essential to an understanding of interpersonal attraction. This argument in turn is aimed at the problem of understanding developing acquaintance. Essentially it claims that individuals' aims, intentions or expectations about acquaintance change and develop as the relationship proceeds; that such things as aims, intentions or expectations are indicated by or translated into overt behaviour; and therefore that the development of acquaintance can be assessed in part through attention to the changing form of overt behaviours that accompany it. However (as is discussed more fully in later chapters) there has been an understandable reluctance, even when the behavioural measures are plainly explicated, for research on attraction to invest the time and effort involved in the completion of the long term studies that are required to tackle the issues raised by such developmental theories as Altman's. The current emphasis of the literature is, it must be admitted, one-sidedly and unevenly placed on the study of attraction responses in initial encounters - and for such studies the methods above often contain more drawbacks than advantages.

Because of this problem of appropriateness and because of the more straightforward prima facie problems of some of the above measures, workers in this area rely heavily on verbal reports of attraction as assessed on duplicated scales - but this is not done simply because of the flaws in other methods. For it is also true, as argued above, that whilst psychology is often right to pay considerable attention to the relationship between verbal responses and actual behaviour (and thus occasionally to pay much attention to behavioural responses) it also has other relationships to examine. The search for variables that relate lawfully to or actually cause overt behaviour is what justifies paying attention to behavioural activities or behaviouroid measures. But psychologists must also find whether the same things cause overt behaviour as cause verbal responses and must therefore examine the relationship between the laws governing verbal responses and the laws governing behaviour. In order to do this we need to know the causal laws governing the responses, and it therefore makes sense to try to establish these causal laws first before going up the chain of complexity to the other relationships above.

Further justification for examining verbal reports or scaled attraction measures rests on statistical and pragmatic grounds. If attitude and attraction scores are measured numerically then they can be arithmetically and mathematically treated (see below) and complex maps of relationships can be statistically analysed. Additonally the data in such circumstances are collected in a manner easy for both the experimenter and subject - in some cases without the experimenter disrupting, interfering with, or unduly sensitising the subject to the processes being examined; or in such a way that he cannot spoil the measure by bias or through causing a subject to feel evaluation apprehension and fear of looking foolish (Rosenberg, 1965). The next section therefore examines a selection of the many methods available, looking at their use in particular circumstances, for what ends and with what resultant deficiencies or benefits.

Techniques of Measurement in the Study of Acquaintance

The attraction literature already contains several extensive reviews of the measurement methods employed in much research in the study of acquaintance (Byrne, 1971; Byrne and Griffitt, 1973; Lindzey and Byrne, 1968). Given the comments above about the global difficulties in measurement and the reasons why precise measurement is desirable, this section will simply aim to illustrate some common practices rather than give an exhaustive review.

Huston (1974, p.14) has argued that there are two assumptions underlying the measurement of positive regard: first, that

> the operations employed to measure attraction define it. Thus the closer one makes one's mark to the positive end of a liking scale, the greater one's liking by definition;

second, that it is this indicator of attraction itself that is the variable of study (i.e. investigators need to show what antecedents lead subjects to indicate certain levels of attraction); the investigation of how far these responses reflect 'real' attraction is a separate issue, and one that is so fraught with philosophical problems as to lie outside the hopes of research to solve it.

These points are more valid in connection with measures of attraction to newly-encountered strangers and less so in the case of measures of actual liking in real life since in the latter case the measures are quite different in form and have different intentions. The purpose is usually the 'nominal' problem of identifying who chooses whom; not the 'ordinal' or 'interval' problem of who likes whom by how much. As such the validity of the choice measure is more readily assessable and can be checked against various behaviours (e.g. the claim by person A to have person B as a friend can be checked by seeing if person B also claims to have person A as a friend). Furthermore, it is true of studies of established friendships that the relationship between liking measures and other forms of behaviour actually constitutes the validation of the <u>construct</u> being measured rather than validation of the measurement technique. Although the term 'sociometric techniques' is sometimes used to cover any measure of liking or of choice, the two can be distinguished since one of them emphasises measures of attraction that are appropriate in the study of brief encounters and the other one emphasises 'maps' of choices made in the study of long lasting and developed relationships.

**Brief encounters** In the study of attraction to strangers, the subject is usually faced with a judgemental task where he is ultimately asked to indicate his liking for some stimulus person. Liking and attraction are thus conceived to be evaluations or attitudes about the stimulus person and can be measured in the same ways as attitudes about other stimuli (for discussion of other methods, see Berscheid and Walster, 1969 and Lindzey and Byrne, 1968. The most frequently used tests have been chosen for discussion here). The most usual form of scale employed in such research follows the form devised by Likert (1932) - that is, it is a simple bipolar scale whose end points are marked with verbal labels (for example 'Do not like at all' and 'Like very much'). The intervals between the two endpoints are usually numbered or otherwise labelled and the subject's task is simply to indicate the position on the scale that reflects his feelings about the person concerned.

Although this technique is sometimes used on its own to assess attraction, it is more usual to assess the subject's feelings about the stimulus on several such scales, all assessing a different feature of the person (how exciting he is to be with; how interesting he is; how well informed, reliable, likeable, ... etc.). The most frequently employed version of this method is the Interpersonal Judgement Scale (IJS) devised by Byrne (1961a). The subject completing the IJS is given six 7-point rating scales which assess different features of the stimulus person including how much the subject would like to work with the other person and how much he likes him and the responses to these two items above are computed into one overall score that is used as the index of attraction. By embedding these two items in the other five (which are used to rate things like knowledge of current affairs) the true purpose of the scale can be concealed from suspicious subjects more effectively and, equally, measures of the relationship between liking and responses to other aspects of the person can be evaluated. This method is the one most commonly used to assess attraction and is clearly well suited to this task which is mainly about immediate responses to a stimulus person - not with developing relationships nor desire to interact with someone which can be assessed by different measures. These include measures of 'social distance' (that is, the degree of closeness which the subject would permit in any relationship involving a given other person) in which the subject endorses one of a range of statements indicating different degrees of acceptance (Bogardus, 1925). Although used primarily as a measure of acceptance/rejection of racial groups, such a measure could clearly be used to assess acceptance of a particular individual.

In an attempt to circumvent some objects to paper-and-pencil measures of responses in brief encounters (e.g. tendencies not to take the rating task seriously, or to give socially desirable answers), Jones and Sigall (1971) devised an elaborate deceptive technique known as the 'Bogus Pipeline'. In essence, the method involves first convincing the subject that 'the electromyograph, a complex psychophysiological monitoring device' (actually a fiction, or course) can measure the subject's true feelings and then getting the subject to estimate the machine's readings as accurately as possible. The resulting scores are assumed to be as accurate a self-assessment measure of the subject's actual feelings as is possible (short of constructing a machine that can really do what Jones and Sigall kid their subjects this one can do). Clearly the value of this technique depends squarely on the efficacy of the deception procedures and its ability to demonstrate clearly that it does avoid the pitfalls of paper-and-pencil measures. Whilst the debate on the usefulness of this method still continues (Gaes, Quigley-Fernandez and Tedeschi, 1977; Byrne and Cherry, in press) those studies comparing it with other procedures for measuring attraction (e.g. the IJS, above) suggest that it is more subject to distortion by social desirability biasses than the other procedures (Cherry, Byrne and Mitchell, 1976).

**Descriptive sociometry of long-term relationships** In order to represent the choices actually made in real-life long term relationships experimenters often choose to supplement the above methods by descriptive techniques that identify 'who chose whom'. Various graphic techniques have been devised, following the work of J.L. Moreno (1934), and two are illustrated in Figure 1.

The target sociogram is a graphic representation of who chose whom and whether the choice was reciprocated or not, and it shows the number of times each person was chosen. The most popular individuals ('Stars') are indicated by positions in the innermost circle and those people placed at increasing distances from the centre are those who are less often chosen, the least popular persons being placed in the outermost ring. This method illustrates clearly certain features of the population concerned: for example, because it distinguishes graphically between reciprocated and unreciprocated choices it can illustrate the extent to which an individual is 'overchosen' (i.e. chosen by people whom he does not choose) or 'underchosen' (not chosen by those he chooses himself). On the other hand it is inconvenient and confusing in use with very large populations that have an intricate structure of choices and for such groups the next method is preferable.

The sociometric matrix is a matrix indicating the same kinds of things as the target sociogram but which is perhaps more appropriate for very large populations of subjects. It illustrates equally well 'who chose whom' (see Figure 1) but avoids the 'spaghetti effect' which a large number of linking lines creates in the target sociogram for a large sample. It is still

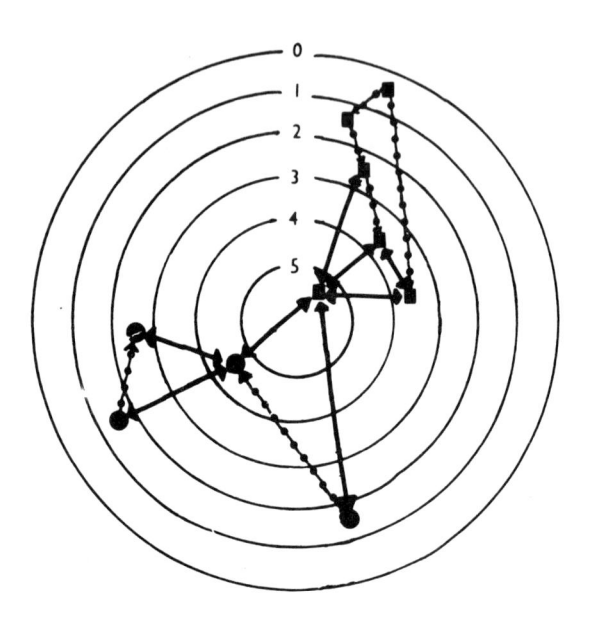

0-5 NUMBER OF TIMES CHOSEN
■ MALES
● FEMALES
•—•—•► UNRECIPROCATED CHOICE
◄—► MUTUAL CHOICE

## Target sociogram

Each individual is placed in the diagram in a position which indicates the number of times that he was chosen by others (the nearer the centre of the target, the more popular the individual). The diagram also indicates who chose a given individual (as indicated by the lines which join the circles and squares) and whether the choice was reciprocated (continuous line) or not (dotted line).

Fig. 1 Long-term relationships: 'who chose whom'

|   | A | B | C | D | E | F | G | H | J |
|---|---|---|---|---|---|---|---|---|---|
| A | ● | X |   | / |   | / | X |   |   |
| B | X | ● | X |   | X | / |   |   | X |
| C |   | X | ● |   |   | / |   |   |   |
| D |   |   | / | ● | / | / |   |   |   |
| E |   | X |   |   | ● | X |   | / | X |
| F |   |   |   |   | X | ● |   | X |   |
| G | X |   | / |   |   | / | ● |   |   |
| H |   |   |   |   |   | X |   | ● | X |
| J |   | X |   |   | X |   |   | X | ● |

CHOICES MADE BY INDIVIDUAL (columns)
INDIVIDUAL MAKING CHOICE (rows)

X MUTUAL CHOICE
/ UNRECIPROCATED CHOICE

**Sociometric matrix**
(not the same data as on page 36)

Each individual's choices are recorded in the row allotted to him and the number of times that he was chosen is indicated in the column allotted to him. In this diagram reciprocated and unreciprocated choices are indicated by crosses and single strokes respectively.

This figure is reproduced from pp. 12-13 of <u>Theory and practice in interpersonal attraction</u> S.W. Duck (Editor) by kind permission of the publishers.
© 1977 by Academic Press: London, New York and San Francisco

possible to derive most of the above information, however. For example by adding the total number of marks in the respective <u>column</u> it is possible to ascertain how often someone was chosen by others; by totalling the marks in the respective <u>row</u> it is possible to find how often he expressed choices of others in the population. The information on 'overchosen', 'underchosen' and 'stars' can thus be obtained from a matrix as well as a sociogram but is more directly extracted in the latter case.

This brief and very selective consideration of techniques of measuring liking and choice serves to show that the research psychologist brings to this area of study a range of tools to apply to the phenomena. However, a framework for application and use of these tools is also required in order to use the tools to make decisions between competing hypotheses about the phenomena.

**Experimenting on Acquaintance**

Traditionally studies in psychology are of an experimental, laboratory-based type, for the familiar reasons that this provides the opportunity for controlled manipulation of variables and close observation of the consequent effects. This method has the advantage that it allows discovery of the direction of causality in any observed relationship between variables whilst simple establishment of the relationship cannot do so. Thus the observation that friends are often similar merely establishes a <u>correlation</u> between similarity and friendship: it cannot tell us (as an <u>experimental</u> study could) whether similarity causes friendship or friendship causes similarity.

A second advantage of the experimental method is that it allows the researcher to remove and control the influence of extraneous factors in a situation in order to establish that the relevant variable (e.g. similarity) is the one responsible for observed differences in, say, friendship level. Thus, in an experiment on the influence of a stranger's attitudes on attraction the experimenter would want to exclude the possible effects of the stranger's physical attractiveness, behavioural style, tone of voice, clothing . . . and all the other things that may otherwise influence attraction. This is not necessarily because he imagines they are unimportant: it is simply because he wants to be able to say with confidence that any influences on the subject's behaviour in this instance are the result of the stranger's attitudes, not something else. Once he has established that influence, he could go on to an experiment on the relative effects of attitudes and physical attractiveness where he controlled only the other variables listed above . . . and so on. In this way he could build up a systematic and reliable base of information about the relative weight of the contributions made by each of the factors to overall attraction score. It would thus be possible over an extended period of investigation to build up an understanding of a complex phenomenon by detailed study of its component parts.

However, it should be clear that adherence to an experimental method is not undertaken lightly, nor as an exclusive means to the achievement of the goals of systematic study even if one believes that experiment and test are an essential part of any final solution of the issues. Clearly, the experimental method is particularly likely to be criticised in the study of acquaintance on three grounds:

1. The artificiality of studying acquaintance in a laboratory;

2. The 'reduction' entailed by laboratory study will omit too much of the relevant detail of acquaintance;

3. The limits on the generalisability of results imposed by the specific studies undertaken in the laboratory ('One cannot always be sure that studies showing some effect in Lancaster will do so on a sample of Londoners let alone Americans').

These three criticisms are advanced with varying degrees of comprehension in seminars - but may all be rebutted on reflection. First, people are not always clear what they mean by 'artificiality'. It is an easy - too easy - criticism to make of laboratory studies and, if true, is fatal; but it is usually made clumsily and without cogency. Duck (1973b) has identified two sorts of artificiality in this context:

1. Laboratory studies may disrupt normal behaviour in some

way (e.g. they may make subjects apprehensive);

2. Laboratory studies may leave normal behaviour relatively unaffected and yet accentuate behaviour which is essentially irrelevant to the topic being studied - so that the researcher may be unwittingly focussed on behaviour that is essentially unrepresentative of what he seeks to study (e.g. experiments may present subjects with questions they do not normally ask themselves in connection with a particular phenomenon - as in the example on affability and physical attractiveness above, p. 29 - or studies may intend to measure liking and actually measure the subject's skill at seeing through an experimental deception).

The first type of artificiality is a familiar part of discourses on experimental design (e.g. Aronson and Carlsmith, 1968). One way to meet this problem is found in the many subtle and elaborate attempts that are made to ensure that subjects are not aware that they are in an experiment at all. For example, Walster, Walster, Piliavin and Schmidt (1973) measured clients' liking for prostitutes by recording how soon and how often they returned after being told about the prostitute's habitual method of selecting clients. Other solutions involve the abandonment of experimental methods altogether and useful work has been done with interviews or role-play studies (e.g. Kleinke, Meeker and Fong, 1974, who studied subjects who were pretending to be engaged couples). Whilst such work provides useful information from time to time it is a supplement to experimental work rather than a satisfactory alternative. Yet it must be conceded that subjects are nonetheless affected in some way when they enter the laboratory - but it simply does not matter in one sense. Whilst every care needs to be taken for the welfare of experimental subjects, any disruption of normal behaviour can influence the interpretation of the experimental results if and only if the disruption is relevant to the variable being studied. Some disruptions or artificiality are as irrelevant as the fact that the subject may have a pimple on his nose. The disruption of normal behaviour becomes important only in relation to the second type of artificiality, i.e. when differences of behaviour attack those processes that are relevant to the topic under study.

The second criticism of laboratory study of acquaintance (that the 'reduction' entailed by laboratory study omits too much) is not a true criticism of studies of acquaintance so much as a limit on their generality. In other words, the criticism that some important aspect had been omitted or neglected would not undermine the study of acquaintance so much as it would point to a new aspect of study or an extra avenue for further research. Too often (as will be argued in subsequent chapters) an interest in certain specific aspects of interpersonal attraction (e.g. concentration on antecedents of attraction) has led a variety of experimenters to ignore aspects of human encounters which have cogency and force in real life. Thus concentration on the influence of first impressions of others, has led to emphasis on impressions formed directly by the subject on the basis of written evidence, whereas in real life a major source of information about potential acquaintances comes from mutual friends: person A may describe person B to person C before B and C meet. Since the gap is so great between the way such information is received in real life and in experiments it remains to be seen whether the psychological principle underlying operation with such information is the same in both cases.

The third criticism of laboratory study (that it limits the generality of results) is true but uninteresting. The study of students at a particular campus is an important limit on the generality of the findings if and only if these subjects differ in some crucially relevant respect from people elsewhere. Otherwise the criticism is as interesting as the complaint that by killing subjects with arsenic from a drinking glass we have not tested the effects of arsenic from plastic beakers. For the same reason, the criticism that psychology knows too much about college sophomores and too little about anyone else is relevant and important if and only if it can be shown that sophomores differ from the rest of the population in some essentially germane manner (e.g. because they process the stimuli differently).

A more sophisticated form of this complaint is the claim that the features of the laboratory study of acquaintance limit the generality of the observed relationship in the same sense that altitude limits the generality of the relationship between temperature and the point at which water turns to steam (Byrne and Lamberth, 1971). Truly, each specific example of an empirical relationship may be different from every other in some trivial sense. The important thing is not to be constrained by this inevitable fact but to take the broader view and see the extent to which a general principle is established or indicated by the combined findings of several investigators in different experimental settings.

All of these discussions and the consideration of the three complaints about laboratory work should not detract from the agreements which exist between researchers about the ultimate goals of a systematic study of acquaintance nor should they disguise the essentially positive side of the quest. However, acceptance of these general aims and purposes does not commit every worker to the <u>same kind</u> of experimental approach and the variety of work reflects this. There are many different facets of the concepts, many dimensions of the problem that need to be fully examined and the ingenuity of researchers has been such that different investigators concentrate on different phenomena and on different ways of exploring the relationships between them whilst still having the same ultimate goal: the lawful explanation of acquaintance.

# CHAPTER TWO

## SOME THEORIES OF INTERPERSONAL ATTRACTION

The lawful explanation of acquaintance or any other behaviour cannot be achieved merely by means of definitions, tools and methods of enquiry alone - any more than it can be achieved without them. These paraphernalia are useful only in the context of theories to explain the phenomena and the theories are useful only when tested out and compared empirically using tools like those outlined in the previous chapter. Common sense 'theories' have already been shown to be chaotic and undisciplined on the one hand, and to be poor yielders of testable propositions on the other. Appropriate and useful theoretical superstructures for explaining acquaintance will need the characteristics of coherence and discipline as well as the ability to yield specific hypotheses and to be translated into suitable operational form for testing the propositions which can be derived.

Fortunately, psychology has many such theoretical superstructures which represent coherent frameworks for interpreting behaviour and explaining its antecedents. In most cases they have been erected as explanations of behaviour as a whole (not just human behaviour and far less human social behaviour) and therefore they do not refer specifically to acquaintance phenomena and indeed may previously have been used most often to explain, say, rat maze behaviour or attitude change or clinical phenomena. However, their usefulness as general explanations for all behaviour may in part be assessed by the adequacy of the predictions that can be derived specifically to apply to behaviour like interpersonal attraction. Therefore several specific approaches have been derived from these general theories (e.g. Psychoanalytic Theory or Learning Theory) to apply to the narrower aspects of behaviour (e.g. social behaviour) and hence to acquaintance, attraction or marital selection.

In the context of acquaintance the explanations of behaviour can be divided into three sets:

1. Those concerned with general reasons why any form of association should occur at all;

2. Those explaining specific selections of associates either

   (a) on the basis of rewards; or

   (b) on the basis of cognitive factors.

   (These latter two sets of explanatory principles need not be mutually exclusive in all cases but it is most convenient to subdivide this way.)

3. Those concerned to explain not the basis for original selection of specific associates but the development of relationships, once the selections have been made. (Again, some of the theories use explanatory principles common to theories in Section 2 of this schema.)

As we proceed, through the rest of this book, to examine evidence relevant to these general approaches and the various aspects of acquaintance, it is important to keep in mind the differences between the three types of emphasis and the inherent difficulties of extrapolating from one of them to another. For example, without some direct explanation of how individual selection or initial attraction transmutes itself into a developed relationship, we cannot assume that the two phenomena are necessarily caused in the same ways. This book sets out to show, however, the ways in which this theoretical integration may be achieved.

# Explaining Affiliation: Why Does Association Occur At All?

As indicated in the Introduction, one set of theoretical principles for explaining social behaviour derives from work on animals. 'Animals' is a term covering many varieties of organism and it is clear that the reasons for association in one species may be unrelated to the reasons that obtain in another case. Equally, extrapolations from 'animal' explanations to 'human' explanations must be looked upon with care.

Wynne-Edwards (1962) has argued that the elementary forms of social behaviour have evolved in the service of homeostasis (that is, as a means of attaining ideal numbers and dispersion, such that as crises threaten or food becomes scarcer or habitats lose their value, so the population decreases or disperses, whereas in times of tranquillity and abundance the numbers increase and tend to concentrate). Whereas some animals achieve this by means of relatively simple processes (laying fewer/more eggs; turning to cannibalism) humans have more complex systems involving birth control or tax concessions for children; immigration or emigration; warfare and slavery. By use of such mechanisms, associations, groups and societies are formed and maintained. Clearly this explanation of association may apply in this limited way to human association, but, if it does, it is more likely to have explained the origin of tribal and national distributions over the earth in the (primeval) past than to account for associations between given pairs of individuals nowadays. However, the proposition may relate to or explain satisfaction with certain aspects of relationships even now, as noted before in connection with work on 'hot and crowded' conditions of interaction (page 4).

A different 'animal' explanation for the origin of social interaction is proposed by Tiger and Fox (1972)! These authors concentrate less on the distribution of food or resources and more on the aggressive or defensive functions served by association with others. Just as wolves hunt in packs and chaffinches 'mob' sparrowhawks, so, too, these authors argue, the evolutionary origin of human friendship may be traced back to needs to aggress or defend. However, as with the other suggestion cited above, such explanations of association appear to be more directly appropriate to evolutionary and historical discussion - although one could use them as analogical or metaphorical guides towards illuminating some of the principles that precipitate certain forms of behaviour, or indicate the origins of present rituals (e.g. behavioural use of space to indicate status; aggressive responses to intrusion into personal space; behaviour in crowds).

Although animals may group together for the various possible reasons offered above this does not, of itself, suggest that there will be 'friendly' behaviour within the group at times when there is no need to co-operate on mutual defensive or hunting/aggressive tasks. However, co-operative and affiliative behaviour will clearly, in certain circumstances, be beneficial to the species. For example, dependent animals like infant monkeys will need to be looked after by their parents until they are mature enough to look after themselves and one would expect that affiliative or nurturant behaviour would be a necessary aspect of that species' behaviour. Similarly, in species with a long gestation period the males may be 'required' to protect gravid females from attack by predators when their pregnancy makes them less mobile or agile. In studies of rhesus monkeys, Harlow and Harlow (1965) have shown how experiences during a monkey's infancy can create or destroy his socialising, co-operative or affiliative/sexual behaviour in adulthood and it appears that co-operation with other members of the species is, to some extent, a reflection of early experience in infancy. Affiliative behaviour in adult monkeys may thus be due in part to the relationship between infant and mother earlier in life. Again, it could be claimed that similar needs and requirements induce social responses in adult humans and that such dependency influences or promotes affiliative behaviour. In Chapter 3 we shall consider work completed on human affiliation.

These explanations of the origins and causes of desires to affiliate are a useful and provocative background against which to study acquaintance. They alert one to the possibility that individuals' selective choices of associates are in part influenced by their personality predispositions, such that one personality will find that certain properties of the Other person satisfy his pre-existing needs whilst the same properties of the same Other do nothing for a second person's needs. The explanation of specific instances of liking and relationship can thus be undertaken only against this backcloth (see next chapter).

# Explaining Specific Selective Choice and Liking

Although psychoanalytic explanations of liking and choice have made little impact on most aspects of the interpersonal attraction literature, Freud (1914) did advance an explanation for the specific choices made by individuals and some of the notions contained in this explanation have been examined by other investigators from markedly different theoretical backgrounds. Freud argued that individuals possess two sexual objects: the Self and the parent who tends and cares for the Self. With age, Freud argues, these two divide and lead the person to seek two sources and two sorts of affection. One kind of love ('anaclitic love') is essentially provoked by a search for a substitute parent and could be described as 'dependency love': that is, a love that is satisfied in the man by finding a caring, succouring woman, and in the woman by finding a man who protects, so Freud argues. The second kind of love ('narcissistic love') is provoked by a search for the other love object: Self. An individual motivated in this way chooses friends or partners who reflect what his own Self is, or what it was, or what he would like it to be. This latter proposition is one that has been investigated by many workers (see Chapter 6) - but for essentially different reasons from those offered by Freud. For example, search for partners who are similar to Self can be explained in a number of other ways (similarity is reinforcing in itself; similarity is reinforcing because it provides a good basis for assuming positive outcomes in subsequent interactions; similarity makes communication easier; similarity 'justifies' the Self), as can search for someone who is like an individual's Ideal Self (such a person would have properties that Self desires but lacks and would thus complement Self; such a person would be more likable than real Self). In short, Freud's proposal here is not uniquely derivable from his theory and observation of the predicted phenomenon does not therefore uniquely confirm his view of love: rather it invites the researcher to test amongst different explanations for the phenomenon. Furthermore, Santee (1976) has shown that attitudes about one's own behaviour are essentially different from attitudes about other people's behaviour and the nature of the relationship between one's own Ideal Self and the actual self of another person may be somewhat more complex than initially proposed (see Chapter 6). Furthermore, the familiar difficulty of specifying from Freud's views the exact nature of the observable events that would confirm his theory against all others is, therefore, one of the contributory reasons why workers have looked elsewhere for explanations of specific instances of liking.

Rewards and Liking

One place where workers have looked for such explanations is in the enormous literature about Learning processes. Derived primarily from the body of work carried out on animals since the start of this century, Learning Theories and associated derivative perspectives focus on the notions of reinforcement (reward and punishment) in describing behaviour and explaining its origins. The emphasis of such theories thus falls largely upon the features of a situation or stimulus which evoke responses in the perceiving organism rather than upon the enduring characteristics of the perceiving organism itself (e.g. its personality traits). In the context of interpersonal attraction the emphasis thus falls heavily upon the properties of the stimulus person that make him attractive rather than on the activities in the perceiver which define his attractedness.

**Classical conditioning**   Classical conditioning explanations for Liking behaviour, derived from Pavlov's work with dogs, has - as Chapter 5 will consider - proved to be a fruitful framework for studying attraction. At first sight there is no obvious connection between salivating dogs and dinnerbells on the one hand and attraction to strangers on the other. However, Byrne (1969; 1971) and Clore and Byrne (1974) have clarified the ways in which the initial dismissal of the connection is superficial. The basic principles of this approach are given here in a general way, whilst the specific development of the empirical base for the theory is given in more detail in Chapter 5.

The basic terms and theoretical apparatus of the classical conditioning position are as follows. In the natural course of events, the organism makes certain Unconditioned Responses (UCR) to objects or situations that it encounters (Unconditioned Stimuli - UCS) and finds reinforcing (rewarding or punishing). Thus a dog may salivate (UCR) when it sets its eyes on a plate of meat (UCS), which will reinforce by providing pleasant food, or a person may blink his eye (UCR) when a puff of air is directed at it (UCS) which will reinforce by providing aversive pain. Pavlov's innovatory discovery was that if a UCR becomes associated with an essentially irrelevant stimulus often enough (e.g. if the dog hears a dinner bell just before the plate of meat appears, or if a light is flashed first when the puff of air is aimed at a person's eye) then the organism begins to react to the irrelevant stimulus in unnatural ways (i.e. salivating when the bell rings; blinking the eye when the light is flashed). Since the latter responses are conditional upon the association of the UCR with the irrelevant stimulus, the term 'conditioning' came to be used to describe the process, and the terms Conditioned Stimulus (CS) and Conditioned Response (CR) to describe the 'irrelevant' stimulus and the response it now evokes. The essential feature of the classical conditioning model is precisely the association of two otherwise unconnected events (UCS and CS) to produce a response (CR) to one of the events (CS) which is, truly, more appropriately a response to the other (UCS).

In the context of work on attraction (and, in case readers have forgotten the special sense of this term here, this refers to initial liking/disliking responses expressed about perfect strangers) the classical conditioning model is developed by Byrne to use the terms in the following ways. In a way analogous to that described above, it happens that certain interpersonal events are reinforcing or punishing - UCS - (e.g. being complimented by someone or being given low ratings on a test). Such events, in the natural course of things, evoke affective responses, feelings, emotional reactions (UCR). Certain essentially irrelevant cues (i.e. irrelevant to the response - they were not what caused it directly) are association with the UCS-UCR relationship (e.g. the person giving the compliment or the low rating - note that it was the compliment or the rating itself that originally evoked the UCR). Accordingly this person becomes associated with the affective response (UCR) and becomes a conditioned stimulus (CS), such that affective responses (CR) are now evoked by the person himself rather than by the compliments or the low ratings that he gives. These CRs are most often manifested in the form of the evaluative behaviour that we call liking or disliking. To echo the final sentence of the preceding paragraph, Clore and Byrne (1974, p.146) state: 'we maintain that people's positive and negative feelings spread from one stimulus to another by association'.

The classical conditioning model of behaviour is not, then, irrelevant to interpersonal attraction as it may seem at first sight. But how far has it been possible to employ experiments to establish the general validity of its proposals in the context of interpersonal attraction? It has been found possible, for example, to use classical conditioning to create associations in subjects' minds between positive/negative creativity ratings and their own evaluations of the experimenter, his apparatus and assistants (Griffitt and Guay, 1969); between positive/negative affect and individuals' first names (Geen and Stonner, 1974); and between rewarding experiences and others who were present at the time simply as observers (Lott and Lott, 1960). Such findings, and many others, indicate the prima facie utility of a classical conditioning approach to interpersonal attraction. One particular advantage that it imports is a large network of concepts and a large body of empirical work which has established the links between concepts in a variety of situations. Although its application in the context of attraction will necessitate the selection of those aspects which have primary relevance rather than the acceptance of the whole body of work lock, stock and barrel, this established theoretical coherence will prove useful all the same.

Perhaps, some readers feel uneasy at this stage that such an approach to liking and to warm personal relationships is too mechanistic, too 'decorticate' a view of man, too visceral in its emphases. Such feelings may be misguided, since there is no reason to maintain that all the associations which occur between stimuli are simple, simpleminded or low level. Nor need the cues which evoke the associations be low grade either. Everyday experience tells us that associations can occur between images, thoughts or recollections - and this can involve a person in many levels of cognitive activity. The very processes of extracting reinforcement or attending to relevant cues or establishing 'the association', may be extremely complex thought processes. There is no need to assume that man is an unthinking puppet just because one takes the view that he responds positively to reinforcement. The intention of this approach is to show <u>how</u> reinforcement may influence attraction rather than simply to show that it does; and <u>how</u> people can come to be attractive rather than just ways <u>in</u> which they are. Thus it is an attempt to explain the <u>origins</u> of the evaluations that characteristics of individuals can be 'good', 'bad', 'likable' or 'unlikable'.

**Exchange theories** Another family of theories of behaviour that has at its roots some hedonistic or 'pleasure' principle is known as Exchange Theory and derives from work by Thibaut and Kelley (1959), Homans (1961) and Blau (1964). It is based upon an economic principle imported into psychology: that people engage in social behaviour in order to maximise profit by achieving the most favourable ratio of rewards to costs. In this context <u>rewards</u> are anything that a person receives - or any activity directed towards him - that is defined by the person as valuable; <u>costs</u> are activities or receipts which are punishing or which involve him in forgoing a possible reward. The <u>profit</u> of a relationship is assessed by subtracting the costs from the rewards.

With this or a similar basic terminology, several theories have been developed to explain or account for social behaviour (La Gaipa, 1977a) and whilst these accounts include the explanation of interpersonal attraction, their primary concern is more general. Thus Homans' (1961) economic model is an attempt to formulate the ways in which individuals in any social encounter (bargaining, decision-making, liking) assess whether the rewards received from a situation are favourable to themselves in the light of costs incurred. An individual has an implicit notion of whether he is getting a 'fair deal' in an interaction and will tend to select those other individuals, situations or behaviours which will attain such an outcome. Adams (1965) proposed a variant of this view in an Equity Theory which concerned the extent to which the <u>individual's perception</u> of his contributions and outcomes corresponds to the perception held by others. In cases where the individual perceives inequity (i.e. perceives that, relative to another person, the amounts received by him are disproportionate to amounts put in) then he will try to resolve the inequity in one of several ways (ranging from a change of input to withdrawal from the encounter). Thibaut and Kelley (1959) developed a similar notion in terms of 'comparison level'. An actor's comparison level (CL) is defined as the minimum level of positive outcomes which he feels he deserves based on his past history and present situation. His Comparison Level for Alternatives ($CL_{alt}$) is his perception of the outcomes in his immediate situation compared with possible outcomes in alternative relationships. A person's CL represents his attraction to the relationship whilst his $CL_{alt}$ represents his dependency upon it.

Whilst there are several versions of exchange theories not covered here (see La Gaipa, 1977a) there are two which are particularly relevant in the context of interpersonal attraction. Resource Theory (Foa and Foa, 1971) represents an attempt to differentiate the classes of reward which are relevant to relationships and thus an attempt to define the content of relationships. The six different resource classes are: love, status, information, goods, services and money. In some relationships individuals will exchange only goods, in some only love: the appropriateness of the items exchanged will also vary and, to some extent, defines the nature of the relationship. Thus a relationship where one party offers love in exchange for money is clearly different from one where love is exchanged for love. Incremental Exchange Theory (Huesman and Levinger, 1976) is an attempt to employ exchange notions to explain the growth of relationships. One assumption here is that individuals expect higher payoffs in interpersonal rewards as the depth of the relationship increases; a second assumption is that the growth of relationships can be viewed as a sequential movement from one matrix or expectation of outcomes to another (La Gaipa, 1977a).

The theories that are known as Exchange Theories are thus focussed both on reward and on the perceptions of individuals involved. As such they form a link between reinforcement theories and theories concerning cognition, perception or thought processes.

Cognitive Factors in Liking

There are several ways in which cognition and liking relate: for one thing my cognition predisposes me to like some things and not others (see Chapter 3); again my processes of cognising are my information processing systems and thus influence the way in which I go about processing information to deduce the likability of things (e.g. by summing or averaging everything I know about it); furthermore, cognition and the reinforcement principles outlined earlier are not necessarily incompatible: not only can certain cognitions, thoughts, etc. be rewarding, but also the association between ideas can follow reinforcement principles. However, the main interest in cognition and liking at this point in the book follows other lines. There are various explanations of Liking which concern the importance for an individual of the relationship between his cognitive structure and his acquaintance's cognition (e.g. whether they share similar attitudes, agree about other people, like the same things). Other views emphasise the importance for the individual of the assessment and evaluation of his own cognition and its utility (e.g. in evaluating his opinions or abilities). Yet others concern the kinds of activities proceeding 'inside' an individual's cognition when he is attracted (i.e. the information-processing mechanisms that he employs in order to arrive at judgements about the other person and his attractiveness).

Clearly, therefore, there is a wide range of theoretical activity gathered together into this section, not all of it concerned with precisely the same things (and therefore not all competing to explain precisely the same phenomena). It is occasionally necessary to remind oneself of this during the subsequent discussion, and one should also bear in mind the degree to which these explanations may conflict with or complement those already outlined.

**Balance Theory**  Balance theory was first espoused by Heider (1958) and deals with the attitudes of person (P) towards another person (O) in the light of their two attitudes about an object or entity (X), e.g. P likes O; P likes X; O dislikes X. These three items are referred to as P-O-X triads. Heider was concerned to examine the presumed psychological preference for 'balance' (pleasant, stable, satisfying) over 'imbalance' (uncomfortable, unstable, unsatisfying). For Heider, a triad is balanced either when the relations between P-O-X are all positive (i.e. P likes O; P likes X; O likes X) or when two are negative and one positive (e.g. P dislikes O; P dislikes X; O likes X). In either of these cases the individuals will not desire change and will let the relations between P-O-X stay as they are. Imbalance occurs when two relations are positive and one negative (e.g. P likes O; P likes X; O dislikes X) and in this case there will be a tendency to change one of the relationships, a strain towards balance (either P comes to dislike O; or P comes to dislike X; or O comes to like X). When all three relations are negative then Heider was unsure whether balance or imbalance obtains, but this is usually treated as imbalanced and the general rule is to work out the algebraic product of the three relations, taking a positive product as indicative of balance and a negative product as indicating imbalance.

This theory can clearly be applied in several fields of psychology, most obviously in attitude change research as an explanation of tendencies to alter opinions and in interpersonal attraction research as an explanation of factors underlying liking and disliking. Here it predicts that agreement about an issue (P likes X and O likes X; or else P dislikes X and O dislikes X) will produce a strain towards balance with, in both cases, P ending up liking O to complete the triad in a balanced way. In one form or another, balance theory has played a part in much research on interpersonal attraction, as shall be seen, but even as briefly outlined above it will be clear to the reader that its original statement involves some difficulties. Why, for example, should we assume that the jealous husband (P) will feel balance if his friend (O) takes a fancy to his wife (X)? Secondly, what about the <u>intensity</u> of the emotion that is felt and its subjective importance not just its sign (positive or negative)? Blumberg (1969) considered the problem of how pleasant or unpleasant it is to be liked more (less) by someone that the person himself likes at varying levels. He found that subjects were happiest when their friends liked them and their enemies disliked them. However subjects also preferred there to be as little asymmetry as possible (i.e. they did not like to be liked 'too much' - even if this entailed being less well liked by a friend). A further problem was identified by Curry and Emerson (1970). They argue that individuals try to create impressions or to project images in interactions and when the image 'received' by the partner is the one they intended to project, then individuals have been effective - but they have been successful only if this image is evaluated favourably. When, in that case, is the interaction triad balanced? When P and O both like X (viz: P's image) or when P and O both like the true P?

Miller and Norman (1976) had subjects rate some hypothetical P-O-X situations involving two persons and an unspecified but important 'thing' for pleasantness and tension and consistency in an attempt to identify what balance meant to observers. The situations varied in the amount of liking that P and O had for each other and in the extent of the agreement/disagreement between them about X. In some cases P and O were described as having to continue to interact subsequently and in some cases not. The results indicated that subjects' ratings of identical situations were different in the two cases and suggested that rating depended on both the preference measures (pleasantness, tension or consistency) and the characteristics of the hypothetical situations being rated, not simply the P-O-X relations themselves.

Newcomb (1971), another balance theorist, has argued that some types of balanced relationship are, in any case, more/less stable than others. In conditions of negative P-O relationships there are other forces than those towards balance which surround the interaction (e.g. a low degree of engagement or interaction is likely with a disliked other). Equally there are some circumstances where a triad may be balanced in some respect and not in another (e.g. two suitors for the same girl may admire each other's qualities and respect her judgement that the qualities are admirable and yet may see each other in terms of competition). Thus many attraction situations are complicated by the fact that a number of role relationships may exist simultaneously, some of which may be balanced and some not. In some cases (especially competitive relationships) it could be argued that imbalance is actually more attractive than balance and that discrepancies rather than similarities will be sought.

**Congruency** A similar and yet subtly different approach from that above is the congruency notion of Backman and Secord (1959; 1962; Secord and Backman, 1961). Whereas balance theories place their emphasis on the means by which an individual achieves satisfying consistency among his opinions or beliefs, etc., congruency theory argues that individuals shape their interactions in order to maintain and maximise congruency between three particular components involved in the interaction: the subject's self-concept; his interpretation of those aspects of his behaviour that are relevant to self-concept; his perception of the behaviours of the other person that are related to this. Thus, if the person (P) holds a particular view of himself and behaves in a manner which he feels reflects that, then he will like the other person (O) if O attributes the same trait to P as P himself does. Individuals would choose to associate with those who appear to be congruent in this way; would evaluate the O favourably or unfavourably as a function of the degree of congruency; and may even misperceive O in order to (re)establish congruency.

Backman and Secord (1962) reported an experiment finding that liked persons, to a greater extent than disliked persons, are perceived by an individual as attributing to him traits similar to those he attributes to himself. Equally, Touhey (1975) has shown that congruency was more important than other forms of similarity (e.g. attitude similarity) and argues that processes of establishing interpersonal congruency are the influences which stabilise developing relationships. In other words, in contrast to balance theorists' emphasis on general agreement about attitudes, congruency theorists specify that particular agreement about three specific components of the interactional matrix will be most important to the individuals involved and emphasise that the locus for stability and change in the individuals' behaviour is in the interaction process itself rather than in the intraindividual or personality structures of the participants.

**Social Comparison Theory**  Just as congruency and balance models emphasise the correspondence between two individuals' cognitions about people or events, so Festinger's (1954) Social Comparison Theory emphasises the importance for an individual of assessing the degree to which others share or accept his view of the world. For Festinger this search is carried on because it serves for the individual the functions of allowing him to evaluate his own opinions, beliefs or attitudes - and hence to test out their usefulness or their strengths and weaknesses relative to those of other people.

Festinger (1954) pointed out that there are certain things that an individual can find out in this world without the help of others: e.g. he can feel that lead is heavy; he can see for himself that glass is transparent; he can smash glass to establish that it is brittle. Similarly when it comes to certain aspects of his own performance, he needs no others to help him assess his ability: e.g. if he wishes to see if he can run a mile in under four minutes he needs only a mile and a watch; if he wishes to discover how far he can jump, then all he needs are some markers and a ruler. However, if he wants to assess whether he is a good athlete, the individual can do so only by comparing himself with the performance of other people (e.g. comparing his time for running a mile with others' times over the same distance). But particularly in those cases where an individual is concerned to form opinions about the world, there is hardly any other way in which he can evaluate himself except by comparing his own views with other persons' views. Thus, if he thinks 'Might is Right', he can assess that view by comparing it to the views of others on that question: if they agree, at least it suggests that the view is an acceptable one whereas if they do not, this very fact casts doubt on the validity of the person's opinion. For Festinger, therefore, it seemed plausible that individuals would seek to evaluate their opinions by comparing them with other people's and would regard the opinions as validated to the extent that other people agreed with them. This notion is referred to as 'consensual validation', i.e. confirmation of the validity of an opinion by the consensus of other people.

This theory has many levels of application to the explanation of social interaction and personal relationships (Duck, 1973b). In particular there is a good deal of evidence that people do seek out opportunities for comparing themselves to other people in a variety of ways on a variety of dimensions (Wheeler, 1974) and do exhibit Liking when they encounter similar others. However, it is possible to evaluate oneself by comparison not only with similar but also with dissimilar others, so why are similar ones preferred? Jones and Regan (1974) attempted to distinguish between the need for accurate self-evaluation (achieved by comparison with similar Others) and the pleasure associated with esteem enhancing self-validation (achieved primarily by comparison with dissimilar others who are 'worse' than oneself). An experiment on ability testing (rather than opinion evaluation) enabled these authors to conclude that individuals like to 'locate themselves on the scale' first (i.e. to find out roughly how they compare with everyone else) before making precise judgements about ability level and its implications for their future behaviour. Comparison with similar others rather than dissimilar ones gives people more information about these implications since they can say to themselves: 'We are similar; therefore what has happened to him probably will also happen to me'. In this book it will be argued that they also say 'We have similar abilities; therefore we probably also have many other similarities and will probably get along well'. As such, this represents a belief about as yet unobservable aspects of the other person - a belief resting on the information that one has about him.

**Information integration**   The previous theories reported in this section have concentrated largely on the interaction between two minds: the next two approaches concern primarily the activity proceeding in one mind when it makes decisions, inferences or attributions about the other person.

Anderson's (1968) information integration model concerns the way in which an individual's information about another person determines his liking for that person.   If the information is generally positive then the person will like the other person and if it is generally negative he will dislike the other person. For Anderson, evaluative judgements about persons or events are reached (and can be completely understood) by means of or in terms of the information that an individual has about something or someone.   In the case of research on interpersonal attraction, such information is usually provided in the form of adjectival descriptions of personality traits (see Chapter 5).   By means of an extended enquiry into the evaluative loadings associated with certain adjectives, Anderson (1968) was able to establish the numerical value that best represents a population's assessment of the value (evaluation) of each item.   Thus the average desirability ratings of 555 adjectives were obtained.   The question for research then becomes one of determining the rule by which people arrive at overall judgements about a person or event when presented with several pieces of information concerning that object or person (e.g. that he is an intelligent, warm, practical, rapist). Do they add it all together, taking account of the sign (positive or negative) that indicates liked or disliked characteristics? Do they average it?   Anderson's (1970) theory suggests a weighted averaging model whereby the scale values of each item of information are modified by its subjective importance (weight) to the person integrating the information, and an overall assessment is thus reached.   Further developments of this basic approach are discussed by Anderson (1970) and Ajzen (1977).

This model could be described as a mechanistic model (Ajzen, 1977) in the sense that it suggests a relatively predictable combination rule based simply on the information provided. In contrast, a constructive model (Ajzen, 1974; 1977) presumes that the evaluations that derive from this process stem not from a mechanistic process but the constructive inferential processes of the observer. In other words, an individual <u>forms</u>

beliefs about the stimulus person on the basis of what he is told. These beliefs comprise not only an estimate of the probability that the information is true (e.g. if he is described as 'reliable' this may be taken to mean that there is an 80% chance he is reliable) but also a set of inferences about what other attributes he may have (e.g. a reliable person may be perceived to be also conscientious, intelligent and considerate). In Ajzen's view, the subsequent evaluation of the stimulus person is determined by the subjective probabilities that the person has certain attributes (whether directly observable or inferred) and the value of these attributes themselves in the eyes of the evaluator.

Further discussions of these approaches will be given in Chapter 5. For the present it should be noted that these models pinpoint two important features of interpersonal attraction activity. First, that individuals process information according to certain rules; second, that information has different weights and values that are determined both by cultural factors and by their significance to individuals. It will be argued later that these processes can apply to several aspects of acquaintance and that the information so processed can be of many types (not just the information about personality traits to which these models usually refer). Readers will be able to judge for themselves whether this approach is compatible or incompatible with other models reported in this chapter.

**Attribution processes** Information integration theories are concerned primarily with the mechanics by which individuals piece together items of information: attribution theories are concerned primarily with the ways in which an individual explains his social environment - particularly with the ways in which he searches out information that will indicate the causes of what he observes. Thus, rather than being concerned with the informational qualities of observations, the attributional literature is concerned with the inferences and deductions that they provoke. Its particular concern is whether, and in what circumstances, an individual uses primarily personal explanations for events (i.e. says they resulted from the personal characteristics of the actor involved) or impersonal explanations (i.e. says they were caused by situational or other factors impinging upon and influencing the actor).

Again, this is a general approach to explanation of several aspects of social behaviour, but it can be seen to have relevance to interpersonal attraction research both directly and indirectly. For example, an individual's attributions concerning an actor's personal responsibility for an event may influence his liking for that person (e.g. Dutton, 1973, showed that individuals who attributed their own persuasiveness to the content or form of the argument they had constructed were attracted to members of the audience who changed their attitude). Conversely, his liking for a person may influence his attributions about another person's responsibility (e.g. Regan, Straus and Fazio, 1974, found that the good behaviour of liked persons was thought to be caused by the internal characteristics of the actors, whilst the good behaviour of disliked others was attributed to external causes like chance or situational factors).

Heider (1958) was the person who first noted the importance of attribution processes in social behaviour. He was concerned to identify the ways in which individuals search for the causes of behaviour when activated by an inability to explain it immediately. He distinguished several levels of responsibility which could link an actor and an event (each progressively more particular in its focus):

1. Association (in this sense we are all responsible for the war in Vietnam, since it occurred during our lifetime);

2. Commission (in this sense of responsibility an individual can be held accountable for things he has actually done - or failed to do - personally);

3. Foresight (in this sense an individual is responsible for those of his acts - or omissions - whose consequences he could have foreseen);

4. Intention (in this sense an individual would be held responsible for those of his acts whose foreseeable consequences he actually intended);

5. Justification (in this sense an observer might hold an individual responsible for those of his foreseen and intended acts which were not justifiable solely on the grounds of external or situational factors - i.e. they

originated from the individual himself rather than from compulsion by others, for example).

The main interest of attraction studies (and attribution as a whole, Eiser, 1976) clearly centres upon the latter three types of responsibility that may be attributed to an individual.

Jones and Davis (1965) attempted to explain how observers made such attributions and they drew upon the 'actor dispositional' model as a means by which individuals are able to observe flux in behaviour yet make inferences about underlying stable structure or dispositions. Since actions have consequences, the observation of an action leads the observer to make certain assumptions about the actor's knowledge and ability, which in turn leads to assessments of his intention, which leads to assessments of his disposition, which amounts to an impression of his stable personality characteristics. Thus from the observation of a single act or a series of different acts, an observer may make inferences about enduring dispositions. According to Jones and Davis's (1965) model of 'correspondent inferences' observers assess the disposition lying behind an act in terms of the context in which it occurs, in the light of the alternative possibilities open to the individual, and the extent to which he chooses to do the same kind of thing that other people would do in similar circumstances. The inference about underlying disposition is likely to correspond to the behaviour it explains or to be a good explanation of the behaviour in so far as the judged position of the actor on the attribute departs from the position of the average person on that attribute. In other words, if the actor does something which differs markedly from what other people would normally be expected to do, then his action probably reflects his personality characteristics.

Taking this a little further, Kelley (1967) argued that individuals use several criteria for deciding whether an act was due to dispositional or situational factors - not simply attending to whether everyone else would be likely to have acted similarly. These criteria are: <u>Consensus</u> (i.e. the amount of agreement about behaviour that others would show in the circumstances - Does everyone act in the same way towards this situation?); <u>Consistency</u> (i.e. the extent to which the person acts in a given way most of the time - Does he always respond this way to this situation?) and <u>Distinctiveness</u> (i.e. the person's discriminations between situations - Does he respond like this to situation A but respond slightly differently to the similar situation B?). Where a behaviour is seen to have Low Consensus, High Consistency and Low Distinctiveness it is, so Kelley argues, attributable to internal causes. When it has High Consensus, High Consistency and High Distinctiveness it is attributable to external, situational causes. When it manifests Low Consensus, Low Consistency and High Distinctiveness it is probably attributable to transient causes. By use of these criteria, Kelley argues, individuals assess the extent to which a person can be seen as responsible for his acts and therefore the extent to which he may be praised or blamed, like or disliked for them.

Just as the attractiveness of another person may depend upon how the observer interprets his responsibility for given events, so too the actor's own interpretation of events may be attractive or unattractive in its own right. For example, individuals may appear to take too much credit for some act which may seem to an outsider to have been an accident. Such a claim by the Actor may be thought unattractive. As a rule, however, it appears that individuals tend to explain their own behaviour in terms of 'external' or situational factors, but to explain the behaviour of others in terms of 'internal' factors, like personality characteristics or moods (Jones and Nisbett, 1971). In the context of attraction this clearly suggests that individuals go about their daily lives attributing other people's behaviour to personality characteristics - which of course could themselves be attractive or unattractive characteristics, just as can the acts which give rise to the attributions themselves.

Such theories present the possibility of forging links between attempts to explain individual instances of Liking on the one hand and efforts to explain the continuance and development of acquaintance on the other. The importance of attributions or inferences for any model of developing acquaintance lies in the fact that beliefs about the future itself or about the future rewardingness of an interaction/interactant or about future discoveries concerning the other person constitute the only reasonable basis for the desire to continue the relationship in cases where the individual has a choice in the matter. Attribution theories thus provide a useful link between this section (explaining specific selective choice) and the broader section that follows (on explaining how relationships develop and proceed once they are initiated) because they involve such guessing processes about what the other person is like, deep down.

## Explaining Development In Relationships

Under a crude heading of 'developmental' aspects of acquaintance there are three forms of phenomena, some aspects of which do not concern us at this stage. For example, 'developmental' is not used here in the sense of 'child development' and the way in which an individual's psychological or ontological development is related to his acquaintance behaviour. This is an important issue (how children form friendships and whether children and adults form relationships differently) but it is a complex one that is most appropriately discussed in Chapter 7. The discussion here concerns the ways in which the development of a relationship may be mapped - e.g. the behaviour that people use, their feelings, their thoughts as they form, nurture and disengage from social relationships - or else the ways in which individuals drift from one level of relationship to another in a 'passive' way (McCarthy, 1976). Equally we are concerned here with the principles by which individuals decide that they want to continue and extend their relationship with someone else and the processes involved in these decisions.

The idea of progression and development in relationships has several aspects: one could be concerned with the ways in which intimacy deepens, or the ways in which this deepening is manifested in behavioural terms, or with the cues which are antecedents of intimacy development. All of these and other aspects have been considered in the theories below. All of the theories therefore concern the middle and end points of relationships as well as the initial points and most are thus 'stage' theories which suggest that relationships progress through different stages where different factors may be relevant to liking. It may be more accurate to talk of them as 'stage and sequence' theories since the implication is that the stages are passed through in sequence and that achievement of one stage entails abandonment of the influences obtaining in the earlier stages. However, for the sake of brevity, the general label of 'stage theories' will be applied to those orientations which begin from the view that different cues are sequentially relevant to different points of a developing relationship. This global label thus subsumes not only those which attempt to account for marital selection and dating but also those which concern the process of long term friendship formation rather than reactions to strangers or behaviour in first encounter. The selected approaches can be seen to share several assumptions, the most basic being in general terms that different cues have salience at different times in acquaintance, that there is a sequence of such cues, and that the original determinants of interaction or attraction may have no effects whatsoever in maintaining or continuing subsequent relationships.

Although the theories below are a selection of those available rather than a thorough listing, they may be adequate to identify some other concerns that seem to characterise the thinking of those who espouse stage theories. First, stage theorists usually point out that a considerable amount of 'sociological sorting' occurs in real life relationships, such that individuals tend to meet more often with others from a similar sociological background (e.g. same race, same economic level). Many studies in interpersonal attraction are forced to omit consideration of such factors although these provide a rich source of variation and differentiation in everyday acquaintance. The stage theorists offer a timely reminder that such information needs to form a part of any thorough-going understanding or acquaintance processes. Second, most stage theorists complain of the one-sidedness of much research inasmuch as it pays attention to A's reactions to B without examining real life parallels of B's simultaneous reactions to A. In short, such theories set out to stress the inter in interpersonal attraction and interaction (Kerckhoff, 1974). Third, whilst stage theorists are not alone in recognising that not everyone achieves the desired one-to-one correlation between liking and association (not all of us ultimately become friends with those whom we find initially attractive), they do place more emphasis on this than some other approaches do. Usually they examine factors underlying such failures and thus stress not only how relationships develop successfully but also how they collapse and deteriorate (see Chapter 7). Fourth, it must be admitted with a sigh that most stage theories are of recent and independent origin - which has meant that, in most cases, systematic empirical investigation of their suggestions is at a very basic stage and evidence for or against them is somewhat thin on the ground.

That said, it is possible to select theories that embody two sorts of approach: those concerned with defining relationship intimacy and what this means to the parties involved; those concerned with establishing the different cues which promote growth and expansion of liking at different points in relationship development.

Mapping Relationship Growth

Several theorists have set out to offer models explaining growth in intimacy levels and how individuals define, refine and extend their relationship. Such theorists who have recently devoted much attention to this problem are not only experimental social psychologists, and sociologists but also communication researchers (Miller, 1976; Roloff, 1976) and this seems to be one area where intercourse between disciplines is necessary to do justice to the complexity of the problem. However the theories reported here have to be selected from that range and considered briefly. More detail is given in Huston (1974) and Miller (1976).

**Pair relatedness**  The earliest progress into this area was made by Levinger and Snoek (1972) and followed up by Levinger (1974). Briefly, this model emphasises the interaction of two individuals and concentrates on more than the simple evaluative responses that may be based on certain cues at certain times. The model outlines the growth of interdependence and identifies four levels of relationship (the last one being a continuum in its own right). Thus the basic (zero) level is Zero Contact where two people may be unaware that each other exists; First true level is labelled Awareness, where each person may have attitudes about or impressions of the other person - but interaction itself has not occurred. At Level Two (Surface Contact) the two persons will be interacting in some unimportant ways, will have attitudes, impressions and minimal information about one another and are not yet much more than mere acquaintances. The Third Level (Mutuality) represents a continuum of degress of relationship and ranges from a very basic level of mutuality to almost total overlap; however, the essential feature of this stage (really a set of stages) is that the partners have deeper shared knowledge about each other, are more concerned to preserve the relationship and more inclined to feel responsible for maintaining the other person's outcomes at an acceptable level.

The important point about this approach is that it accepts time as only a very poor indicator of the strength of a relationship and sets out to identify the behaviours that help to define the level of relationship for the participants and for outsiders. Thus for example, the types of communication that are appropriate to each level of relationship have been suggested by Levinger and Snoek (1972) to be: Unilateral (Level 1); Defined by role requirements only (Level 2); Self disclosure about personal feelings (Level 3). The suggestion is also made that attraction at different levels will be defined by, and dependent on, different things (e.g. at Level 2 P's attraction to O may depend on O's image or reputation but at Level 3 it would relate to the information disclosed by O about himself). Various factors will affect the transition from one level to the next and these may differ between different pairs of levels (e.g. transition from zero to 1 may be affected by climate or affiliation need, whereas transition from 1 to 2 may be affected by time and opportunity, whilst transition from 2 to 3 may be influenced by attitude similarity). For Levinger and Snoek (1972), initial liking for a stranger is not an end in itself but amounts to 'permission' to ourselves to continue the interaction a stage further to see if this is profitable.

**Relationship definition**  An independent approach with some similarities to this one is proposed by Altman and his co-workers. The intention of this proposition is rather to define the behavioural means by which increasing intimacy or desire for intimacy is communicated between interaction partners, and the work of Altman (1974) in this regard has been briefly noted in Chapter 1 (p. 31). However, Morton, Alexander and Altman (1976) have very recently extended the proposals. These authors claim that interpersonal communication is a transactional procedure where individuals attempt to achieve mutuality of (or consensus about) relationship definition. In other words, 'the key ingredient to understanding social ties between people is reflected in the properties of their relationship to a degree equal to or greater than in their characteristics as separately functioning individuals' (Morton, Alexander and Altman, 1976, p. 106). These authors argue for a distinction between the content of a relationship and its form (thus the same request can be made assertively or submissively) and they explore the ways in which communication processes are employed to define the form of the relationship in multi-modal, multi-level ways (including both verbal and nonverbal means, and extending to the way in which interpersonal space is used in interaction to define status - Altman, 1975). To use Morton et al.'s own example, a teenager may ask for the loan of the father's car by saying either 'May I have the car?' or 'I am taking the car'. Whilst both statements express the same content (acquisition of the car) a different form of relationship is implied between parent and teenager in the two statements. Essentially the different forms depend on the balance of influence and control of resources. If the parent responds to the assertive request in an accepting way (e.g. 'Have fun') he is indicating acceptance of the form of relationship and the teenager's option to control resources. If, however, he counters with 'Have you finished your homework?' he is redefining the relationship in terms of his own control of resources and his ability to distribute or withhold them as a function of satisfactory performance by the teenager of certain prerequisites (Morton, Alexander and Altman, 1976).

Because of the many forms of communication that are possible (e.g. verbal, nonverbal), relationships can be defined (and relationship development can be understood) in terms of the ways in which diversification takes place. Thus strangers adopt a relatively superficial and stylised communication system, placing considerable emphasis on 'tit-for-tat' types of reciprocity (which may be why the buying of 'rounds' in bars is banned in some countries which fear the growth of alcoholism). However, individuals who are better acquainted seem to be able to employ a much wider range of behaviours to maintain mutuality and they place considerably less weight than strangers on short-term tit-for-tat reciprocity in the same mode or range of behaviours. For Morton, Alexander and Altman (1976), satisfactory development of relationships is contingent upon such diversification and expansion occurring in the cause of maintaining mutuality of relationship definition. Development of the relationship is thus to be mapped according to the behaviours and communication processes that are exchanged by the participants as definitions of their relationship.

**Proactive and retroactive attribution**   Berger and Calabrese (1975) have attempted to explain the development of interpersonal communication between strangers who have just entered a relationship with one another. They distinguish between three phases to such an interaction: <u>entry phase</u>; <u>personal phase</u>; <u>exit phase</u>. The entry phase tends to concern normative communication content and 'demographic conversation' - that is, conversation directed rather by norms of politeness, or focussed on issues of low consequence or relatively low involvement for the interactants. The personal phase concerns attitudinal issues, personal problems and other more central issues. This phase appears only after several interactions at the entry level and is characterised by conversation less governed by social desirability or normative considerations - indeed socially undesirable aspects of self may be discussed. The exit phase concerns the future of the interaction and its probable continuation. Examples range from departure to divorce, and at the point of study by researchers some relationships may never yet have reached the exit phase. Seven axioms and 21 theorems are derived from the study of the development of interpersonal relationships and these concern amount of uncertainty in the relationship as an influence on information seeking and communication behaviour. Thus, for example, it is predicted that high levels of uncertainty tend to produce greater amounts of information-seeking and greater amounts of reciprocity concerning the type and extent of information revealed.

In an attempt to extend this model beyond the initial encounter, Berger (1975) reports a series of experiments which attempted to explore 'the processes of proactive and retroactive attribution in ongoing communication transactions'. In other words, he was examining the ways in which individuals (a) predict likely future behaviour of interaction partners; and (b) explain past behaviour post hoc in the light of subsequent evidence. From a series of experiments it emerged that perceived background similarity led to assumptions of attitude similarity and that, if later behaviour was consistent with earlier information then the early information was used to explain the later behaviour. (Of course this work was concerned with the form of such attribution processes rather than with their accuracy.) On the basis of this model, then, it would be predicted that uncertainty motivates individuals to seek more information, to assume certain things about the other person and to seek explanation of both past behaviour and present behaviour in terms of what is gradually discovered about the other person. Thus the process of relationship development is based on attribution and communication processes in the service of uncertainty reduction.

Stage and Filter Theories

A second set of theories could be identified as those which relate to the processes by which individuals decide to engage in, continue or disengage from relationships. They concern either the stages through which relationships pass (and the cues that reflect this passage) or the factors which individuals regard as necessary conditions for the progress of a relationship - and they thus often contain a basic 'filter' principle.

**The filter principle** In a study in 1962, Kerckhoff and Davis found that at early points in relationships couples tended to be similar in values (value consensus) but subsequently manifested need complementarity. In other words the basis for choice of the partner changed as the relationship developed, and Kerckhoff and Davis argued that individuals probably operated filters as criteria for judging the suitability of allowing a potential acquaintance to proceed to a deeper level of intimacy. If the potential partner failed to satisfy one of these criteria he was filtered out and never got as far as being tested up against the next criterion. This filter principle is now implicit or explicit in much work on acquaintance even though Levinger, Senn and Jorgensen (1970) failed to replicate the Kerckhoff and Davis (1962) study.

For example, Lewis (1972, 1973) developed a filter model of heterosexual relationships with its emphasis placed on the sociocultural background of such relationships. On the basis of a questionnaire study of dating couples during 1965-66 (and followed up two years later whether the relationship was still in existence or not) Lewis proposed a sequence of six processes in courtship: perceiving similarities; achieving pair rapport;

inducing self disclosure; role taking; achieving interpersonal role fit; achieving dyadic crystallisation. Perceived similarities can be of various types, of course, and Lewis proposes that similarity of sociocultural background precedes similarity of values which in turn precedes similarity of interests and of personality. In Lewis's formulation strict filtering occurs such that the subsequent stages are not entered unless the preceding ones are completed satisfactorily. Whilst the evidence presented by Lewis (1973) is supportive of this theory, independent evidence is lacking and Lewis's own data do not claim to test the validity of the whole model.

A further stage theory that embodies a filter principle is, however, one that has considerable empirical support: the Stimulus-Value-Role theory of Murstein (1971a; 1976; 1977). Since it is so well tested and since it is primarily concerned with courtship development, it is reserved for further discussion in Chapter 7. However, the basic principle is that beginning courtships are based upon the Stimulus properties of the individuals concerned (e.g. physical appearance) whilst Values begin to become more important as the relationship proceeds and the ultimate 'fit' that determines satisfaction with relationship is centred upon Roles (see pp. 187-8).

**Predictive filter model**  A model with several similarities and commonalities with the theories outlined above has been suggested by the present author (Duck, 1973b, c; 1975a; 1977a, b) and forms the basis for the structure of this book. Essentially, this model argues that individuals seek the rewarding experiences of consensual validation (see above) for their cognition or view of the world (involving attitudes, personality, etc.). In this formulation the personality is seen at one level as composed of personal constructs (or hypotheses) about reality and the people or events it contains (Kelly, 1955). It thus embodies and represents the individual's characteristic approach to his environment (and hence requires test, evaluation and validation) just as much as his attitudes do (see section on Social Comparison Theory, above). Indeed, 'attitudes', 'beliefs', 'information', 'hypotheses', 'personal constructs' and 'personality' are all seen, in this view, to be complementary and not necessarily exclusive ways of describing an individual's cognitive structure and content - <u>all</u> of which requires validation. An individual is therefore motivated to establish the validity of these several aspects of his cognition. Since they all represent (different) cognitive features, the appropriate method of validation is through social comparison with the cognition of others. There are good reasons (Duck 1973b, pp. 144-150) for supposing that similarity (of cognition at its various levels) is usually but not always attractive, and circumstances can be conceived where dissimilarity or complementarity may offer the individual 'better' validation or support for his cognition than similarity would do (e.g. as a relationship progresses then individuals may seek to <u>develop</u> or change their view of the world - their cognition - in ways suggested by their partners, in discussions or conversations).

How does this relate to relationship development? Given that the individual has the goals stated above, it is clear that he cannot achieve them immediately he meets a new acquaintance for two reasons. <u>First</u>, the information is not directly available: we do not normally gain direct access to a stranger's attitudes, beliefs or deep-structure personality on the first occasion when we meet him. <u>Second</u>, any information available in such encounters is unreliable as a means of validating one's own cognition: we simply do not have enough contextual information about the stranger to know how much confidence to place in the support or validation that he may be able to offer. For example, he may be mad: similarity would therefore <u>not</u> be reinforcing. The individual therefore has two parallel tasks: <u>one</u>, to assess the value of the other person as a 'comparison other' - i.e. someone to whom he could usefully compare himself and his cognition; <u>two</u>, to assess the amount of support or validation that the other actually does provide. In the service of both of these aims he needs to find out as much as he can about the other person to aid his interpretations. To do this, the individual needs to employ the proactive and retroactive attributional processes identified by Berger (1975; Berger and Calabrese, 1975) above. The model is thus developmental because it argues that people attend to different aspects of the other person as the relationship progresses and as they wish to test out their models of the other person or explain his past behaviour in order to establish his value as a comparison and his contribution to one's personality support.

The model is also a 'filter theory' in that it makes the

following assumption: continuously throughout a relationship each individual reviews his model of the other person and scrutinises it to assess the probable or actual level of support that it offers to his own personality. Those who do offer enough of the right kind of support are allowed through to the next stage of the filter process, where different aspects of the person are scrutinised, 'better' aspects of the person are attended to, more safe and reliable indicators of his personality structure are examined. Those who do not pass through a given stage of the filter process are normally ruled out as more intimate associates (Duck, 1973b; 1977a, b, c).

## Some Observations and a Plan of this Book Henceforward

As may be clear from what has been noted so far, the work on interpersonal attraction differs in several ways. First, different workers attend to different aspects of interpersonal attraction: some look at antecedents and some at consequences of liking; some (below) look at loving; some look at physical attractiveness; some at personality similarity; and so forth. Second, different workers give different interpretations to words like 'attraction', 'relationship' or 'liking' and they differ correspondingly in the way that they measure these things. Marlowe and Gergen (1969) have commented upon this relatively chaotic state of affairs but, nearly ten years later, there has still been relatively little systematic progress in identifying the nature of the attraction response itself (McCarthy, 1976). Third, different workers examine (largely on intuitive grounds) different points of relationship (e.g. first encounters; long-standing friendships) as well as different qualities of relationships (e.g. same-sex friendship; courtship). Whilst (again on intuitive grounds) it may be argued that at the start of every long-standing friendship there must have been a first encounter, intuition is not an adequate basis for us to decide whether this means that the factors that cause initial attraction are the same factors that cause long-lasting friendships. Yet there has been a paucity of both empirical research and theoretical speculation concerning the ways in which different aspects of acquaintance relate to each other. Fourth, a variety of theories at a variety of conceptual levels has been constructed to explain a variety of (perhaps) independent events and observations. The theories listed earlier are apparently different in several ways, but two points should be noted: if they relate to different aspects or points of acquaintance then the differences are not necessarily theoretically significant; the theories are often reconcilable in various ways even where they appear to conflict. Thus a theory dealing with initial attraction is not necessarily in conflict with one addressing relationship development; a theory concentrating on balance between two individuals is not necessarily incompatible with one concentrating on the way an individual makes associations between events that he observes. Of course in some cases there will be a direct conflict, but in others there will be no contest - just as Newtonian Laws and Einstein's notions make the same predictions in some cases, address the same phenomena in some cases and consider widely different events in some cases.

This book is organised in such a way as to structure the research that has been done in interpersonal attraction so as to provoke consideration of these four issues. It is structured to reflect a particular view of how people get acquainted. It is assumed, therefore, that different workers studying essentially different things have nevertheless got something to say to each other in the sense that their work can be organised to reflect the dimensions along which a relationship may develop. It is assumed that individuals take certain personal and cultural beliefs into any interaction; that they respond first to the outward appearance of each other; then to behaviour, gesture and the like; then to the content of conversation like attitudes; and then to personality structure or content. At each point, it is assumed, individuals use these bits of evidence in the service of model building: i.e. they make initially shaky but progressively more stable and constellated models of each other's personality as their acquaintance proceeds. This model of the Other is compared at each point to their own beliefs about their own personality - as outlined earlier.

Thus the first of the next few chapters looks specifically at work on the context or background to encounters - things like cultural and sociological factors - which may influence an interactant's beliefs about his partner and his evaluations of the partner's initial attractiveness. Chapter 4 then examines evidence compiled by workers investigating the influence of interaction behaviour upon participants' liking for each other. Chapter 5 examines what are the effects of direct exposure to a partner's particular cognitive processes (his attitudes) whilst

Chapter 6 reports the work on broader aspects of individuals' cognition (i.e. personality). Chapter 7 considers how these processes relate to special forms of relationship like children's friendships, courtship and love - as well as to breakdown and failure in relationships. By taking this approach it is hoped to clarify some of the processes uncovered in the Study of Acquaintance by structuring the findings in a way that mirrors relationship development.

# CHAPTER THREE

## THE BACKGROUND TO ACQUAINTANCE

A person does not start an acquaintance as if he were an animated blank tablet: he imports certain things to interaction. He has a personality of his own which influences his responses to other people and affects the ways in which he evaluates other people. He comes from a cultural and sociological context which influences his beliefs about human relationships and affects the ways in which he conducts these meetings. He has certain observable static characteristics (like height, dress, physique) which influence the responses of other people towards him and affect the ways in which other people evaluate him. In a sense this observation emphasises two aspects of an individual's behaviour which occur in interaction with others. On the one hand he is an information receiver and on the other an information transmitter: his reception of information is modified by his personality (next section); his transmission of information is effected by various means including his clothing, his physique, his attitudes and his behaviour (subsequent sections and chapters). Although this receiver-transmitter dichotomy is rather simplistic when one considers all the complex information being emitted by both participants in an interaction, it is useful to start out employing it - as if the individual was either transmitting or receiving exclusively in his interactions - before we look at a more complex picture in Chapter 4.

Since we have adopted a primarily developmental approach to acquaintance it makes sense to look at the personal, static imports (e.g. clothing, physical attractiveness) before we examine the dynamic cues available in interaction (e.g. posture, gesture) - Chapter 4 - and proceed to look at work on the attractiveness of cognitive attributes in themselves - Chapter 5 - or personality - Chapter 6. It just is the case that in the normal development of acquaintance individuals find out about these latter aspects of other people <u>after</u> they can observe physique, dress and so forth. It is <u>also</u> the case that an individual's evaluation of the attractiveness of a given stimulus depends not only on the cue itself but also on what he, the observer, <u>makes</u> of that cue. In this latter respect, he may be influenced by his assessment of the attractiveness of the cue itself or by his judgement about the implications that it has for future interactions (i.e. it affects both his attraction towards the other person and his desire to acquaint further). The reason why it is important to consider the attractiveness of the static cues available to interacting individuals when they first meet and before they interact is therefore that these represent the first evidence that the individuals have about each other. They are the first evidence that each interactant can use as a basis for deducing what the other person <u>will be like</u> to talk to, or what his personality <u>will be like</u> or whether the other person <u>will</u> like him . . . and so on. They are thus available in the present - but their significance lies in the future: in terms of what they lead each interactant to <u>expect</u> about the other.

### What the Observer takes into Interaction

An individual's mechanisms for deducing what to expect about other people are influenced by two things: <u>first</u>, his own personal past history of interactions where he has learned how other people respond to him personally; <u>second</u>, his cultural/social/sociological contextual history which tells him how individuals treat one another in his society, prompts him to place significance on certain things and not others, and instructs him on how to manage, promote or cancel any developing relationship. For example, Hall (1963) has noted that whilst Western cultures habitually regard punctuality for appointments as polite and tolerate lateness of up to 5 minutes without apology or remark, the Arab culture operates on a different time scale such that a late arrival of two or three hours would not occasion any comment at all. Whilst a westerner meeting an Arab may deduce (wrongly) that a long-overdue Arab did not like him or was intending to insult him or ruin a promising relationship, the Arab would make the same deductions only if the westerner left the appointed place before the end of the following day! In his turn, the Arab would make the (wrong) inference that insult was intended if a gift was offered with the left rather than the right hand - a distinction with no significance to westerners. Other examples of latitudes of tolerance for certain behaviour within a given culture (given below) are significant backcloths against which an observer makes deductions or attributions about the motives, intentions and dispositions of the people that he meets. They therefore exert an influence over his willingness to interact just as his own personal expectancies about other people do.

The Influence of Observer Characteristics

In this content an observer's deductions about the attractiveness of other persons are affected firstly by his willingness to interact with others to start with (if an individual deliberately chooses to shun society or be ascetic then even very attractive other individuals will exert no influence over his acquaintance behaviour) and secondly by his inherent propensities for processing information (e.g. if he is a poor judge of character he may be continually involved in 'bad' or doomed relationships).

**Tendencies to interact** Some people enjoy social interaction more than others; some are able to forgo it entirely. Explanations for these types of individual differences have been sought by appealing to the concept of 'need for affiliation'. Hardy (1957) has argued that those who score highly on measures of need for affiliation are positively motivated toward affiliation and will seek others' company very frequently, taking pleasure in it. Those who score medium or low on such measures are hypothesised to be ambivalent or unconcerned about affiliation with other people. In presenting evidence that high and low affiliators (as measured by TAT techniques) actually do seek high and low amounts of interaction with others, Byrne, McDonald and Mikawa (1963) have claimed that an individual's past history of experience with social interaction leads him to a generalised expectancy that other people will be rewarding (high affiliators) or punishing (low affiliators). Accordingly, the individual's tendency to interact with other people at all (i.e. before, and independently of, any individual's selections of particular associates) is guided by his beliefs about whether other people as a rule are trustworthy, accepting of him and 'enjoyable'. Mehrabian and Ksionzky (1974) have developed and extended this view in a series of experiments which suggest that - against this background of a general expectancy about the rewardingness of other people - an individual chooses to affiliate with particular others 'from whom he has already received positive reinforcements or evaluations or when he expects to co-operate rather than compete' (Mehrabian and Ksionzky, 1974, p.149).

Such an explanation seems to point to individual differences in anxiety about social interaction which could exert powerful contextual or background effects upon an individual's acquaintance behaviour in general. The relationship between anxiety and affiliation has also been discussed by Schachter (1959; see Introduction) whose work has revealed the general tendency for first born or only children to respond more markedly to increases in anxiety by seeking the company of other individuals. Interestingly, this has implications concerning their suitability for co-operative/team tasks as opposed to individual tasks and first born children are more effective members of bomber aircrews than they are as individual fighter pilots. Equally, first borns tend to seek psychotherapy more (a 'social' or affiliative response to anxiety) whilst later borns have a greater tendency to alcoholism (a non-affiliative, non-social response)!

What might be the basis for the relationship between anxiety and affiliation? Nowicki, Nelson and Ettinger (1974) have noted that need for social approval in initial interactions is related to need for affiliation and have suggested that this predisposes individuals to respond positively to similar strangers. Independently, Goldstein and Rosenfeld (1969) have shown that initial dissimilarity is threatening to individuals and that highly anxious persons are prone to seek out similarity between themselves and a stranger. Thus anxiety relates to affiliation by predisposing individuals to be attracted to similarity, and an individual's anxiety level influences the kinds of things he looks for in prospective interactants - and therefore affects his responses to the particular characteristics possessed by those interactants.

These 'predisposing' effects of anxiety levels probably have a relationship to an individual's level of self-esteem or SE (the positive or negative affective component of beliefs about the self). Stroebe (1977) argues that individuals need to evaluate themselves in various ways and, over a period of experience of the results of self-evaluation, individuals build up a picture of their likely success at given tasks and an impresssion of their own worth or abilities on various dimensions. An individual with low self-esteem (LSE) could be predicted to be more anxious in new social encounters than someone with high self-esteem (HSE) - especially when he imagines that the interaction is likely to result in interpersonal evaluations (as, for example, a competitive task might do) and that the evaluations may be unfavourable to him (as a low level of self-esteem might predispose him to expect). It is therefore likely that self-esteem (SE) level can both be influenced by past experience and be an influence in a person's characteristic manner of choosing associates. For instance, Guthrie (1938) reports an unexpected influence on a girl's SE (and subsequent dating behaviour) in the following way: a rather unattractive girl from his class was selected as the unsuspecting object of a practical joke by the boys in his class. The boys (at first reluctantly) drew lots to see who would date the subject, who rapidly found that she was the centre of attention and had gained a full social diary. Slowly her behaviour began to change: she took more care over her appearance and began to wear different, more attractive clothes. Eventually the boys found they were reluctant dates no longer and competition to date the girl became real enough as she had become a star attraction on campus in reality.

The inference from the study seems to be that a person's attractiveness to others is mediated by SE, which in turn is mediated by how others have treated the person in the past. Stroebe, Eagly and Stroebe (1977) tested this inference rather more directly. These authors obtained samples of low self-esteem (LSE) and high self-esteem (HSE) subjects and told them that they would be evaluated by some judge who was either telling his true opinion or role-playing a predetermined script. The subject's task was to identify whether the judge was role-playing or not. It was found that LSE subjects assumed the judge was role-playing when he evaluated them positively and truth-telling when he gave negative evaluations. The reverse was true of HSE subjects.

Thus it seems that an individual's SE influences his beliefs about the genuineness of attractive or liking responses made by other people - and this will presumably influence his behaviour towards them and his desire to continue an acquaintance. In support of this view, work by Dittes (1959) showed that LSE subjects responded much more markedly to fluctuations in a group's acceptance or rejection of them. In a study refining this position further, Snoek (1962) distinguished invidious rejection (i.e. rejection for reasons reflecting on a subject's SE - such as derogation of his task competence) and non-invidious rejection (i.e. rejection for incidental reasons which had no implications for self-esteem - such as the need to reduce a group's size by one member, selected by lot). One finding was that willingness to join another group was increased after strong rejection - a finding interpreted as due to a sharp temporary increase in need for social reassurance. This points to an important fact to be borne in mind in deciding the place of SE as an influence on acquaintance behaviour (Stroebe, 1977): individuals have a relatively stable and enduring level of self esteem but are also liable to experience sharp fluctuations on a temporary basis - just as someone could be generally a happy and even-tempered person on the whole, but may one day feel sad or grouchy. In a test of whether stable or temporary manipulations of SE influence liking for potential dates of varying degrees of social desirability, Walster (1970) obtained measures of subjects' SE level using three different measures and then gave subjects 'a psychiatrist's ratings of their scales' (actually rigged by the experimenter) in an attempt to exert a temporary influence on their level of self-esteem. For one third of the subjects the report was intended to raise SE, for one third to lower it and for one third it was intended to be neutral, as a control. Subjects were then exposed to the problem of choosing potential dates varying markedly in social desirability (i.e. either very attractive or very unattractive) and it was expected that LSE subjects would choose less attractive dates whilst HSE subjects would choose more attractive ones (i.e.

that subjects would relate the physical attractiveness of the date to their own level of self-esteem and be happy to choose a date when these two variables 'matched' but not otherwise). No support was found for this matching hypothesis. However, it could be argued that this and other studies on the matching hypothesis (discussed in Stroebe, 1977) fail to maximise or emphasise the fear of rejection by the potential date which is an essential feature of the argument for a relationship between SE, anxiety and tendencies to choose particular partners (Stroebe, 1977): only if a subject fears rejection should he choose someone who matches himself. In many studies however the subject is more or less guaranteed that the date will accept him - whomever he chooses - and it is less surprising therefore that physically attractive dates are preferred even by LSE subjects in these circumstances. Furthermore, the emphasis on the matching of SE and physical attractiveness has permitted too ready a neglect of other ways in which matching could occur (e.g. between SE and dominance of stranger; or between SE and preference for similarity in strangers; or between SE and preferred level of sociability or extroversion or social 'grace'). The suggestion here is that SE level exerts a significant effect on an individual's choice behaviour as a whole rather than merely in one specific way, i.e. in respect of choices related to the physical characteristics of the other person. For example, several theorists agree that those with HSE are more likely to enjoy good social relationships whilst those with LSE are likely to be more self-protective, untrusting and derogatory about other people (Adler, 1926; Fromm, 1939; Horney, 1939; Rogers, 1951; Maslow, 1953). In essence the argument runs that those who are more accepting of themselves are better able to be accepting of other people also.

Clearly, therefore, SE level is one characteristic of an observer which combines with other features of a situation to be a substantial influence on the individual's general tendency to interact with others - as well as influencing specific choices that he makes. It is also likely to have an effect on the course of his interactions (especially the amount of trust or intimacy that he permits) as well as his general style of behaviour and interaction (e.g. his friendliness and warmth). Ehrlich and Lipsey (1969) examined the influence of an individual's affective style (that is, his characteristic mode of affective response to people in first encounters) on his subsequent interactions and on his acceptance or rejection of other people on the basis of first impressions. They found that strong reactors (i.e. individuals scoring high on a measure of affective style) formed more stable first impressions on the basis of less information and were alert, vigilant and somewhat defensive in first encounters. They were very concerned about self-presentation in interaction (i.e. concerned about the image they were creating in the other person's mind) and had a preference for more structured interactions. They were much more likely to attempt to form structured impressions from first encounters than were low scorers - who preferred to concentrate on enjoying the social encounter itself rather than coming away with any fixed impressions of the other person. In this latter case, then, both the individual's tendency to interact with others and his enjoyment of the social interaction are substantially influenced by his perceptual apparatus and his beliefs about the nature and function of interaction. Equally, Holmes and Jackson (1975) have shown that Internally Controlled Subjects (i.e. those who tend to see events or reinforcements as largely the result of their own behaviour) attend primarily to rewards available in interactions, while Externally Controlled Subjects (i.e. those who tend to see events or reinforcements as largely determined by luck or factors outside their control) attend primarily to punishments. In an experiment that operationalised 'punishment' and 'reward' in terms of the positive or negative evaluations made about the subject by a discussion partner, these authors found the predicted individual difference and showed that they influenced attraction responses: to attract an internally controlled person rewards should be offered and to attract an externally controlled one it is best to avoid punishment (i.e. remain neutral, since he does not respond to reward but does respond negatively to punishment). The other studies reported below have concentrated more directly on these and other ways in which perceptual mechanisms, cognitive structure and personality influence the observer's reactions to attractive or unattractive stimuli.

**Mechanisms for processing stimulus input** At first sight it may seem that an individual's cognitive structure and stimulus processing 'equipment' is irrelevant to any consideration of the attractiveness of stimuli: they either are or are not attractive. However, this is only superficially true. There is considerable evidence in the interpersonal attraction literature that an individual's thought processes affect not only his assessments of the attractiveness of certain stimuli (and hence his liking for the person manifesting them) but also his ability to perceive and infer from certain types of stimulus (such as, for example, the significance of certain facial expressions or fluctuations in the tone of voice of another person). From this literature it could be deduced that individuals have different levels of ability to notice and make use of all the cues that other people provide - so that they may actually fail to realise that someone likes them, and hence they may fail to respond appropriately and initiate an acquaintance.

Consider some of the evidence. Kaplan (1973) examined the effect of personality dispositions on the judgement of persons described by inconsistent stimuli and found that subjects discounted the importance of information when such information was incongruent with their own disposition. He concluded that a subject's disposition affected the pattern of weightings that he ascribed to incoming trait descriptive stimuli and thus influenced the overall judgements made about another person. In examining a similar problem from a different perspective, Robbins (1975) showed that dogmatic subjects were prepared to form lasting and fixed impressions of stimulus persons on the basis of much less evidence than other subjects, gave more extreme ratings of the probable stability of their impressions, expressed greater liking for a source that agreed with them and were more likely to try and explain away information that was inconsistent with their impression rather than withhold judgement. This appears to mean that some individuals would be more influenced by first impressions than others, would express liking or disliking on the basis of less evidence, would order their social relationships on the basis of 'snap' judgements and would be less affected by subsequent evidence about the other person. It is tempting to suggest that it was someone like this who first coined the phrase 'love at first sight'.

Dogmatism is usually tested in reference to a particular emphasis within a cognitive system - that is, it usually identifies particular beliefs and is usually limited to political, racialist or sexist areas of thought and is unrelated to other aspects of cognition (which can be conceptually partitioned by researchers in an infinite number of ways, not mutually exclusive: using terms likes attitudes, personality, intelligence, creativity, and so forth). There is, however, some evidence that general cognitive style - irrespective of particular aspects of thought - influences an individual's responses to attraction stimuli. Johnston & Centres (1973) proposed that differences in cognitive systemisation as a whole - but particularly in the context of need gratification - constitute one of the significant variables which determine individuals' attraction towards other people, particularly since it is likely that such systemic differences affect the way in which individuals structure their evaluations and discriminations between people. In other words, they suggest that differences in cognitive system lead not only to different evaluations of the same other person or stimulus, but also to variations in the ability to detect discriminable differences between people and to evaluate such differences. Similarly, Leonard (1976) has shown that cognitively complex judges (i.e. those whose conceptual structure is comprised of many, rather than a few, central organising concepts) were more likely than cognitively simple judges to perceive and evaluate dissimilarity or similarity in other people - whilst cognitively simple judges just did not notice it. Complex judges evaluated individuals who were similar to themselves more positively than dissimilar individuals, whilst simple judges evaluated them both the same. Craig and Duck (1977) also found differences between complex and simple judges - but complex judges were here found to be more accepting of strangers who used different trait dimensions from the ones they themselves employed to describe other people. Goldman and Olczak (1976) have further shown that psychosocial maturity (as assessed by scores on an inventory of psychosocial development) was related to an individual's reactions to attitude similarity between himself and a stranger. High maturity subjects responded most extremely to different levels of similarity: the high similarity level producing high attraction and the low similarity level low attraction.

The above findings relate specifically to the ways in which the observer's personality or cognitive structure and way of perceiving/thinking influence his ratings of the attractiveness of certain stimuli. However, these things can influence other components of liking responses which are particularly relevant to the development of acquaintance rather than responses to strangers. Fiedler (1953) for example, has suggested that individuals differ in their ability to predict other people's behaviour as a function of their tendency to assume that they themselves are similar to those other people. He argued that therapists who assumed that the patient was similar to themselves were better at producing patient improvement. He also showed that an individual's ability to differentiate between the characteristics of liked and disliked persons (and to assess accurately the extent to which they were similar to self) was a predictor of his effectiveness in informal task-oriented groups. Clearly, an assumption that someone is similar to oneself is an important factor in acquaintance since it presumes that one will find it easier to communicate with that person and to understand that person and that one will likewise be intelligible to him (Duck, 1973b). The ability to detect accurately the extent to which someone is actually similar to oneself is a necessary one, which determines the course of a developing acquaintance by indicating the likely profitability of continued interaction with that person.

Another similar influence is likely to be an individual's ability to perceive whether someone else likes him or not, since the correct response to this event will need to be exhibited. Those who are incompetent at making these discriminations will presumably suffer rejection or embarrassment more often than those who are not and it is therefore important for smooth social interaction that there should be congruence between the amount of liking presumed to exist and the amount that actually does. Backman and Secord (1959) undertook a study of congruency - the tendency to like and feel liked by or to dislike and feel disliked by another person - which attempted to show which was cause and which was effect: did people come to see disliked persons as disliking them or did they come to dislike persons who seemed to dislike them first? The experiment was a longitudinal one, that is, it assessed the changing likes and dislikes of persons in a given group over a period of some weeks. It was found that individuals expressed more liking for other individuals who seemed to like them (in other words, an individual's liking for someone was the result of believing that the other person liked him). However, this was only true of early sessions in the study and the effects of this variable decreased as time went on. Presumably this was because individuals responded at first to what they had been told (viz. that X, Y and Z liked them) and subsequently began to perceive more accurately whether or not they had been told the truth. Equally they may have become better at telling whether only X, Y and Z out of their 10-man discussion group liked them or whether the others did too.

One way of deducing whether someone likes us or not is from his facial and vocal expressions. Zaidel and Mehrabian (1969) investigated the extent to which individuals were able on the one hand to detect positive and negative attitudes from the behaviour of other people ('decoding'); and on the other hand to represent their own positive and negative feelings in their own outward behaviour ('encoding'). It was found that the facial channel was generally more effective than the vocal channel in transmitting attitudes about people whilst the vocal channel transmitted information about things. Individuals were more effective at communicating subtle degrees of negative feelings than subtle degrees of positive feelings, and low social-approval seekers were better at encoding variations in negative attitudes than were high approval seekers. In view of the social taboos that surround overt expression of intense emotion and the tendency for people to have a more differentiated negative vocabulary than a positive one (Koenig, 1971), it is not surprising that negative attitudes about others are more easily detectable. However, this study does serve to emphasise that there is an element of skill involved in both the encoding and decoding of such attitudes - and therefore that individuals in the same culture can be expected to exhibit different levels of ability or skill in these respects, with consequent effects on their ability or skill at forming relationships.

Work by Mehrabian (1970) also indicates the relative influence of the vocal and facial components of a message in transmitting various facets of an inconsistent message. Thus in sarcasm or teasing (where a negative statement is intended to be read positively) it seems that the facial channel is used to convey the assessment of the person (smile) whilst the vocal channel conveys the assessment of his acts ('That was stupid, wasn't it') - giving an overall impression of friendly criticism, whereas the same phrase said with a frown would create an impression of hostility. The ability of an individual to understand these social subtleties (which escape some schizophrenics at least) would influence his reaction to the utterance and hence his response to the other person - and the other person's interpretation of him. It is plausible to suggest that such interpretations and responses are influenced by a knowledge of the usual ways in which individuals in that culture conduct the business of negative and positive expressions of feeling and that in this instance the observer's reaction will be influenced by his cultural background.

Effects of Cultural Sociological and Incidental Factors

What is attractive in one culture is not necessarily attractive in another; what is permissible in one culture is not necessarily permissible in another. Equally, any interacting individual is constrained by the beliefs of his culture about how relationships should be conducted and is subjected to (usually hidden or nonobvious) pressures to select his friends, acquaintances or, more especially, his marital partner in a way consistent with his status in that culture. The more obvious form of this pressure is the limit imposed on his choices by his socioeconomic status or religion; the less obvious form is represented in the fact that a given culture usually agrees about what criteria or properties qualify someone as desirable and cultural agreements about the attractiveness of certain cues or properties will influence an individual to pay most attention to those cues in his choice behaviour.


**Cultural and sociological influences on acquaintance** It will be evident to most people that the choices open to an individual who sets out to find a marital partner are not unrestricted. In such cultures as India, the choices are predetermined (either specifically by the parents or generally by the bounds of caste); and even in western cultures it is evident that more marry within the same social/economic class than stray outside it. It was argued by Winch (1958) that an individual's choices were invariably placed within a 'field of eligibles', that is, that the individual was not allowed a totally free choice but was constrained by social convention to limit his choices to those who were in some major respects similar to himself. Thus it is found that individuals tend to marry others who are similar in terms of wealth, social position, intelligence, educational background, religious beliefs and age. Kerckhoff (1964; 1974), however, has pointed to an inadequacy in Winch's hypothesis in that a pattern of similarity in marriage (homogamy) could arise because of the simple <u>statistical distribution</u>

of certain types of characteristic or types of people in the population on the one hand, or because of <u>preferences</u> of people for those characteristics on the other. He thus distinguishes between the 'field of availables' (i.e. like marries like because they are the only ones around) and the 'field of desirables' (i.e. like actually seeks out and prefers like). Whilst the social delimitations on choice are relevant here (especially in a consideration of the background to acquaintance) the interesting question is whether like <u>seeks</u> like or not - and if so why. It is not invariably the case that people of similar background are mutually attractive in the long term: but it is usually true that people of basically similar origin are more attractive than those of markedly different origin <u>in first encounters</u> (Berscheid and Walster, 1969). The reason is not hard to find: at the initial stages of interaction, when one knows virtually nothing about a stranger except what is visible to the naked eye, one is likely to use those naked eyes carefully and to draw inferences from what is observed - as we have already seen that people do draw inferences from cues they are presented with. In that case, any cues suggesting similar social status (cues like clothing or poise) or similar cultural background (cues like style of dress) will encourage observers to draw inferences that similarity exists at other levels - simply because this is the most likely and parsimonious inference to draw. In other words, as a 'best guess' in first encounters it makes most sense to assume that someone who <u>looks</u> as if he is from a similar contextual background to oneself probably <u>thinks</u> similarly too. Certainly he is statistically more likely to have had similar experiences of upbringing, education and so forth. Brickman, Meyer and Fredd (1975), for example, have demonstrated experimentally that people who gave familiar associations to a set of word-association stimuli were liked more than those who did not. They suggested that a preference for the <u>familiar</u> is one factor in the widely observed preference for similar others. That is what is suggested here - only in more wide-ranging terms. The similarity and homogamy observable in general terms may therefore be due in small part to the fact that individuals are likely to look harder for cognitive similarity to apparently similar strangers than they are to do so with apparently dissimilar strangers. Since cognitive similarity (it is argued here - see Chapters 2 and 6) is what is most important in relationships it is this rather than the originally observed superficial similarity that promotes the development of subsequent acquaintance - just as it is the ensuing ball game that causes crowds to congregate at a sports stadium and not (as a visiting Martian sociologist may incorrectly assume) the similar dress or team support emblems that the crowds wear, or the songs that they sing.

If it is the case that individuals are limited in their choices by certain characteristics of the field of desirables, and if this is due to cultural agreements about what is desirable and appropriate for them, then it should also be predicted that cultural agreements exist about the attractiveness of certain properties. Since the present account places much emphasis on cognition and personality it should be predicted that certain kinds of personality type will be generally regarded as more attractive than others - irrespective of the extent to which the person doing the rating of its attractiveness is similar to the personality rated. Posavac and Pasko (1974) found that individuals responded not only to the extent of similarity between themselves and a target personality but also to the social desirability of the target personality. In other words the subjects reported greater attraction to strangers who endorsed and exhibited 'popular' characteristics as well as being attracted to similar others who were not necessarily endorsing popular characteristics. (At first sight it may appear circular to claim that people are attracted to popular personalities - viz. they are attracted because the personality is popular; it is popular because it is attractive to a lot of people. However this is a 'cultural circularity' rather than a logical one: individuals respond with attraction to a given personality because as members of a given culture they recognise it to possess culturally desirable properties and adopt the cultural desires as their own.) Two other studies report more specific types of personality which are generally attractive. Hendrick and Brown (1971) have shown that extroverts are generally preferred to introverts; Nowicki and Blumberg (1975) have found that internally controlled strangers (i.e. those appearing to believe that they control their own 'destiny', reinforcements, outcomes on the basis of permanent, stable, internal characteristics) were generally preferred to externally controlled strangers (i.e. those who seem to believe that their reinforcements, outcomes and destiny are the result of chance or factors outside their own control). It thus appears that certain cognitive properties predispose their possessors to be liked by others just as certain physical or other properties may do.

In an early study of the origins of liking and disliking, both Perrin (1921) and Thomas and Young (1938) have looked at the noncognitive properties which make people attractive to others. Perrin was primarily concerned with a detailed analysis of the physical characteristics of individuals which caused others to be attracted and repelled. This work is discussed more fully in the next section, but here it can be said that a part of his study concerned the discovery of cultural agreement about certain aspects of physique and their significance in judgements of attraction/repulsion. He found that, in relation to intimate acquaintances, the importance of static, structural aspects of physique (as opposed to movements and gestures) was minimal as a correlate of liking, but that there was considerable agreement about the attractiveness of clean hair, teeth and breath! Thomas and Young (1938) on the other hand found that intelligence was the most commonly agreed cause of liking, although college men put physical beauty ahead of intelligence as the most commonly agreed cause of liking for women. By far the most common reason for disliking is conceit, and this - like most of the other reasons for liking or disliking - was commonly agreed to apply to disliking both men and women.

Two themes of this chapter (an individual's ability to detect certain cues; cultural agreement about the evaluation and significance of cues) can be tied together here. Not every individual from the same culture will have the same criteria nor the same ability to detect nor the same interest in attending to some of the subtler forms of the culturally approved or disapproved behaviour or characteristics (e.g. not everyone will always agree or care whether the same individual is conceited: those who do agree and care will probably dislike him). It is thus possible to explain why not every ugly, conceited or poorly-toothed individual is a social outcast in his own society, even where there exists agreement about the attractiveness of these cues.

Agreements about acceptable behaviour take two forms, however. There is, on the one hand, agreement about what constitutes attractive or unattractive behaviour; and, on the other hand, there is agreement about the acceptable ways for public indication of liking or disliking. Since the decline in frequency with which swords are worn, the thrusts occasioned by dislike, for example, have tended to take a less visible and more subtle form. However, we do still recognise when someone is indicating dislike or hostility by 'looking daggers' rather than using them.

Such indicators are usually either verbal, non-verbal (gestural) or elaborate ritual indicators of degree of liking and they are important here because they are culturally or socially prescribed to a large extent and provide a general background against which particular instances of others' behaviour can be interpreted. (Thus there arise circumstances where intimacy allows one to call a friend 'an old bastard' without him taking the offence he might reasonably take if a stranger used the expression.)

Verbal social indicators of liking or disliking are usually conveyed by different degrees of 'immediacy' (Mehrabian, 1968), that is, the degree of intensity and directness of interaction between a speaker and the object he speaks about. For example, 'X is my neighbour' and 'X and I live in the same neighbourhood' or 'I visited X' and 'I visited X's house' each describe the same relationship or event but would convey to the listener different degress of relationship between the speaker and X. Equally, in languages employing different forms of address for 'you' (e.g. France where 'Tu' or 'Vous' can be used to address a single other person; cf. German 'Du' and 'Sie') one form is usually an intimate form and one a more 'distant' form. In such languages, changes of liking can be rapidly conveyed by the sharp adoption of one form in preference to the other.

In investigating such differences in immediacy as indicators of liking, Anthony (1974) showed that observers were able to judge the amount of liking between two individuals on the basis of statements made between them. Furthermore, Mehrabian (1968) showed that untrained observers consistently interpreted speech immediacy to indicate a more positive speaker attitude. However, relevant to the arguments earlier is the finding, reported in that same study, that when subjects were provided with information about the degree of speech immediacy appropriate or expected in a given context there was considerable agreement amongst judges about the interpretation to be made. In the absence of such information about appropriateness judges were less consistent. It is worth speculating, therefore, that an individual's ability to draw the correct inferences about 'appropriate' verbal indications of liking/disliking will influence his ability to perceive the extent to which strangers like or dislike him and hence will be a background influence on his interpretation of their behaviour and their suitability as acquaintances.

Non-verbal social indicators of liking usually take the explicit forms of touching, gazing at one another and social distancing. Thus Goffman (1971) has pointed out that behaviour in public places is often characterised by signs which indicate to other people that the individuals involved are to be seen as a unit (a 'with', as Goffman calls it). The devices for indicating a 'with' are referred to as 'tie-signs' and range in subtlety from, for example, the holding of hands to extremely subtle differences in spacing (people stand closer to those they like), similarity of posture, similarity of dress (e.g. football scarves) and so forth. Harré (1977) has ventured the suggestion that tie signs at the beginning of a relationship are blatant and overt in the service of a conscious need for public display, whilst more intimate or routine relationships are characterised by more subtle and less obvious ones. Harré (1977) also notes how research work has concentrated on the positive side (liking) rather than attending also to the negative (disliking). 'What,' he asks, 'are the untie signs by which one broadcasts 'I'm not with him'? Perhaps some budding ethogenist can record the means by which a respectable citizen dissociates himself from a 'with' thrust upon him by a persistent and importunate drunken beggar.' (Harré, 1977, p.348). The real life relevance of this remark is illustrated by the study by Shotland and Straw (1976) who showed that if observers are given no information about a man and a woman seen to be having a violent argument (in which the man physically assaults the woman) then the onlookers will assume that the pair are a married couple and will not intervene or help her. The ability of a woman to demonstrate convincingly to onlookers that she is not part of such a 'with' could thus become a highly salient (not to say literally vital) part of her social performance.

Ritual social indicators of liking and disliking are also culturally implicit. People know, on the whole, how they should treat friends; for example, how often they should invite intimate or less intimate acquaintances out for a meal. Harré

(1977) gives an extended treatment of this problem - much neglected in research on acquaintance - of how people make friendships <u>work</u> after the relationship has been started off. This is relevant here because it not only cements a relationship but also determines the form it shall take in the future. It is also relevant to later chapters and will be reserved for fuller discussion there.

The cultural and sociological context of acquaintance is thus, as this section shows, an important factor to bear in mind in the interpretation of the significance for individuals of certain cues and behaviours. It is as influential a factor in their interpretations of other people as is the factor of their own personal cognitive processes reviewed at the start of this chapter. One factor brings their own personal history into any relationships: the other imports the frameworks of their social history and cultural emphasis.

**Incidental influences on acquaintance** Relationships are occasionally initiated by factors outside the individual's control (e.g. two people may meet first through the coincidence of their housing positions in an estate) and it is important to consider the influence of such factors and to evaluate their significance. For, just as people are limited by the fields of eligibles, availables or desirables so too their relationships may be limited by accidental or incidental constraints on the range of others that they encounter. The important question for the researcher is what people <u>do</u> in such circumstances and how significant a long-term influence such incidental factors are on individuals' final choices of associate.

In a series of studies to test the effects of 'mere exposure' (that is, the hypothesis that simple frequency of exposure to a stimulus or person makes people more accepting of or attracted to it) Zajonc and his co-workers have attempted to demonstrate that exposure is <u>sufficient</u> for enhancement. This would explain, for example, why people tend to be friends with those they meet most often (Gullahorn, 1952). However, one would expect the context of exposure as well as the content of any ensuing interaction also to be significant influences on subsequent liking, for which more exposure simply provides the opportunity. Accordingly, Saegert, Swap and Zajonc (1973) attempted to determine the effects of mere exposure in negative or positive contexts and the effects of this on interpersonal attraction. Two experiments showed that, whether the context was negative or positive, frequency of exposure enhanced liking. However, it should be noted that the negative and positive contexts here were unpleasant or pleasant experiences of tasting liquids rather than the kinds of context normally experienced in everyday interaction and the authors themselves are loath to extrapolate too wildly from the findings.

A more developed view of the nature of limits imposed on interaction frequency, contextual influences on interpretation and opportunity for interaction is provided by Murstein (1971a; 1977). He distinguishes between the concepts of <u>open</u> and <u>closed fields</u>: in an open field two individuals are not forced to interact even though they occupy similar spaces (e.g. two members of the same university, working in different departments); in a closed field the individuals, through their relative roles, occupations or duties are forced to interact (e.g. the lecturer and students on the same course; the Department Chairman and his secretary). Whilst these fields are not 'contexts' in precisely the same sense as used by Zajonc (above), nor 'fields' in the same sense as used by Kerckhoff earlier, they are another level at which both context and field influence an individual's choices and acquainting. For example, Willerman and Swanson (1952) reported that within an organisation (actually a college sorority) where some of the members live in the residence while others live outside of it, those living within the residence tend to have, proportionate to their numbers in the group, many more friendships among themselves than non-resident members. Thus one would expect, as a general rule, to find that individuals' choices were more frequently made in the context of closed rather than open fields - although this should also be true of his strong rejections and dislikes (Warr, 1965). Indeed, the highest percentage of murders takes place within the immediate family group!

Other evidence also suggests the importance of such incidental factors. Festinger, Schachter and Back (1950) found that those who lived near the postbox on a housing estate also had more friends. Those whose respective houses faced one another directly were more likely to be friendly with one another than were those whose houses faced in non-parallel directions. Thus it seems that <u>functional</u> proximity or opportunity for interaction rather than simple proximity itself are important incidental constraints on choices of associate. Similar findings with schoolchildren by Seagoe (1933) and Byrne (1961b) suggest that propinquity of living space on the one hand and of classroom seating arrangements on the other account very largely for children's friendship patterns. However, as with the Festinger et al. (1950) work, it should be noted that functional distance rather than physical distance was the most important factor in determining interactions.

It may be, therefore, that an important incidental influence on a person's decision to interact or acquaint with another person is his expectancy of <u>further</u> interaction. The fact that two people meet for the <u>first</u> time today does not of itself guarantee they will ever meet again, so any strenuous attempt to start a relationship may be wasted effort. Berscheid, Boye and Darley (1968) investigated the effects on subsequent voluntary choices to associate of being forced to associate with someone. They found that subjects who had been forced to associate with an unpleasant person actually chose that person more often in the free choice situation subsequently. On the other hand, Sutherland and Insko (1973) manipulated both the interestingness of an expected future interaction and its probability and found that strong expectations of interacting on an interesting discussion topic produced a marked generalising effect on attraction and significantly increased liking for the interactant. Layton and Insko (1974), who manipulated probability of future interaction with a stranger and the attitude similarity of the stranger to the subject, found that attitude similarity was a most powerful influence on attraction scores only where no interaction was expected.

More direct studies by Lerner, Dillehay and Sherer (1967) found that when subjects anticipated competition with a prospective partner rather than co-operation they preferred the partner to be dissimilar to themselves rather than similar. When a partner was better liked, or was likely to be co-operative, subjects tended to perceive him as more similar to themselves. This finding should be seen in the context of the evidence discussed above which indicates that individuals assume similarity where none exists: or, more accurately - and this has often been ignored - assume <u>cognitive</u> similarity where only <u>superficial</u> similarity exists. This tendency, as will by now be clear, is proposed to be a central and important determinant of the decision to acquaint. It is all the more important because its effects are most strong at that early point where individuals have before them only the superficial evidence of a stranger's cultural or social origin and those static cues such as dress, physique or appearance (see below): the most basic and trivial stimulus material on which to form judgements of initial liking.

## The Stimulus Person's Properties

Unappealing though it may seem at first sight, there is some sense in believing that at the most early points of an encounter, the two people in an interaction are stimulus objects for each other rather than stimulus persons. It is not until later that their personalities emerge for one another and they become people rather than things or role-occupants or stereotypes. Equally, it is not until later that the 'vibrant reciprocity' of warm human interactions (Levinger, 1974) begins to characterise the encounters. At the moments of first acquaintance and before they begin to slip into the rituals of greeting or polite conversation (Harré, 1976), the two parties in an interaction are simply agglommerations of static cues: what each person sees is the other's physical appearance rather than his deep personality structure (although, as we have seen already, individuals are prepared to draw inferences from the first of these to the second). This account of acquaintance therefore considers these 'static' cues and their importance first before (Chapter 4) considering the significance of the cues that follow immediately in interaction, viz. the 'dynamic' cues provided by posture, gesture and interaction behaviour as a whole.

Static Cues

There are two sorts of static or unchanging cues that an individual may present to others: first, the associated cues that indicate his social status, or embody his reputation; second, the direct, mainly physical cues mentioned above.

**Associated cues**     An individual's reputation often but not always precedes him into his interactions: indeed, acquaintanceships often start through mutual friends bringing two individuals together. On such occasions, part of the greeting ritual (Harre and De Waele, 1976) is concerned with indicating to each of the participants their relative status, the key stereotype information that will facilitate the subsequent interaction, and the depth of acquaintance that each shares with the person doing the introducing. For example an introduction may go like this:

> <u>Sponsor</u>: Peter, I'd like you to meet an old friend of mine, John Brown, who travels in cosmetics. John, this is a colleague from the office: Peter Smith. He has recently joined our staff.

The two individuals then greet one another and proceed to explore each other's 'selves' as indicated in the introductions they have received. Thus in this example they are likely to talk first about one another's jobs.

The clearer experimental example of those 'reputation' phenomenon was provided by Kelley (1950) who, by distributing apparently similar but actually different sheets of information to the members of a lecture class, led half of the class to believe the new lecturer they were about to hear was a warm person and the other half to believe he was cold. All subjects then, of course, heard precisely the same lecture. However, the reputation of the lecturer (established in the prior manipulations) had extensive influences on the class's subsequent ratings of the lecturer, his competence and the lecture itself: the 'warm' lecturer was seen as more considerate, more sociable, more popular, good natured, humourous and humane. His 'reputation' (warm/cold) thus influenced perception of his character. Further, in general terms, the work of Miller, Campbell, Twedt and O'Connell (1966) supports the view that pairs of friends are likely to be similar in reputation. Such contextual influences upon impressions and interpretation of individuals are hardly as striking as those in real life but are nonetheless more often present there than they are in laboratory studies of acquaintance.

One other cue which hovers over the distinction between associated and direct cues is socioeconomic status. Occasionally, this is inferred from observable phenomena, occasionally it is directly observable. As Byrne, Clore and Worchel (1966) have shown, it is a significant factor in attraction, and individuals at the extremes of the socioeconomic continuum respond most sharply to similarity/dissimilarity of socioeconomic status. One interpretation of this finding would be, as above, that economic similarity implies, as a 'best guess' in the absence of more safe information, that other forms of similarity may be revealed on closer inspection or - at the very least - that the similar individual is comparable to oneself in some very important ways.

**Direct cues**   Socioeconomic status can occasionally be observed directly from such cues as dress or accoutrements. However, these direct cues are not always reliable indicators of the true state of affairs, since they form a part of self-presentation techniques designed to create positive (and unbalanced or misleading) impressions in observers' minds. Thus people wear smart suits to suggest success (even if they are not successful) and buy flashy cars to suggest wealth (even if they cannot afford it) and carry leather-and-gold executive briefcases (even if these contain only the lunch packet). These observations serve to illustrate that individuals know that other people make inferences on the basis of static cues; therefore they set out to manipulate or direct these inferences by their choice of cues to present or emphasise. What about those cues over which they have less control?

Physical attractiveness is one such cue that is modifiable only within limits. In a very early study of what physical properties make individuals attractive to other people, Perrin (1921) constructed a rating chart to discover those aspects of other people's physical appearance which were relevant in deciding their physical attractiveness. This highly detailed survey broke cues down into <u>static cues</u> (further subdivided into head and face, arms and hands, trunk, etc., each category further detailed and subdivided), <u>Personal habits</u> (e.g. care of hair, care of teeth), <u>Expressive behaviour</u> (e.g. general poise, pleasingness of handshake), <u>Voice</u> (e.g. pitch, modulation) and <u>Dress</u> (e.g. taste, neatness). Judges' ratings of the rank-order importance of the items on the list were correlated with their rank-order of liking for intimate acquaintances with the intention of showing which characteristics were related to liking (as argued in Chapter 1 here, such a correlational method cannot expose cause-effect relationships, but this early study is admirable for its thoroughness even if more modern readers would criticise its design from other viewpoints). The findings revealed that static beauty correlated lowly with liking, but dynamic, expressive beauty correlated highly. In an attempt to generalise this finding beyond intimate acquaintances Perrin then required judges to identify the general characteristics which they found attractive or repulsive. This part of the study showed that attractive individuals tended to be rated near the mode or average for each characteristic whereas unattractive ones were rated as deviating from the mode. Put into other words, with a slightly increased risk of misunderstanding, these results mean that attractive people were seen as more 'normal' than unattractive ones, although our everyday experience tells us that both attractiveness and unattractiveness occur in the normal population. The proportions of legs and feet (and, in females only, characteristics of hips, mouth and lips) were what repelled students in 1921, whilst they were attracted by clean hair, teeth, breath and general appearance. As a general finding, physical attractiveness was explained by dynamic, expressive behaviour such as gestures ('Beauty is as beauty does') whilst unattractiveness was explained in terms of static cues (physical structure). Alert readers will know how this finding fits into the argument developed here: those who have an unattractive arrangement of physical structures will be presumed by observers to be unexciting, uninteresting and not worth getting to know - so they are filtered out early; those with attractive physical structures are interacted with and, after a time, their physical appearance becomes less significant than how they behave.

This speculation is borne out not only by a final part of Perrin's study but also by more recent work. Perrin examined the correlations between attractiveness/repulsiveness and other traits. He found no correlation between attractiveness and intelligence, but a correlation between ratings of attractiveness and the belief that attractive individuals had better attitudes to life, were more aware and sophisticated. More recently Dion, Berscheid and Walster (1972) found that physically attractive individuals were generally believed to lead better lives, to be more interesting people and to do more exciting things altogether. Other work by Dion (1972; 1974) and Dion and Berscheid (1974) has built up a compelling picture of the way in which the physical attractiveness of children influences (1) observers' judgements of how naughty they are (beautiful ones are seen as inherently less malicious); (2) females' punitiveness towards children (females punish physically attractive boys more leniently than they punish attractive girls or unattractive boys); (3) children's judgements of the likability of their peers (physically unattractive children are liked less). In the latter case, unattractive children were attributed with more antisocial behaviour, whilst attractive ones were seen as more self-sufficient and independent in behaviour - a finding that mirrors those above (Perrin; Dion et al.) that dealt with perceptions of attractive adults. Also, Cavior, Miller and Cohen (1975) found support for the hypothesis that individuals make assumptions about likely attitudes held by an attractive person: specifically they found that people who were rated as physically attractive were assumed to have attitudes that were similar to the rater.

Clearly, then, _in initial encounters_ it seems likely that physical attractiveness influences observers to make assumptions about the type of personality structure and content they are likely to discover if they proceed to join in an acquaintance with the attractive (or unattractive) other. Kleck and Rubinstein (1975) showed that the effects of physical attractiveness outweighed the influence of an attitude similarity/dissimilarity manipulation, a result which is perhaps clarified by the independent study by Duck and Craig (1975) who found that information about physical _appearance_ (not simply or exclusively information about level of _attractiveness_) similarly swamped any effects of attitude information. They interpreted this finding as due to the point of relationship studied (initial response to a stranger) where physical information provides a necessary context for interpreting cognitive information (just as aggressive behaviour from a midget and from a giant may be differently interpreted and treated). Whilst these authors might hold that this is generally true of all encounters, there are special reasons for believing that it is true of dating encounters. Krebs and Adinolfi (1975) found a positive relationship between physical attractiveness and dating for females but not for males, whilst Curran (1973) found that the most significant predictor of interpersonal attraction was the date's rating of his partner's physical attractiveness.

In relation to the significance of physical attractiveness, then, a complex picture has been shown to obtain, but it has been argued that physical characteristics are attractive in part because of their aesthetic appeal and in part because of what they imply or suggest about the 'owner's' personality. However, there is another side to physical characteristics which occasionally needs to be managed in interactions: stigma. 'Stigma' has been used by Goffman (1964) to refer to 'spoiled identity', i.e. deformity, abnormal size or shape of organs, amputation of limbs, deafness and so forth. How do people respond to stigmatised others? Goffman argues that they are at a distinct disadvantage in encounters, since they are 'liabilities', and lead to increased 'costs' for the partner (see Chapter 2). Another side to this is the following: as we have seen earlier in this chapter, certain behaviours and responses are required or expected in any friendship or social interaction - yet people with some stigmata may be physically incapable of performing such behaviours. So there are two facets to stigma and acquaintance; first, the physical handicap may strain the interaction by preventing expression of normal behaviour by the stigmatised person; second, it may do so by evoking abnormal behaviour from the non-stigmatised partner who strains 'not to notice' the affliction or manifests overcontrolled or patronising behaviour - thus creating a 'spurious interaction' (Lemmert, 1962). For these and other reasons, Kleck, Ono and Hastorf (1966) found that individuals interacting with disabled others were more likely to express opinions not representative of their actual beliefs in order to create fewer arguments with the disabled person and to give a spurious appearance of 'smoothness' in the interaction. This behaviour was also observed by Cooper and Jones (1969) who noted a subtle form of ingratiation involved in the expression of false opinions. Just as individuals tend to withdraw from interactions with stigmatised others, so too, when in the presence of an authority figure as observer, subjects tended to try to dissociate themselves from an obnoxious but otherwise similar other, Cooper and Jones report. They did this by expressing false opinions so that the actual similarity to the obnoxious other was falsely minimised. Cooper and Jones suggest that the explanation is to be found in a desire to avoid being 'associatively miscast' by a person whose approval he seeks. ('Associative casting' is the assumption that people who have common positions or similar orientations or equivalent backgrounds will have the same beliefs and values - one notion extended in this book to include 'the same beliefs, values, attitudes and personality structure'.)

Although this section has concentrated on static cues, there are also dynamic physical cues that are relevant to attraction and acquaintance. These include nonverbal expression, gesture, eye movements and a whole selection of other things like management of space in interactions. All of these will be considered in the next chapter. At this point, however (since this is the first chapter where the attractiveness of cues has been considered directly) let us ask the question why these things matter in the development of acquaintance. It is asked here directly to provide an example for the future since it could be asked at the end of every subsequent chapter, where it may occasionally be revived as a reminder.

## Why Do These Cues Matter in the Development of Acquaintance?

Most workers on the above topics have asked themselves the important question: how can the attractiveness of these cues be explained? They have therefore produced explanations of the significance of these cues for attraction (see Chapter 1 for the usage of this term) and have done so in terms of, say, the rewardingness or the balance or the informational qualities of the properties. However, there is much to be gained also from the not incompatible question: how do these cues fit into Acquaintance (as the term is used here)? Can their attractiveness be seen as a primary cue in the development of relationships and if so, how? All of the above cues can be factors in an individual's decision to interact further with the Other person (who possesses them) as much as they are a factor in the assessment of the Other's initial attractiveness. Perception and interpretation of these cues may be influences on the subject's decisions to proceed to develop a relationship at all.

The cues are thus important for three reasons:

1. Of and in itself each cue may be attractive, pleasant, rewarding, affectively positive;

2. Each cue can be used as a basis for forming impressions of personality, beliefs, attitudes - in short it can be used

as a basis for guessing at the cognitive structure that lies beyond it, created it or chose to display it.

3.  Cues that induce feelings of attraction have implications about the future existence, form and nature of deeper or less superficial relationships. Thus an attraction response to a given cue can have (but does not invariably have) an implication about future relationships with the attractive Other <u>either</u> because an attraction response is an expressed choice or commitment to associate <u>or</u> because it leads the observer to expect <u>future</u> reward ... etc. in the shape of personality/cognitive similarity.

This latter distinction may be hard to grasp and an example will help. If I 'come forth' at a Billy Graham meeting, any subsequent religious behaviour may be due to the fact that I do not want to renegue my expressed commitment or choice (e.g. I might feel foolish if I did: I had made a public choice and others would expect me to live up to it) <u>or</u> because my new beliefs led me to expect future rewards for the religious behaviour (e.g. secure afterlife; greater feelings of goodness). Analogously, an attraction response to a given cue could lead to further interaction with the possessor because my expression of liking now commits me to follow it up and live up to it; <u>or</u> because I deduce that the cue means I can expect future rewarding discoveries (for example, that the attractive stranger and myself have similar personalities). In any case, an initial attraction response in real life has implications if further interaction is at all likely. It implies choice of and preference of that person as opposed to all others; this in turn implies association with him in a friendly way; this implies further contact during which exploration of each others' Selves can be predicted - so each person must be prepared to disclose his Self - and it creates a need for ritual maintenance of the relationship and display of it to the outside world.

The simple response to a given cue thus has many implications for an individual's willingness to interact and for finding out more about the other person. In short it leads to attributions about the suitability of the other person for further social interaction and acquaintance. An individual's success in making these attributions will depend on his skill at attending to significant cues and his ability to make use of them by drawing valuable inferences. Thus Berscheid and Walster's (1969, p.3) argument that 'we can predict future behaviour only from observable events' can be seen as a beguiling but incomplete hypothesis. An individual is presented with many observable events during acquaintance and he must select those that seem relevant or meaningful. Furthermore, he can predict future behaviour in many ways on the basis of only one observable cue. His task is actually to differentiate those future behaviours that are likely from those that are not and hence to form an impression of the Other's personality as a basis for predicting the likely behaviours. From this impression or model it is possible for him to assess or predict the extent to which the Other's personality is likely to be found to be similar to his own. An attributed model of the other person's personality is thus an essential mediator of any predictions about his future behaviour. As we have seen in this chapter, models or inferences can be erected on the unsafe basis provided by single, static, observable cues or by context. In the next chapter we will examine the surer basis provided by the wider range of cues and observables available as the encounter proceeds.

But the above reasons are the essential basis for deciding why these cues matter in acquaintance.

# CHAPTER FOUR

## LIKING BEHAVIOUR DURING INTERACTIONS

The deliberate ambiguity in the title to this chapter is intended to emphasise that there are two aspects to the behaviour in an interaction: on the one hand the behaviour is either likeable or not likeable, attractive or not attractive, intended to appeal or to repel; on the other hand, the behaviour can indicate degree of liking for the partner in various quite subtle ways. The developmental structure of this book has required that we postpone until now the examination of the effects of such interaction behaviour upon acquaintance. In the previous chapter the discussion centred on the interpretation of certain static stimuli and treated the two acquaintance partners as objects for each other. It was suggested that at the point of initial encounter the 'external' characteristics of each interactant were most important as scene-setters and the previous chapter proceeded as if one individual was a transmitter of information and one a receiver. Whilst this remains partially true when interaction itself begins, it is unsatisfactory to cling too tenaciously to the distinction between the 'receiver' and 'transmitter' functions of individuals once they start to behave in a meaningful way towards one another. It is at the point of interaction that each person most clearly begins to serve both receiver and transmitter functions simultaneously and to need to monitor his own performance as well as that of the other person. In other words, he more clearly requires to ensure that his own feelings towards the other person are manifested or encoded in socially acceptable ways whilst at the same time he is concerned to assess the other person's liking for him. Those cues, actions and behaviours that were discussed in Chapter 3 are then placed in new lights, and may lose their primary significance in determining attraction responses or initial impressions as they become enmeshed as part of the dynamic processes of acquaintance.

In the dynamic context of an interaction such things as physical appearance (e.g. spectacles) lose their impression-forming powers (i.e. implications of intelligence) as other factors become available (e.g. conversation) which provide better evidence about the truth or falsity of the original impression (i.e. expressed opinions are a better basis for judgements of intelligence - Argyle and McHenry, 1972). The setting of the interaction (e.g. co-operative or competitive) becomes more salient and the sequences of behaviour more significant than the static aspects of the interaction. The argument of this chapter thus fits into the book at this point by attending to the behaviours that people exhibit at the start of an interaction, or the sequences they begin to follow. However, as in the previous chapter, the significance of these behaviours lies in the interpretations of intention, causality or underlying personality structure which they promote. A cognition or belief about why someone did something can be formed and translated into an affective evaluation of the person. But if intention and liking can be deduced from behaviour, it follows that behaviour can likewise be used to encode intentions. As in the last chapter, therefore, we shall discuss the extent to which individuals exhibit different levels of ability at decoding other people's intentions from their behaviour and at encoding their own intentions in their own behaviour. The importance of these two abilities can be gauged from the study by Jones and Panitch (1971) which showed that when an individual believes that another person dislikes (likes) him, his consequent behaviour can actually produce feelings of disliking (liking) in the other person - even when the original belief was totally incorrect. The self-fulfilling prophecy is, they argue, essentially a false definition of a situation which evokes new behaviour that makes the originally false definition into a true one. An individual's beliefs about his own likability, or his discriminative skill at perceiving whether someone truly likes or dislikes him could result in striking influences on his acquaintance behaviour and its success or failure.

**Behaviour In Interaction**

There are three aspects to behaviour in an interaction which affect the progress of acquaintance and individuals' willingness to enter into more intimate relationships on the basis of what they observe early on: first, the setting of the interaction and relative status of the two interactants determines how each prepares to handle the ensuing interaction, since, for example, competition requires different behaviours from those exhibited in a co-operative situation; and, again, certain things may be said and done to inferiors but not to superiors. Second, the actual sequences of behaviour shown by each interactant have culturally-coded significance and consequent effects on the liking of acquaintances for each other. Third, as argued briefly in Chapter 3, relationships and interactions require to be 'managed' in various ways which indicate both to the interactants themselves and to the outside world just what is to be made of the relationship. An individual's responses to these three aspects determines his willingness to involve himself further in the interaction.

The Role of Setting: Interaction Type and
Status Differences

Just as the reputation of a new acquaintance may determine an individual's responses to that person (Chapter 3), so certain 'situational' aspects of the encounter will determine his interpretation of the other person and his intentions, attitudes or personality structure. For example, in an interview probing questions are permitted and are not therefore offensive or indicative of over-intrusiveness on the questioner's part; in a chance encounter with a stranger the opposite would usually be true.

**Co-operation or Competition**   The evidence concerning the effects of task upon attraction to a task-partner is somewhat contradictory. On the one hand, Senn (1971) showed that similarity of task performance was an attractive event; on the other hand, Harvey and Kelley (1973) demonstrated that attitudinal similarity was more significant an influence on attraction than was the comparative success or failure of two individuals at the same task. Clarification of these two apparently divergent findings may be sought in the work of Anderson (1975) who conducted a study in two sessions: one where attraction levels were shown to be determined by value similarity; the second where the latter cause of attraction was overridden by goal-path clarity on a specific task (i.e. the ability of the group to define a mutually agreeable goal and reach it by one sequence of actions performed co-operatively by all group members). In certain types of group (those concerned more with task completion than the social-emotional atmosphere in the group) the individuals will be attracted to other members of the group as a function of their ability to help the group to reach the task-goal rather than as a function of their individually attractive qualities. In some cases conflict will therefore promote attraction to other group members (particularly if that group is in conflict or competition with another group); in some cases it will reduce attraction (when it hinders achievement of group goals) and in some cases it may be irrelevant (e.g. emotional conflict in a task-oriented group). In a study of some of these hypotheses, Wheaton (1974) distinguished different types and sources of conflict as a means of illustrating the different senses in which conflict could have either negative or positive effects on group cohesiveness and member attraction. A distinction was made between 'principled' and 'communal' conflict such that the former refers to conflict over principles whilst the latter refers to conflict which assumes adherence to the same basic principle (e.g. at its simplest, conflict which accepts the nature of a group goal and merely disputes the manner of its achievement). Two sources of conflict are internal (over principles or issues concerning the structure, function and nature of the group itself) and external (over principles or issues unrelated to the nature of the group). Wheaton found that principled conflict decreases the attractiveness of individuals for each other, whilst communal conflict increases it beyond even the level before the conflict began. This latter work may be taken with the findings described above (and more thoroughly in subsequent chapters) that, in general, similarity or agreement over values and principles is attractive whilst, in general, disagreement is not.

In two-person 'groups' the competitive and co-operative aspects of interaction are obvious to both interactants, whereas in a larger group a person need not necessarily interact with all the other members of the group. In such circumstances, and at the earliest points of a relationship, a salient feature in the attraction felt towards the other person may thus be the extent to which equity is attained - the extent to which benefits are reciprocated in kind and at an equivalent rate. Stapleton, Nacci and Tedeschi (1973) induced liking or disliking for a confederate and then arranged for confederates to confer benefits on subjects at different rates. When subjects were given the chance to reciprocate these benefits they did so at a rate equivalent to the one they had received irrespective of degree of liking. However, those subjects who had been induced to dislike the confederate increased their liking for him as a direct function of the amount of benefits received whilst those induced to like the confederate decreased their liking the fewer benefits they received. The authors suggested that the subjects tended to make estimates of the degree of 'true' benevolence lying behind the amount of benefit actually bestowed and related those estimates to their expectations about the 'correct' amount they should receive to match their liking level. In the context of longer term acquaintance, La Gaipa (1977b) has argued that individuals have a similar kind of expectancy about the level and nature of the benefits that they become entitled to as an acquaintance develops and proceeds. He suggests that individuals decide whether to continue a relationship as a function of their expectancies about it and the degree to which these expectancies are satisfied in the event. Clearly the relationship between expectancy and level of liking is one which will have an influence upon a Subject's interpretation of another person's motives and 'true' likability. In support of this, Regan, Straus and Fazio (1974) present evidence that good or skilled task-related actions by liked individuals or bad actions by disliked persons (i.e. actions consistent with the affect felt for the person) are interpreted by observers as caused by the nature of the actor (his personality) whilst actions inconsistent with the affect felt for the actor (e.g. bad actions by liked people) are attributed to causes external to the actor (chance, situational factors).

An individual's assessment of the nature of the task, his expectations concerning appropriate actions and his beliefs about the likely causes of another person's task performance evidently influence, predispose and determine his assessments of the other person's attractiveness - and vice versa. These factors are thus incidental influences exerted on his interaction with the other person. A second such factor, related to the inference processes underlying the first, is the relative status of the two interactants and the different kinds of action which this renders appropriate for each of them.

**Power, status and prestige** How is attraction related to power, status and prestige? From what has been said already, the reader may have deduced that there is some link, but what is it? As argued above, attraction is related to expectancies about appropriate behaviours and these appropriate behaviours are often concerned with the reciprocation of benefits in a way that is expected. Again, the behaviours could concern assistance toward achievement of goals or could depend on the power of the other person to provide reward via attractive (similar) personality characteristics. Since we have already seen that co-operativeness, bestowal of benefits, and rewards are all attractive, it is clear that the power of someone to provide these things will act to enhance his attractiveness. Since people of higher status do, by definition, have more control over some resources, we should find that liking is related to status.

Tedeschi (1974) has argued that the relationship between attraction and power stems directly from the ability of one person to reward the other, whilst Kelvin (1977) on the contrary claims that power and attraction are parallel rather than causally connected phenomena. For Kelvin, both power and attractiveness depend on predictability: an individual is <u>attracted</u> to someone who confirms the predictability of the universe for him by agreeing with his predictions about it; someone gains <u>power</u> over an individual to the extent that he can predict what the individual will do. However, there is another important parallel between power and attraction that is suggested by Kelvin (1977). When a person claims to be attracted to someone he is admitting that he accepts the attractiveness of that person; when someone admits that another person has power over him, he is also admitting that he allows it to be exerted, that he accepts it. Thus both the attractiveness of another person and his power over an individual depends on the acceptance of him by that individual or on continued willingness to interact (Homans, 1971). Becoming attracted and allowing someone to have power over oneself both amount to an increase in tolerance for vulnerability (i.e. an increased permission for the other person to know private things about oneself).

In the context of attraction and power, however, it should be noted that power depends on reward (see above) and there are two types of reward-power: power that is *internal* to the interaction (where A specifically rewards B during the interaction) and power that is *external* to the interaction (where A rewards B by directing him towards some reward in the external environment, or by showing him how to achieve a reward). For example, in crude terms, the giving of money to B in an interaction is internal reward; the giving of a list of reference books where B can discover how to turn lead into gold is an external reward. This latter form of reward power is important in the conception of acquaintance since it suggests the possibility that whilst we may initially be attracted to someone on the basis of expectations of internal rewards, acquaintance is prolonged by expectations of external reward (e.g. an expectation that the new acquaintance will be able to demonstrate new, stimulating or exciting ways of looking at the world, or new, rewarding aspects of arguments or issues).

Reward power can normally be expected to relate to Status since those with higher status will have more control of resources, and attractiveness presumably relates to the effectiveness with which such reward power is used. Hollander and Julian (1969) have noted that the attractiveness of a group leader is related to his ability to assist the *group* toward the achievement of its goals rather than to gain superior outcomes for himself alone. However, before an individual's ability to promote group achievement can be assessed directly people are likely to base their judgements on his actual or apparent status, prestige or power. In accordance with previous arguments here, people should expect high/low status persons to do some things and not to do others - and judgements of attraction should be influenced by these expectations. In a study of the effects of hierarchical relationships upon attraction, Ring (1964) argued that if subjects observed high or low status persons complying or not complying with a request from an individual of different status they would like these persons to different extents as a function of their status and their action. High status compliers were predicted to be most attractive and high status non-compliers the least attractive - because of the presumed causes of these actions (in the former case the person is demonstrating an 'honest evaluation' of the request, in the latter he could merely be giving a perfunctory demonstration of his status and power). Although results largely supported such an hypothesis, it was also suggested that observers 'distrusted' individuals who departed too sharply from expectation about what was 'proper' for a person of a given status to do. DeCharms, Carpenter and Kuperman (1965) support the principle of this argument by showing that a person seen to be persuaded by someone that he likes will be seen as acting voluntarily, whilst a person persuaded by someone that he dislikes will be seen as acting unwillingly.

A further influence on interactions, expectations and attractiveness might be supposed to derive from a person's prestige (e.g. his occupational prestige, or, in the army, his military rank): but research does not confirm this. Byrne, Griffitt and Golightly (1966) found in two studies that prestige had little effect on attraction as compared to the influence of attitude similarity and they concluded that 'general effects of prestige are operative only in relatively ambiguous situations lacking in other specific informational cues' (p.442). Such situations are more likely to obtain at the initial points of interaction before a more personal picture of the prestigious individual has been assembled. In view of the multi-dimensional nature of the attraction response (Chapter 1) the claim that individual factors like prestige can _determine_ attraction can be entertained only when it is the only variable manipulated or when the point of attraction under investigation is so primal that other influences have not yet come into play. Clearly in the complexity of factors that influence liking and help to promote acquaintance, power is only one of many. In any case, its 'primal' influence will be moderated by the interpretation put upon _sequences_ of behaviour in which different power or status roles may play only a small part.

Sequences of Behaviour

Just as individual static cues may promote attraction responses in themselves (cf. Chapter 3) so too dynamic sequences of behaviour involving those cues can produce effects on liking. Thus whilst an individual's status power is largely determined by events prior to the meeting of two individuals, it can nonetheless exert an influence over the course and nature of the meeting. For example, during the actual sequences of interaction, the ability to exert power over another person may be demonstrated personally and cogently. Equally, other cues examined in Chapter 3 can be manipulated during sequences of interaction behaviour.

**Esteem and Liking** In a provocative study in 1965, Aronson and Linder examined the effects of personal evaluations made by a stranger about a subject. In some cases these evaluations were negative and in some cases positive, but the interest of the study stems from the predictions made about different sequences of such evaluations. What are the likely effects of a positive evaluation followed by a negative one, a negative one followed by a positive, or two evaluations of consistent nature? Common sense is quite clear about this: someone who evaluates a person consistently positively will be preferred most of all by that person and someone who is consistently negative about him will be most disliked. From the point of view of Self Esteem, however, different predictions can be derived. Aronson and Linder (1965) hypothesised that an individual's self esteem is likely to be enhanced more sharply when a judge changes from a negative opinion to a positive one and dented most severely when someone who was positive about him changes to negative. They predicted, therefore, that these two conditions would produce the most extreme liking and disliking responses. They found that the subjects in the 'gain' condition (that is, those who overheard a confederate change from a negative to a positive evaluation) liked the confederate significantly more than subjects in the consistent positive condition. Equally, the subjects in the 'loss' condition (where the confederate changed from positive to negative) had a slight and entirely non-significant tendency to dislike the confederate more than the subjects in the consistently negative condition.

Like many of Aronson's studies, this one has proved to be as controversial as it is stimulating and many subsequent researchers have taken issue with the findings and their interpretation. Tognoli and Keisner (1972) were unable to replicate the Aronson and Linder findings and found results themselves which suggested several other explanations for the original findings, such as a recency phenomenon (i.e. the most recently-heard remarks are those that determine attraction level) or a quantity phenomenon (i.e. that attraction was determined by the number of positive or negative remarks heard rather than simply the degree of negativity/positivity they contained). Some combination of these last explanations was eventually preferred by these authors. Other explanations involve contrast effects (Clore, 1977): just as warm water seems warmer after cold water, so the positive feedback in the gain condition may have seemed more positive simply because it was preceded by negative feedback and the gain effect occurs simply because subjects perceived the positive feedback as more positive than it really was - because of this contrast. In an attempt to resolve some of these issues, Mettee, Taylor and Friedman (1973) suggested that it was important for the subject to believe that the evaluator had really changed his mind, rather than simply made an additional, different assessment which represented no change of opinion - merely a capricious judgement or extra source of evidence. The term 'affect conversion' was used to describe the case where an evaluator overturned and replaced his original judgement with a new one rather than simply added extra affective information. The findings of two experiments combine to suggest that the gain-loss of esteem model can account for observed phenomena when affect conversion is regarded as stable and permanent.

In a different form of 'sequence investigation' Jones and Wein (1972) investigated the effects produced on attraction ratings when a person expressed similar (dissimilar) opinions to the subject's own and subsequently expressed others which were dissimilar (similar) to subject's own. The authors found a general preference for receiving agreement from a previously dissimilar Other and a pronounced disappointment when a previously similar Other disagrees with one. This was interpreted as showing that the early opinion statements made by an individual establish an expectancy in terms of which later opinions are interpreted. If, however, it is the case that similarity of opinions is, as a general rule, one type of reinforcement that causes liking (Byrne, 1971 and Chapter 5), and if the subjects held a belief that the other person in this experiment was also finding out about them, then it is plausible that a relationship between self esteem and liking is mediated by implied evaluation. In other words, when an individual manifests similarity to another person, he assumes that the other person will evaluate him positively, because, in general, similarity is attractive. In a test of such an hypothesis, Insko et al. (1973) distinguished between three possible models to explain the linkage between implied evaluation and liking. They concluded that similarity causes liking; liking causes subjects to assume that the other person will like them (compare this step with the work of Jones and Panitch reported at the start of this chapter); this assumption of implied evaluation causes further liking. A complex relationship between variables is, at any rate, the most likely explanation for the equally complex behaviour observable when social interaction first occurs between strangers.

**Self Disclosure and Ingratiation** Other complex sequences are also proceeding during acquaintance, and they serve to emphasise the multi-dimensional nature of the acquaintance process which contains so many components and such complex interactions between variables. Two of these sequences relate to the gradual increase of intimacy in acquaintance and its manifestation in the gradual disclosure of information about oneself, on the one hand, and the specific handling of negative information in this process on the other hand. During these processes appropriate levels of intimacy for the interaction are negotiated and over-intrusive discussion is treated negatively. The appropriate amounts of disclosure of the right kind of information thus play a very large part in the satisfactory development of an acquaintance and a certain amount of 'skill' is implicit in the ability to decide what is 'the right kind of information' and when is the appropriate time to release it. A new acquaintance who tells you that he likes watching horses mate (as Queen Victoria apparently did - Murstein, 1977) should be treated with caution; but the same information from an old acquaintance need not cause as much alarm.

In a review of the literature on Self-Disclosure, Cozby (1973) discusses the principal variables that appear to facilitate disclosure. Among these are reciprocity, liking, and certain social situational circumstances. However, besides these considerations and those relating to an individual's habitual level of disclosure (considered more fully in Chapter 6), there is the more pertinent question (at this stage of our considerations) about how individuals negotiate the level of intimacy appropriate to their encounter and the factors that determine their acceptance of intimate questions. Kaplan et al. (1974) examined the effects on attraction scores of intimate or non-intimate questions in three settings of varying degrees of formality. In all settings, probing questioners were disliked but this was especially pronounced in highly formal settings. The authors suggested that negative attraction (i.e. dislike) resulted from disclosure at too rapid a rate or from too intimate a probe. Clearly the study indicates the important point that permission of intimacy and consequent liking vary with the type of context in which the interaction occurs. In brief encounters, such as those studied by Kaplan et al. it seems most probable that probe intimacy is more likely to induce disliking than it would be to do so in rather more extended interactions. Further evidence is provided by Davis (1976) who examined the ways in which people in brief encounters contrive to structure and define the level of intimacy that is appropriate to their encounter or relationship. Amongst several major findings was the discovery that, against the background of the predictable increase in intimacy of disclosure as the relationship proceeded, it was invariably the case that one partner assumed major responsibility for prescribing levels of intimacy whilst the other person largely reciprocated, such responsibility being assumed by the more disclosing of the two. The establishment of a level of intimacy thus appears to be attributable to the level adopted by the most extreme partner, and so it would seem to follow that - in brief encounters at any rate - a given individual would disclose more to some partners than to others as a function of the lead provided by the other person.

What about negative information? When and how should that be disclosed? Jones and Gordon (1972) conducted an experiment where an individual disclosed either a pleasant or a traumatic experience from his past which was either entirely his own responsibility or entirely outside his own control. In addition, the experience was reported either at the start or at the end of an interaction. Which is more attractive, a modest success or an immodest one; a person responsible for his outcome or not? Findings suggested that it is unattractive to disclose good fortune early in a relationship, but that if the experience is a traumatic one, the observer will find it (un)attractive as a function of whether the individual was responsible for it or not. A responsible person should disclose bad fortune early rather than late, it seems, but someone who was not responsible for bad fortune should keep it quiet until the end of the interaction! The results of this experiment thus make the important point that the nature of an experience is less significant an influence on attraction than is the manner and timing of its disclosure to the other person, and the consequent deductions that he makes about it.

The phenomena of self disclosure are variously explained (cf. Chapter 6) but one view of the attractiveness of disclosure suggests that people like others to disclose to them because it suggests that the discloser has a healthy personality (Jourard, 1971). The importance and relevance of this claim is the implicit suggestion that it is the intent behind disclosure which is important rather than the information that is disclosed per se (although these two things presumably interrelate). A similar assessment is involved in deciding whether someone's behaviour is genuine or caused by ingratiation: 'ingratiation' is a judgement of the intent behind an act. Liking for an ingratiator is correspondingly reduced when his deception is discovered as opposed to when it is not perceived (Jones, Stires, Shaver and Harris, 1968). However, this experiment also suggested that it is harder for the targets of ingratiation to detect it than it is for uninvolved bystanders or observers.

**The influence of affective states**   Just as the interpretation of observed behaviour can influence the observer's assessment of its attractiveness, the relevance of the behaviour to the observer and his affective state can influence his response to observed sequences of behaviour. Johnson, Gormly and Gormly(1973) examined the affective responses of subjects to disagreements from a stranger and were concerned to establish whether negative responses were mediated by a loss of self esteem caused by the apparent threat to one's personal competence that is implied when another person disagrees with oneself. It was found that decrements in Self Esteem were most pronounced among subjects expressing the greatest dislike for the disagreeing stranger. In a further investigation of a similar hypothesis, Baugher and Gormly (1975) demonstrated the ways in which disagreements promoted physiological arousal in subjects (as measured by electrical skin conductance) and showed ways in which such arousal was translated into action as an influence on attraction responses. They were concerned to examine the effects of sequences of agreement/disagreement (that is, changes from or reiterations of an original agreement or disagreement with the subject). When subjects felt they were competent to discuss the issue involved, then hearing disagreement from the other person was highly arousing.

This work looks primarily at how physical/affective states are created in individuals by sequences of cognitive input received from the environment and the people in it. Whilst this is an important question, another important issue is the implication that such affective states may be perceptible to interaction partners (e.g. the partners may see that X is aroused by the disagreements he is experiencing), since this in turn may produce affective states in them. They may become uneasy, elated, aroused, relaxed when they detect emotional turmoil or arousal in the interaction partner.

Equally, affective states can be created by observing the interest, boredom, liking or disliking that another person manifests toward oneself. Clore, Wiggins and Itkin (1975) examined the effects of observing sequences of nonverbal behaviour which indicated 'warmth' and 'coldness' about another person. Subjects were shown a videotaped conversation between a male and a female. The sound was, however, turned off, and subjects could see only the nonverbal behaviour performed by the female. Two half-tapes were made, one in which the female was behaving 'warmly' (e.g. smiling and nodding affirmatively) and one in which she was behaving 'coldly' (e.g. looking distractedly round the room, frowning). These could then be combined to produce four experimental conditions: warm-warm; warm-cold; cold-warm; cold-cold and the interest of the experiment focusses particularly on the effects of the warm-cold and cold-warm sequences. However, the subjects' task was to make ratings of these tapes from three points of view rather than just one: 1. how much the male liked the female; 2. how much the female liked the male; 3. how much they themselves liked the female. Note that in the first of these tasks they are taking the role of the person on the receiving end of the warm and cold behaviour: this person's reactions to the behaviour are likely to reflect his affective state since they reflect his interpretation of the behaviours directed toward him personally. He is affectively involved in the interchange in the sense that the female's behaviour to him indicates her feelings about him. The study revealed significant Gain-Loss effects (see above) only in this one of the three tasks. In other words, a person's affective involvement determines his responses to Gain-Loss sequences, rather than this being simply due to the sequence itself (as seen by outsiders). Clearly, therefore, such sequences of nonverbal behaviour are often seen as pleasant or unpleasant by individuals because the <u>sequences</u> of cues imply some evaluation of the person at whom they are directed.

**Nonverbal sequences** Various sequences of nonverbal behaviour are more attractive than others, just as certain static nonverbal cues are (e.g. dilated pupils, cf. Chapter 1), but it is by concentrating on this type of behaviour that it is easiest to blur the distinction between behaviour which is attractive <u>in itself</u> and behaviour which is attractive <u>because of what it implies</u> or because of the message it conveys (as above). In this section we will concentrate upon the attractiveness of such behaviour for itself and later in the chapter will consider again the way in which nonverbal behaviour is used to <u>indicate</u> liking for the other person. The most frequently studied behaviours in this context are Gaze (i.e. steady looking at the other person), Eye Contact (i.e. looking the other person straight in the eye) and Spatial Relationship (e.g. closeness of seating position, or conversational distance).

Kleinke, Staneski and Pipp (1975) examined the effects of Gaze, Distance and Physical Attractiveness as factors in the first impressions formed by males about females. Subjects talked to female confederates who gazed at them either 10% or 90% of the time and moved their chairs either towards or away from the subject during the interaction. Main effects on attraction were not observed for either the distance or the gazing manipulations but there was a significant interaction indicating that highly attractive females were liked more when they gazed longer and unattractive females were disproportionately disliked when they gazed at a 10% level. In a further study, Kleinke, Staneski and Berger (1975) showed that nongazing interviewers were rated least attractive, particularly if they were physically unattractive. Additionally, individuals with a high rate of talking were preferred over those with low rates. On the other hand, Stang (1973) found that liking was an inverted U-shaped function of interaction rate - that is, those who interacted most and least were evaluated less favourably than those whose interaction rate was of moderate magnitude. It is arguable whether these two studies were actually measuring precisely the same kind of interaction rate (one measured talking in an interview, one measured length of utterance when reading a prepared script) and the apparent differences in findings may be attributed to this fact. However, it seems indisputable that a number of nonverbal behaviours mediate initial liking responses.

In a theory designed to account for factors contributing to the level of intimacy in a given situation, Argyle and Dean (1965) examined two such factors known to be influences upon attraction: distance (closeness implies liking) and eye contact (more eye contact implies more liking). They proposed that amount of eye contact would interact with distance to produce a constant: in other words, as distance increased (decreased) so individuals would increase (decrease) the amount of eye contact to produce an equilibrium level of intimacy. Whilst this is an interesting suggestion in itself, the authors (and also Argyle and Kendon, 1967) suggested that nonverbal behaviours such as gaze, eye contact and distancing serve not only to attract or repel another, but also to regulate social interaction. The sequencing and timing of nonverbal behaviour, particularly eye contact, is used to maintain a smooth interaction and to indicate various things about a relationship. Thus, on the one hand, speakers tend to gaze less than listeners; there tends to be more eye contact during discussion of 'easier', less personal topics; there is more gaze if A likes B. On the other hand, eye contact is also used to seek information (is the other person bored?); to signal that the other person may begin to speak (for example, at the end of sentences or utterances) and to initiate social encounters (as when a barman lets one 'catch his eye').

Such behaviour is thus highly salient to acquaintance: for one thing it is used to convey friendliness or willingness to interact; for another it helps to sequence and regulate social encounters so that individuals do not continually interrupt one another's speeches. Both of these functions require an amount of skill on the part of the behaving individual. An individual who does not have the skill to signal friendliness will not be approached (Cook, 1977); individuals who cannot regulate their interactions properly will be continually offending others with apparently 'rude' interruptions or will fail to recognise that they are required to speak next (Argyle, 1967). However, in relation to the other evidence presented above, the skill model of social behaviours suggests several other levels at which skill is also required - particularly a skill in regulating self disclosure, encoding and decoding affective states, and regulating agreement/disagreement or interpersonal evaluations.

Interaction and Relationship Management

There is also a further level of skill required - one that was mentioned in the last chapter: the management of the relationship and 'exhibition' of it to the outside world. In some cases there is also the problem of managing specific facets of the interaction itself (e.g. a dynamic stigma like a stutter).

The evidence earlier in this chapter suggests that not only are there ritual aspects of a relationship to manage (cf. Harré, 1977, and the discussion in Chapter 3), but more personalistic ones. Kelvin's (1977) arguments on tolerance of vulnerability (see above) indicate that an individual needs to bear in mind the extent to which he admits the other person to private information as well as, and as opposed to, the extent to which he discloses the general layout and geography of his self. The latest section might indicate that the individual needs to regulate his tolerance for touching, gazing and proximity to the Other, not only because different degrees of relationship necessarily carry different implications about permitted activities but also because he needs to demonstrate both to the other person and to other observers that a given level of intimacy exists in the relationship. For example, Kleinke, Meeker and Fong (1974) showed subjects videotapes of actors playing the role of engaged couples in an interview with a research psychologist. Couples either gazed at each other or did not gaze, used each other's first name five times or not at all and touched each other or did not touch. Subjects watching these tapes rated the couples on a range of scales and it was found that gaze made the most significant difference to their ratings of the couples, with touching couples rated more favourably than non-touching ones. The conclusion that would be drawn from such analysis is that the proper regulation of these revelatory and indicative behaviours is therefore an important determinant of other people's responses to a forming or formed relationship. Possibly - especially during the early points of relationship formation - the regulation of such cues is also an important signal to the relationship partner. If so then some skill in their regulation would be a pre-requisite in the development of a satisfactory acquaintance: the ability to perform them appropriately is a necessary - and under-researched - aspect of the formation of personal relationships.

## Assessing the Interactant

To a large extent the above behaviours are attractive or unattractive in their own right or they influence the course of acquaintance because they indicate certain states or feelings in the performer. However, whilst such behaviours often have agreed cultural significance (Argyle, 1969), interactants are also guided, one presumes, by the individually characteristic ways in which the other person performs these behaviours. In other words, interactants probably look for likely causes of observed behaviour, levels of skill in performing them, intentions lying beneath the acts, and the extent to which the behaviour indicates a stable personality characteristic or a merely temporary mood. By this means they may seek to 'clarify' a partner's behaviour by deducing the personality structure which gave rise to it (and hence his personal likability, as opposed to the general likability of his behaviour - since apparently likable behaviour can be performed for unlikable motives) at the same time as they are assessing his own degree of liking for themselves. The behaviour itself is thus only a guide to the underlying 'person' beneath it. In the development of acquaintance, the likely personality of the other person can be progressively deduced both from his behaviour and from the systematic search for the causes and intentions which gave rise to it (see Chapter 2). Thus from observable behaviour can be deduced not only the Other's feelings for oneself but also a basic model of his personality.

Behaviour

**Deducing liking from behaviour** Liking may follow from certain nonverbal behaviours either because they convey directly the message that the other person likes oneself or because they simply suggest warmth and closeness rather than a distant unfriendliness. Thus Mehrabian (1968) has shown that individuals sit closer to people that they like - and presumably the second person is able to deduce the extent to which the first one likes him from the distance at which he chooses to sit. Byrne, Baskett and Hodges (1971) took this a little further and showed that seating position could be influenced indirectly by manipulating similarity levels between subject and a confederate. Now, as the next chapter will show, attitude similarity is, as a general rule, attractive: therefore, a similar confederate should be liked more; therefore the subject should choose to sit closer to a similar confederate. Byrne et al.'s findings were largely consistent with this prediction, although the authors were cautious enough to suggest that physical distance cannot be used as the sole measure of degree of liking since liking is not the sole determinant of proximity. They are however able to cite the unpublished work of Efran who showed that, as the level of attitude similarity between subject and a stranger was manipulated, so there were variations in IJS score (see Chapter 1) and nonverbal behaviour simultaneously. However, Latta (1976) supports their general caution by indicating several respects and dimensions on which the verbal and nonverbal measures of attraction are unrelated. Furthermore Tesch, Huston and Indenbaum (1973) have shown that in interactions in a dynamic space (as opposed to the relatively static nature of experiments on seating behaviour - once you have chosen your seat you do not usually move from it) the physical proximity of interactants is unrelated to attraction levels or level of attitude similarity. Schiffenbauer and Schiavo (1976) have shown, however, that quality of interaction (positive or negative) modifies the influence of physical distance such that positive close interactions induce considerable liking whilst negative close interactions induce considerable disliking.

The hypothesis that liking is clearly related to nonverbal behaviour seems not to have fared well - but two things need to be said. First, in some of the experiments above subjects' liking for confederates was assessed by use of nonverbal measures above and as noted by Byrne, Baskett and Hodges (1971) it is likely that this is unreliable on its own. It is more likely that in normal interactions nonverbal and verbal factors <u>interact</u> to produce liking. Second the experiments do not always assess the extent to which subjects deduce a confederate's liking for them from various nonverbal activity on the confederate's part: rather, it is the simple likability of the confederate as indicated by subject's nonverbal behaviour that is assessed (i.e. the confederate is treated as a stimulus object). However, as we have already seen, a powerful influence upon other attraction responses is implied evaluation, or what subject thinks the other person thinks of him. Presumably he can deduce this from a confederate's behaviour just as he can from anyone else's. If the above workers are correct in assuming that nonverbal behaviour indicates liking then it could also be serving two roles in the experiments since subjects are deducing things about the confederate's liking for them - they don't know he is a confederate. The influence of implied evaluation is thus not ruled out in these studies; nor is nonverbal behaviour used as an independent variable as often as it could be.

Taking up the first point, it has already been shown that the nonverbal (paralinguistic) properties of speech can affect the way in which emotions are deduced or the speech is interpreted (see Chapter 3). Scherwitz and Helmreich (1973) have shown how such factors interact with the other nonverbal activities of individuals such as eye contact. When a confederate gave negative evaluations of the subject, increasing levels of eye contact led the subject to greater liking, whereas positive evaluations led to greater liking when there was a <u>lower</u> level of eye contact. In a second experiment it was shown that these effects were influenced by the extent to which positive verbal content was either personal or impersonal (i.e. with personal positive evaluation low eye contact levels were preferred but with impersonal positive verbal content, high eye contact levels led to greater liking).

Taking up the second point above (use of nonverbal cues as independent variables), Argyle et al. (1970) have investigated the relative impact of verbal and nonverbal style. It was found that nonverbal expressions of superiority-inferiority were far more powerful than verbal expressions of the same thing. A superior nonverbal performance was judged more unpleasant with all verbal messages (superior, neutral, inferior). However, judgements that the stimulus person is unpleasant are not necessarily the same as inferences that the stimulus person dislikes oneself, and this study therefore illustrates a principle that supports the points made earlier (about use of nonverbal cues as independent variables) but it does not answer it directly. In an experiment by Argyle, Alkema and Gilmour (1972) on the conflict between verbal and nonverbal indicators of friendliness-hostility, however, it was again found that nonverbal indicators had a far greater effect on subjects' rating than verbal indicators. There was also some evidence that subjects were confused by inconsistent nonverbal/verbal components of the message (which was not found in relation to superior-inferior behaviour) and rated inconsistent stimulus persons as insincere or unstable. It is particularly interesting that the latter finding should occur in an experiment on friendliness-hostility. However, it indicates the need for further work to establish the significance of friendly-hostile dimensions as behavioural indicators and particularly points up, as noted above, the need to examine the effects of _personal_ messages of liking-disliking in the two channels as opposed to the relatively general and impersonal friendliness-hostility conveyed by the videotape presentations used in these experiments.

This is all the more important since inconsistent personal messages of liking-disliking in verbal and nonverbal channels present the recipient with a highly complex social problem in everyday encounters: how should the inconsistency be construed? What is the true meaning of the message? This, of course, is particularly salient when meeting a new acquaintance whose underlying structure of beliefs, habits and 'style' is, as yet, unknown. In a study of contradictory meanings in different channels, Bugenthal, Kaswan and Love (1970) presented videotaped messages containing conflicting inputs (friendly or unfriendly) in different channels - viz verbal (content); vocal (tone); and visual (facial expression) to children and their parents. Joking messages (e.g. criticisms said with a smile) were interpreted more negatively by children than adults (especially if the joking person was female). Evidently children resolve incongruity by assuming the worst! Yet in this, as in the previous experiments, the stimulus material was _generally_ friendly or _generally_ hostile rather than particularly friendly to the person himself. 'Friendliness' to one-and-all is different from 'liking' for a particular person and in everyday encounters the individual's quest is precisely a quest for the extent to which he is getting special treatment from the Other (i.e. is the other person friendly to everyone or just me?). Additionally the design of these experiments is calculated to assess general agreement about the general components of general behaviour rather than examining individual differences in the particular abilities of individuals to detect the 'true' meaning or true amount of liking felt for them by a given target Other.

**Assessing the person from behaviour** The assessment of the 'true' meaning of behaviour is really a judgement about the personality lying beneath the observed behaviour, or the intention that the person had in doing what he did - or both. We have already seen several examples of behaviour that are not simply taken at face value by observers but which prompt a search for more evidence. A person's attractiveness can be assessed on the basis of judgements about his behaviour rather than simply on the basis of his behaviour alone: generous gifts may be seen as unattractive if their ultimate aim is perceived to be self-serving. Such judgements are presumably conducted on the basis of the appropriateness of the act to the situation and the extent to which one is justified, on a given piece of evidence, in making any inferential leaps from it about the underlying personality or intention. Clearly, some pieces of evidence will be better bases for such judgements than will others.

Whilst, as we have already seen, people do deduce attractiveness from the most insignificant of cues (dress, spectacles, etc.) such deductions can only be regarded as unsafe 'best guesses'. As an interaction proceeds, however, interactants are gradually exposed to safer bases for judgement, culminating in exposure to attitudes, beliefs, personality and cognitive structure itself. At the stage of interaction considered in this chapter (i.e. encounter with a stranger) is there any evidence that can be used as a relatively reliable indicator of personality? Argyle (1967; 1969; 1975) has indicated several ways in which individuals deduce personalities from posture or gesture or eye movements, although the question of the accuracy and reliability of such inferences is not one that is thoroughly settled yet. The problem is complicated by the fact that both permanent personality characteristics (e.g. dominance) and also temporary mood states (such as fear or aggression) are assessable from nonverbal behaviour and different judges have different abilities at performing the different judgemental tasks (Argyle, 1969). Libby and Yaklevich (1973) have also argued that permanent dispositional features of the person, rather than temporary affective states or moods, could be communicated by nonverbal behaviour such as eye contact. Three types of need (nurturance, that is need for affection and control; intraception, that is thoughtful analysis of others' feelings; abasement) were examined as contributors to eye movements during interaction; and various distinguishable patterns emerged. Subjects high in abasement looked away from an interviewer more than those low in abasement; subjects high in nurturance maintained eye contact more than low nurturant subjects. The authors concluded that the face 'leaks' information to observers about personality. But this presumes that observers are looking for it, that they actually make judgements like the experimenters did, and that they have the same acute observational techniques and the same personality variables in mind. Studies testing the ability of subjects to detect, interpret and assess the impact and meaning of the various nonverbal cues emitted relative to attraction are less frequent than those indicating how different degrees of attraction evoke different nonverbal behaviours. Presumably people would not emit these behaviours if they served no function, so presumably other people can detect them and interpret them correctly. But even so, people may manifest different levels of abilities at doing so.

It seems likely that individuals will respond to others' behaviours in these terms according to their expectations as to the type and amount of certain types of activity they should 'receive'. In a study of the effects of being ignored (i.e. when amount of attention is deficient), Geller et al. (1974) found that ignored subjects did not react by leaving the interaction or by expressing anger but by evaluating themselves and the ignoring confederate less favourably and by rewarding confederates less. If it were safe to generalise from this finding to other forms of behaviour one would be tempted to suggest that inappropriate behaviour (or violation of expectations) yields dislike of the person acting inappropriately. If interpersonal disagreement were construed as violation of expectations (since one expects not to be challenged too consistently, to be wrong too often or to be confronted with evidence of incompetence too frequently) then the experiment of Gormly, Gormly and Johnson (1972) is relevant. These authors exposed subjects to moderate amounts of disagreement on social attitudes, answers to IQ test questions and their own personality characteristics. Individuals tended to respond in different but relatively stable and consistent ways to such disagreement (even when responses were assessed in three different ways) and these involved various forms of derogation or rejection of disagreeing persons. Individual differences, in terms of differing levels of expectation about likely outcomes, and about how to interpret or respond to departures from expectation seem to indicate the fruitfulness of further examination of individual abilities to interpret the behaviour of others specifically in attraction and acquaintance contexts.

Intentions

The ability to interpret a behavioural sequence 'correctly' and hence to make the correct assessment of the intended likability of the behaviour depends in part on the ability to perceive the intention behind the act. This depends in turn on a model of the other's personality ('I know he seemed to act unfairly, but he isn't really like that, so there must be another reason') and on the ability to observe differences between the way he treats oneself and other people. It is unfortunate that there are currently very few studies investigating an individual's perceptions of another person's interactions with third parties and the literature is currently overbalanced in favour of studies assessing an individual's perceptions of another person's interactions with him alone. Yet the interpretation of a given level of friendliness to oneself can be clarified by observing the habitual level that the other person bestows on others that he meets.

**Observing the Other with Self** Since many examples of this kind of observation have already been presented, this section will confine itself to those additional instances which illustrate the processes whereby an observer assesses the 'interpersonal intent' of the other person in respect of the observer (e.g. his hostility, his intention to influence or persuade). Naturally such observations will influence an individual's willingness to interact with the Other - but it does so not only at a simple level of reaction ('He is being hostile so I will withdraw') but also at a more complex level ('He is being hostile, so it is unlikely that we shall reward one another now; it is, furthermore, unlikely that we shall communicate rewardingly in the future; there is therefore no likelihood of a satisfactory future relationship').

As a result of one's interpretation of the Other's motives, feelings and intentions, one is likely to behave in certain ways towards the Other (e.g. one is less likely to take the trouble to find out about people one does not expect to form a relationship with). For example, Stephan (1973) encouraged subjects to imagine that they would be paired with another subject who was either similar or dissimilar to themselves and either liked or disliked them. Subjects then took part in an interview with this person (so they believed: the person was actually an experimental assistant), during which they stated their attitudes and the (unseen) other person responded either similarly, dissimilarly or neutrally. It was found that the amount which the subject afterwards felt he knew about the interviewer was affected by his beliefs about the partner's similarity and liking. Subjects in the 'dislike' condition felt they knew less about the person than those in the 'like' condition.

Equally, one's interpretation of another person may be moderated by the extent to which he appears to want to dominate or persuade. Mehrabian and Williams (1969) examined whether liking for a partner was related to the ability to perceive his degree of intended persuasiveness. It was found not only that this was largely the case but also that observers were able, as a general rule, to detect the true intention of the communicator and perceive the extent to which he did actually <u>intend</u> to influence or persuade. There is also some connection between this work and that indicating a relationship between influence in a small group and preference for individual group members. Tagiuri and Kogan (1960) examined <u>perceived</u> influence and the extent to which individuals preferred those who influenced them or those whom they themselves influenced. The authors distinguished four types of relationship between liking and influence: Type I subjects liked those whom they felt they influenced <u>and</u> those who influenced them; Type II subjects liked only those whom they influenced; Type III subjects liked only those who influenced them; Type IV subjects showed no appreciable relationship between liking and influence. However, Brickman and Seligman (1974) have shown that judgements of influence (competence) and attractiveness are intertwined with perceptions and private expectancies about performance and effectiveness. Their study concerned subjects' reactions to 'public' stories about a stimulus individual's competence when they were also informed about his own private feelings. Stimulus persons who were inclined (privately) to overestimate their own competence vis a vis the 'public' estimate were invariably rated lower in attractiveness (but not necessarily lower in competence). On a related point, Norman (1974) has shown that highly competent sources (experts) are rated more influential than highly attractive sources when each presents a battery of supporting arguments for a given belief. Evidently people respond differently to attractive and expert/competent individuals in a way which reflects the behaviour which is 'appropriate' in the two cases: experts are supposed to have lots of supporting arguments for their beliefs; other people are not.

A further influence upon attributions of intent (and of likability) is the judgement of the extent to which a person intended to be hostile. If he acted aggressively from carelessness or lack of thought rather than from hostility, then presumably his aggression would be regarded in a different light. Palmer and Altrocchi (1967) examined the extent to which individuals were judged as acting in hostile fashion unconsciously, and found that the personality characteristics of the judge were largely responsible for the different levels of unconscious hostility attributed to others. Since the attribution of unconscious hostility does, to an extent, absolve the person from the responsibility for his actions, the fact that there are individual differences in tendencies to excuse or condemn 'hostility' is as significant as the fact that there are differences in assigning given behaviour to the category 'hostile'. Some people perceive others as less hostile, whatever; some people excuse it more when they think they see it. Clearly this will affect their levels of liking for the 'hostile' others. However, the stimulus material in the Palmer and Altrocchi study was a film containing professional actors. It may be that actors encode 'hostility' in ways that differ from other people. In an investigation of the relationship between hostility and nonverbal action in college students, Freedman et al. (1973) tested the hypothesis that individuals using 'object-focussed movements' (i.e. those gestures that punctuate and qualify speech) would be construed as showing overt hostility whilst those using body-focussed movements (i.e. activity that is continuous in nature and apparently split off from speech - such as playing with the hair) would be construed as avoiding overt expressions of hostility. These predictions were confirmed.

Observation of an individual's behaviour with self thus provides several pieces of evidence relating to his intentions, his desires to influence, his level of hostility whether overt or covert. However, from the individual's point of view it is important to establish whether such intentions and hostility are due to dispositional (personality) factors, casual (situational) factors, episodic factors (such as mood fluctuations, internally caused) or particular features of the other person's response to the individual as a person. As the individual interacts more with the other person as the acquaintance proceeds, he can gather more information to help him clarify such things. One way of doing this is to observe the other person's characteristic mode of behaviour with other people.

**Observing the Other person with others** If a person is hostile to me, the chances are I will not like him. If that person is then hostile to someone else (so argue Aronson and Cope, 1968) the chances are that I will like that third person - even if I know little about him. My liking for him is solely due to the fact that he is my enemy's enemy. Results supported the prediction even when the only similarity implied between the subject and third person was that they were both treated harshly by the same person!

Scott (1973) and Touhey (1974) have both examined the extent to which subjects could deduce P's liking for O (or P's attractiveness to O) simply from observing certain facts about the relationship between P's and O's attitudes. Touhey's experiment also included a task where subjects indicated their own liking for P. This was done in a design where subjects were asked to ascribe personality characteristics to P on the basis of his level of liking for O! Put into other words, subjects were asked to observe a relationship between P and O, to deduce the personality structure which P probably had if he reacted to O in a given way, and then to rate P for attractiveness on this basis. Among the results were the findings that two consistent sets of undesirable personality characteristics were attributed to Ps who displayed inappropriately high or inappropriately low ratings of attraction for specific proportions of similar attitudes with O. Thus observers appear to have some notion of what treatment someone 'should' get in certain circumstances - and they condemn those who do not oblige.

Another related aspect of this problem is the ability of subjects to differentiate between the treatment they receive at the hands of another and the treatment others receive. Jones and Archer (1976) arranged for subjects to perceive a target Self-Disclosing to two other people and either disclosing or concealing a particular stigma. Subjects then met the discloser and he either did or did not disclose the stigmatising information about himself to the subjects. What happens if the discloser reveals a stigma to others but not to the subject? Or if he does not disclose stigma to others - only to the subject (personalistic disclosure)? Results showed that personalistic disclosers were preferred to someone who did not reveal the stigma to anyone but that revelation of stigma to others rather than the subject did not make the subject like him less. This latter result is only surprising if one assumes that personal revelation of such material is much more important than any other evidence which could be used to form an impression of the other person - wherever the evidence originates from. In other words, it is surprising if it is permissible and safe to make the assumption that disclosure of stigma is an invariable indication that the discloser likes oneself better than other people - in short, if his intention in revealing stigma is to bestow increased liking.

Evidence from Walster et al. (1973) suggests that where an individual has proof that a person likes him <u>more than other people</u> he will like that person better. In a series of experiments on the attractiveness of 'playing hard to get' using a variety of experimental situations concerned with aspects of dating and a variety of experimental confederates from prostitutes to college students, results of varying cogency were obtained. The upshot of the series of experiments could be summarised as the findings that a woman's desirability is a combined function of how hard she is for the subject to get and how hard she is for other men to get. A selectively hard-to-get woman (easy for the subject, hard for everyone else) was strongly preferred to uniformly hard-to-get or uniformly easy-to-get women. The <u>selectively</u> hard-to-get woman was attributed with all the assets of the uniformly hard/easy-to-get woman (selectivity, friendliness, warmth, easy-going nature) but none of these persons' liabilities.

Once again, therefore, it seems that several important and interactionally-salient consequences follow from the ability to distinguish one's behaviour towards a given person from one's behaviour toward another. The ability to indicate liking for someone else seems to depend on such an ability to differentiate effectively; the ability to assess whether someone likes one or not depends to an extent on similar skills.

Skill?

The above evidence contributes to the view that the ability to encode his own emotions in his behaviour, to decode other people's emotions and intentions from their behaviour and to respond appropriately will jointly have substantial effects on an individual's desire to acquaint, his liking for particular others and his willingness to become involved. Equally his ability to differentiate his treatment of another person from his behaviour towards others in general will affect that person's willingness to interact with him. So too his ability to detect when he is getting special treatment at the other person's hands will affect the likelihood of his personal involvement with that person. These discriminative abilities may well be found to differ from one individual to another, just as some people are notably worse at construing the emotional content of messages than others (pathologically so in the case of schizophrenics: McPherson et al. 1971).

In the context of nonverbal behaviour it has been argued (Argyle, 1969; Argyle and Kendon, 1967) that certain aspects of social behaviour amount to a skilled performance with many of the properties of analogous skills like typing or driving a car. Responses must be sequenced correctly; they must be appropriate to the situation; they must reflect changes in the environment and so forth. Using this model it has been possible to detect individual differences in the ability to perform certain nonverbal skilled sequences (e.g. Libet and Lewinsohn, 1973 who examined the behaviour of depressed patients). Such differences are usually related to failures in encoding or decoding emotion or intention, or to failure to realise the dynamic significance of certain sequences of behaviour.

Could the development of acquaintance be conceived to be a skill? At the level considered so far, it clearly involves not only adequate sequencing of the appropriate behaviour (ranging from nonverbal activity to Self-Disclosure) and appropriateness of behaviour to situations (ranging from how to indicate or negotiate degree of intimacy to ignoring of others) but also the correct response to changes in the atmosphere surrounding a progressing, dynamic interaction (ranging from evaluations of Self Esteem to interpretation of Others' behaviour in relation to oneself and other people). Superficially, then, acquaintance does amount to a skill in some sense. However, the suggestion at this point of this book goes further. It starts from the view that one complex component of acquaintance amounts to the process of erection of models of the other person's personality and cognition on the basis of observed behaviour. The ability to erect accurate or useful models will depend on the ability to detect signs in behaviour that are relevant to the erection of the models; and this will depend on all the features of interaction that have been discussed in this chapter. The skills involved here are more than those surrounding management of the nonverbal content of the interaction and will entail the release of information at the correct rate, reliance on different cues at different points in the interaction, and so forth. It is also a safe bet that individuals will differ in their abilities to make useful deductions from the facts that they observe in interaction and therefore that they will differ in their ability to make models of their partner's personality and hence will differ in their ability to make appropriate and attractive responses to his behaviour in ways that would encourage greater intimacy in the interaction. This is especially likely to be true of those cues discussed so far, since they provide at best shaky and unreliable evidence about the detail of a person's thinking or personality. It is plausible, however, that one could talk of different levels of acquaintance skills and one would mean more than simply the management of the nonverbal content of interaction. Indeed, as an interaction proceeds and acquaintance develops, individuals will be exposed more often and at greater depth to the attitudes, beliefs and thought processes of the other person. These provide greater insights into his personality but represent a different sort of evidence upon which to found a model of it, and therefore may require different types of skills to process it and use it most effectively. Accordingly, the next chapter considers the place of attitudes in acquaintance.

# CHAPTER FIVE

# ATTITUDES AND ACQUAINTANCE

Whilst the previous two chapters have concerned aspects of individuals which incidentally may prompt observers to make evaluations or assessments of attractiveness, they have primarily concerned external cues: that is, cues which are not directly concerned with an individual's cognitive structure or content nor with his personality nor his beliefs. It has been argued, however, that observers nonetheless make use of such cues as dress, nonverbal style and so on in order to make inferences about the individual's cognition, beliefs, personality - albeit unsafe inferences.

## Influences of Attitudes

At some point in an interaction it becomes possible for interactants to make rather safer explorations of each other's cognition directly as, for instance, by discussing contentious issues, by asking each other's opinion or by offering comments about other people or events. In these cases the interactants' beliefs, personality and cognition are explicitly laid open for scrutiny and individuals therefore have the opportunity of access to new aspects of one another. Where previously (Chapters 3 and 4) they have been restricted to inference about the general nature of each other's cognition now they are exposed to it more directly. Where previously they have been unsure, now they may directly test out their model of the other's cognition. Whilst such direct evidence is therefore different in level, in nature, in quality and in reliability than the 'earlier' evidence, processes of inference and judgement may still attach to it. For instance, even when someone expresses a given attitude one may still ask oneself whether it is his true opinion or one made for the benefit of the audience in order to ingratiate or present himself in a socially desirable way. Inferences about personality structure could still be made erroneously on the basis of attitudes, therefore, but one might expect that their status as direct evidence about cognition would still make them significant factors in the acquaintance process. This chapter examines some of the evidence: however, as will become clearer later in the chapter, most of the work on attitudes in this context is explicitly concerned with their role as determinants of responses to strangers rather than with their role in the development of acquaintance and this should be borne in mind during what follows. Later on we will examine the possible ways in which the work on attraction (as defined in Chapter 1) could fit into the process of acquaintance (ditto) and into the processes of development of a relationship.

It may be immediately clear that there are three aspects of 'attitudes' that may be relevant to acquaintance: attitude type; attitude structure; and attitude content. All three have been investigated but most emphasis has fallen on attitude content, which is therefore reserved here for a whole section on its own. However, the other two aspects are also important in their own right and will also illuminate some of the issues that will be discussed in relation to attitude content.

Attitude Type

Under the general label of 'attitude' are concealed several subtly different aspects of evaluative and descriptive processes - both in the layman's and the research psychologist's vocabulary. Sachs (1975) reports work on a distinction between _attitude_ (value) - that is, the degree of positivity or negativity that is felt about a given object, event, person, state of affairs - and _belief_ - for example, whether God exists, whether politicians really care about people. Thus one could have a belief about politicians (that they do care) and an attitude about them (degree of feeling towards them). Sachs showed that both similarity of beliefs and similarity of attitudes influenced subjects' liking for a stranger, but that attitude similarity exerted the greater influence on other aspects of interpersonal evaluation. In teasing apart other aspects of this same distinction, Goethals and Nelson (1973) tested the hypothesis that when a belief was at issue, agreement from an otherwise dissimilar Other would increase judgemental confidence more than agreement from a similar other; whereas when a value was at issue, agreement from a similar other would be more influential. The reason is that when (belief in) the existence of some attitude-object is in dispute, agreement from a dissimilar other shows that even those people with different perspectives can accept the truth of the belief, whereas agreement from a similar other cannot make an equal contribution to one's confidence. (Perhaps this is why there is more joy in Heaven over one sinner that repents...). In the case of attitude values, however, a dispute merely emphasises the different views that can be taken and support from someone else (i.e. the observation that someone similar to oneself makes the same evaluation) is encouragement that one's evaluation is substantially correct. Craig and Duck (1977) made further examination of the evaluative and descriptive elements of attitudes about other people and found that certain personality characteristics predisposed observers to be more (less) influenced by these two components of attitudes. Evaluative aspects of attitudes had greater influence on attractiveness than descriptive aspects did, but complex judges were more accepting of strangers who used different descriptive attitudes.

There are other ways in which the concept of 'attitude' can be split up, however, and several other types of attitudes have been investigated in the context of interpersonal attraction. Batchelor and Tesser (1971) follow Katz (1960) in identifying four distinct motivational bases for holding attitudes (and thus they divide attitudes up into 4 types on the basis of the function that they serve). These are: value expressive (i.e. attitudes that embody the individual's evaluation of some attitude-object); need for cognition (i.e. attitudes that help the individual to impose order on the world); utilitarian (i.e. attitudes that are held solely to facilitate the achievement of some objective and may be used ingratiatingly or for strictly practical purposes); ego defensive (i.e. attitudes held as a means of defending the self against attack). Working with these distinctions, Batchelor and Tesser (1971) found that strangers holding value-expressive attitudes were best liked and those holding ego-defensive attitudes were least liked. These authors suggested that value-expressive similarity provides stronger support for subjects' own attitudes than does similarity of any other kind. A recent study by Duck (1975a) provides strong conceptual support for Batchelor and Tesser's findings if one makes the not implausible assumption that individuals believe their own attitudes to be value-expressive (McCarthy, 1976). Duck found that both similarity of attitude content and similarity of reasons given for holding the attitude affected ratings of a stranger's attractiveness. As may be guessed from earlier comments here, this result was interpreted as indicating that dissimilarity of reasons for holding the attitude indicates deeper dissimilarity existing beneath the surface appearances of agreement - and hence the relatively negative response of subjects to such a combination of information items.

The latter finding and the next distinctions about attitude type will play a role much later in the chapter when we discuss the relationship between attitudes and personality and the significance of this link for acquainting individuals. These final distinctions about attitude type concern the extent to which the attitude relates to impersonal or personal objects and whether they refer to one's own behaviour or to other people's. McCarthy (1976), Duck and Craig (1977) and McCarthy and Duck (1976) have all pointed out that attitudes may refer to things, events, objects, political parties and the like or to people, character and personality. What may be the significance of this for acquainting individuals? Casual observation makes it clear that personal comments about others are usually taboo in early encounters or are reserved for discussion between friends. On the other hand, attitudes about things and events are the familiar fodder of casual discussion and are not taboo. McCarthy and Duck (in prep.) have shown that disagreement about things and about people has different significance to pairs of long-established friends (12 months' acquaintance) and pairs of forming friends (4-6 months' acquaintance). Tentative friends (4-6 months' duration) reacted more positively than Established friends (12 months or more) to attitudinal disagreement, but they were also more influenced by attitudes about objects than by attitudes about persons. Equally, Santee (1976) has distinguished between attitudes that are intrapersonal or reflexive (e.g. 'I enjoy drinking') and those that are interpersonal or relate to other people (e.g. 'I am in favour of women pursuing careers'). Since attitudes to self and attitudes to others are not necessarily the same, Santee tested the extent to which each of them influenced individuals' attraction to one another and found that similarity of intrapersonal attitudes was unrelated to attraction.

From this collection of evidence it would be safe to conclude that the type and focus of an attitude is a significant determinant of its salience in evoking liking and that its place in an acquaintance process may be likewise determined. However, before this can be decided conclusively, the relative significance of attitude structure and attitude content must also be determined. The above section looked at the classification of an individual attitude: the next two sections look at the influence of the relationship between attitudes and at the overall amounts of similarity of content that is implied.


Attitude Structure

In a series of papers Tesser has argued that whilst the evaluative nature of attitudes has received considerable attention in attraction research, the structural relationship between an individual's attitudes has been overlooked (Tesser, 1971; 1972). Johnson and Tesser (1972, p. 154) elaborate this latter concept in the following way: 'Attitude structure refers to the relationship an actor sees among his attitudes. To the extent that an actor sees a relationship between two attitudes it implies that if he changes one attitude he will also change the other'. It is possible, Tesser argues, for two individuals to be evaluatively similar (by rating a number/proportion of attitude objects similarly) or structurally similar (by having similar structural relationships between the component attitudes making up their cognitive space). Evidence in support of this proposal has been presented in the papers listed above, and it is found not only that individuals are able to perceive differences in structural aspects of strangers but that attraction is positively related to structural similarity and evaluative similarity (Tesser, 1971). Johnson and Tesser (1972) elaborated this finding by means of a study showing that structural similarity was preferred in situations where the individual was faced with a task involving predicting a partner's attitudes. Evidently knowledge of structure makes people feel more confident about working out the likely content of the other person's attitudinal complex. This is an especially relevant finding to bear in mind when considering the influence on attraction that is exerted by attitude content itself.

Attitude Content

There are several studies that have looked at the relationship between attitude content and attractiveness, ranging from those studies that examine attitudes expressed in the service of creating a good impression (e.g. studies of ingratiation - Jones et al. 1968; social desirability - McLaughlin, 1971; Stalling, 1970; obsequious misrepresentation of beliefs - Cooper and Jones, 1969; and attitude 'popularity' - Posavac and McKillip, 1973) to those where features of individuals' attitudes or opinions are related to their sociometric activity (e.g. Newcomb, 1961). Such research has a long - indeed, ancient - history which goes back beyond Aristotle, through Dale Carnegie (How to win friends and influence people) to early studies in the psychological research literature (Winslow, 1937; Richardson, 1939, for example). However the main impact of research on attitude and attractiveness has come since 1961 when Byrne first published a study showing that similarity of attitudes (an example of reinforcement, as is described below) promoted attraction to strangers. The rest of this chapter will examine his approach, but it should be noted throughout that Byrne's work is concerned with attraction (i.e. initial encounter - see Chapter 1) and whilst we shall examine the ways in which such work may fit into the present conceptualisation of the acquaintance process this is not necessarily the main concern of Byrne himself. There are accordingly two utterly distinct features of the work to be appraised: the extent to which Byrne's work explains attraction behaviour (or a part of it); and the extent to which the principles identified by Byrne could explain or be incorporated into an explanation of acquaintance. The confusion of these two issues has often misled critics, as shall be seen.

## The Attraction Paradigm

The work within the framework known as 'The Attraction Paradigm' (Byrne, 1971) is extensive and has occupied a book on its own. The purpose of this section is to examine the main principles of the work, to give the flavour of the approach and to evaluate its contribution in the context of the present outlook rather than to give an exhaustive review. Fuller details of the supporting research are available in Byrne (1969, 1971), Byrne and Griffitt (1973) and Griffitt (1974). Furthermore, readers can remind themselves of the basic theoretical tenets of this outlook by consulting Chapter 2 of this book: 'Classical conditioning', beginning on page 48.

Outline of Methods and Principles

The work on the attraction paradigm is almost unique in social psychology in its strict adherence to one systematic method of enquiry with three main features. First, the approach has, to date, been concerned primarily with the effects of similarity-dissimilarity of attitude content. Second, it is concerned with the influence of this upon ratings of attractiveness made about strangers in an impression-formation task. Third, it most usually assesses these ratings by means of one particular paper-and-pencil method known as the IJS (Interpersonal Judgement Scale) which has already been described (p. 34).

The requirement to measure the manipulated effects of attitude similarity may have struck some readers as puzzling. How can one manipulate similarity of attitudes between two people? More especially, how can it be done in a precise and controlled manner in an experiment? The answer to these queries provides also the answer to the question of why attraction to strangers is the keystone of Byrne's approach. As noted in Chapter 1 (p. 19) it is difficult to manipulate subjects' beliefs about what attitudes their friends actually possess, so, after Smith (1957), Byrne uses the following approach. Individual subjects' attitude profiles are obtained some time before the experiment proper (or else as the first stage of the experiment). During the intervening period between the session and the true experiment, the experimenter completes another attitude scale in such a manner that it is similar/dissimilar to the subject's own to a precise degree (say 25% or

50% or 75% similar). This scale is now presented to the subject as if it had been completed by another person in the experiment, who, because he is non-existent, is known as the Fictitious (Bogus, Hypothetical, Simulated, Standard) Stranger. Subjects' attraction responses to the Fictitious Stranger on the basis of this attitude scale are assessed by means of the IJS. This whole method is usually referred to as the Fictitious Stranger (or Bogus Stranger) Technique. Using this method Byrne (1961a) first demonstrated a causal relationship between level of attitude similarity and amount of liking.

Before proceeding to discuss the implications of this, let us pause to consider certain points whose disposal now may cause avoidance of misunderstanding later. Research, as Chapter 1 suggests, is a dynamic business and so is theory building. As each new study is completed, so its results may modify parts of an approach or strengthen others. It may cast up new proposals or techniques just as it may cast down old ones; it may cause the emphasis of one aspect of an hypothesis or neglect of another. However, no single study has ever solved all the problems associated with a given research issue. The problems are usually convoluted and extensive so that a series of studies may be required to clarify all the points. It is therefore no criticism of a given study (assuming that it is sound methodologically) that it does not solve all the problems or that it raises other questions: indeed, it should rather be seen as praiseworthy if a given study is sound and yet still indicates the need for and fruitfulness of further work. Accordingly, a good way to proceed, given the establishment of a causal relationship such as that found by Byrne (1961a) is first to examine the nature of this relationship more closely and then to perform factorial experiments which place it in context, show how it is affected by other factors and generally establish its status. Since Byrne has chosen to proceed in this sytematic way, it should be borne in mind that aspects of his theory still remain to be explored - but this does not necessarily mean that they have been overlooked. Equally, since theory development is also a dynamic process, certain aspects of Byrne's approach to the attitude-attraction relationship have been reconsidered in the light of empirical evidence and certain features of the original statement have been brought into greater prominence than they were given to start with.

The basic finding (Byrne, 1961a) was that attitude similarity caused attraction. This could be explained in terms of Balance Theory (see Chapter 2) but Byrne chose to develop an argument following Learning Theory and Festinger's (1954) Social Comparison Theory (see also Chapter 2). Byrne argued that every person wishes to interpret and respond to the environment logically and looks to other people for a means of assessing the logic or acceptability of his interpretations and responses. When other people manifested similar attitudes therefore, they were assumed to be indicating that they interpret the environment in the same way as the person himself and the person thus felt supported or reinforced. Such interactions thus become rewarding. Since the proportion of times that another person rewards like this is theoretically more likely to be important than simply the total number of times, Byrne and Nelson (1965) compared these two things and found that proportion rather than total number was indeed the vital feature of the stranger that determined attraction level. Indeed, a formula was derived empirically from the study to embody the authors' view that attraction was a linear function of the proportion of similar attitudes (i.e. the higher the proportion of similar attitudes, the higher the subsequent level of attraction expressed on the IJS). This law, derived empirically rather than hypothetically, described how people had actually behaved and the interesting question that it naturally raises for subsequent research is the extent to which it predicts how other people will behave in other studies. The law is represented in the formula:

$$Y = m \left[ \frac{\Sigma S}{\Sigma(S + D)} \right] + k$$

where Y is attraction, S and D are similar and dissimilar attitudes, respectively, and m and k are empirically derived constants (Byrne, 1971).

It was subsequently found that this formula was inadequate on its own in view of the fact that it took no account of the subjective importance of the attitudes involved. Clearly it is likely to be more significant for an individual to find that a stranger is similar on an attitude that the individual rates as personally important than on one that he does not. Byrne and Rhamey (1965) produced evidence to support this proposal and modified the Byrne-Nelson formula to read:

$$Y = m \left[ \frac{\Sigma (PR \times M)}{\Sigma (PR \times M) + \Sigma (NR \times M')} \right] + k$$

where Y is attraction, M and M' are magnitudes and m and k are the slope and Y intercept respectively. In other words, attraction 'is a positive linear function of the sum of the weighted positive reinforcements associated with [a person] divided by the total number of weighted positive and negative reinforcements associated with him' (Clore and Byrne, 1974, p. 152).

This version of the formula takes account of the subjective weight of the attitudes involved. As Byrne, Nelson and Reeves (1966) subsequently showed, the importance of an attitude could also be related to the difficulty with which it could be validated by means other than social comparison (e.g. value-expressive attitudes about highly complex issues). Clearly the more difficult an attitude is to validate by non-social means, the more impact will attach to the discovery that someone else shares that attitude and thus 'validates' it.

Up until this point, although Byrne's formulation of his proposal had received considerable attention, it became necessary for Byrne to re-emphasise the nature of the explanation that had been offered for the observed relationship between attitude similarity and attraction. For one thing, attitude similarity had been conceived to be rewarding since it offered evidence of consensual validation. Byrne and Clore (1967) elaborated this notion by discussion of the Need for Effectance (i.e. the need that is satisfied by evaluating and finding consensual validation for one's view of the world). An inverted U-shaped function was discovered in which both very highly and very lowly aroused and confused subjects responded less markedly to attitudinal similarity-dissimilarity than did moderately-aroused subjects. Once a need like this has been postulated, it is easier to be clear about the other aspect of Byrne's formulation that was found to need re-emphasis about this time: namely, that it is essentially a classical conditioning model. In other words, Byrne argues that an individual finds the experience of consensual validation rewarding or reinforcing; associates the positive affect so produced with the person who provides the reinforcement; and manifests this association in the form of a positive evaluation of the person (liking) or favourable treatment of him (thus Golightly, Huffman and Byrne, 1972, showed that attitude similarity affected the amount of cash that one person would approve as a loan to another person even when relevant financial information, such as income and debts, was held constant. Equally, Mitchell and Byrne, 1973, showed that attitudinally similar defendants were given lighter sentences by authoritarian jurors). It is in this context that the effects of attitude similarity should be seen: attitude similarity is one form of reinforcement or reward and others could be found - it just happens that Byrne is interested in examining attitude similarity. Equally, the theory is about reinforcement not attitude similarity and it could be the case that there are circumstances where dissimilarity is reinforcing. In support of the first of these claims, Golightly and Byrne (1964), Lombardo, Weiss and Buchanan (1972) and Kian, Rosen and Tesser (1973) have successfully used attitude similarity as a reinforcement to condition subjects in learning experiments; on the second point (reinforcement from dissimilarity) evidence will be presented later.

**The basic strategy: objections and ripostes** For Byrne and his co-workers attraction is a response conditioned to the positive affect induced to the reinforcement provided (by and large) by attitude similarity. Dislike is a response conditioned to the negative affect induced to the negative reinforcement provided (by and large) by attitude dissimilarity. Attraction depends on reinforcement and if the degree and direction of this can be assessed, then the degree of attraction is predictable by means of the empirically-derived laws of Byrne and Nelson and Byrne and Rhamey.

The approach has several characteristics - both implicit and explicit above - which have been criticised by other workers. For one thing the methods are very precise and controlled. This has led to various forms of the complaint that the laboratory study of attraction is therefore artificial. Whilst it is best to reserve general discussion of this until we have looked at the extent to which Byrne's findings are generalisable (next section) there is a point to discussing certain limited aspects of the methods here. Most forms of this criticism of

Byrne amount to the claim that systematic study of one aspect of attraction behaviour is too narrow a view of the purpose of scientific endeavour and that attempts to set up a paradigm for research are invitations to the fulminations of critical attacks (Levinger, 1972). Thus Levinger criticises Byrne because his subjects and the strangers rarely interact (whenever the bogus stranger method is used clearly they cannot). Similarly, Wright and Crawford (1971) argue that in focussing on attitude content Byrne overlooks the different types of attitudes on which males and females may focus in 'real life', or assumes that all subjects will place equal emphasis on attitudinal agreement/disagreement. However, it is not quite fair of such critics to attack Byrne for failing in what he has never attempted. As noted at the start of this chapter, Byrne is concerned with attraction - initial responses to strangers - and not with acquaintance, as these critics are. To make this particular criticism is to beg precisely the question that Byrne has never yet attempted to ask: namely, whether the behaviour observed in attraction is the same as (or even the basis for) the behaviour observable in acquaintance. These critics assume that Byrne assumes that it is - but he does not (Byrne, Ervin and Lamberth, 1970, p.158). It seems that he would allow, however, that it is a legitimate focus of concern and we shall proceed to examine a way in which it could be incorporated into enquiries on acquaintance. The difference, therefore, between the present approach and those of Levinger and Wright and Crawford is that this approach broadly accepts that Byrne's work on attraction is relevant to and assimilable within a conception of acquaintance development. To prepare the way for a consideration of this conceptualisation, however, it is necessary to examine the status of Byrne's work in terms of its generalisability and limitations.

Findings Relevant to the Basic Position

As indicated above, the studies by Byrne are tied closely to the laboratory and focus on strangers. There are thus a number of issues that they raise, as the position has been outlined so far. How far are the findings generalisable to 1. the world outside the laboratory; 2. other populations than the students who are invariably the subjects in such experiments? How far do the processes reflect initial attraction as it occurs in real life (as distinct from the question of how accurately they actually concern the early points of an extended acquaintance process in real life)? How far are the findings influenced by the temporary states of subjects in the laboratory and how far are they indicative of general, stable relationships?

**Generalisability**  Any work conducted systematically in the laboratory over a period of years runs the risk of finding out too much about student subjects and too little about anyone else.  An important question is therefore the extent to which laboratory findings on students (who may be a group particularly concerned over attitudinal issues) are representative of the processes shown by other groups of individuals.  A study by Byrne, Griffitt, Hudgins and Reeves (1969) examined the responses within the Bogus Stranger Method of schizophrenics, surgical patients, alcoholics and corpsmen.  The relationship between attitude similarity and attraction was found to hold as true of most of these subjects as it did of the college students used in previous work.  The only exceptions were the schizophrenics (who yielded a linear relationship between attitudes and attraction - but one that differed in degree from that usually found) and the job corpsmen with low educational attainment (whose abilities were perhaps not suited to the tasks set them during the experiment).  Further studies by Byrne and co-workers have indicated the replicability of the earlier and usual findings when other groups of subjects are employed, including primary and secondary schoolchildren (Byrne and Griffitt, 1966b) and elderly subjects (Griffitt, Nelson and Littlepage, 1972).  A study by Byrne and many others (Byrne et al., 1971) further demonstrated the predicted linear relationship between proportion of similar attitudes and attraction in 6 different cultural/ethnic groups: Texans; Chinese- and Japanese-Americans in Hawaii; Japanese; Indians and Mexicans.  McCarthy (1976) has found the same to be true of British subjects.  It does seem on this evidence that Byrne is justified in referring to this as 'the ubiquitous relationship'.

**Possible limits on application**  As indicated in Chapter 1, an empirical law or a theoretical viewpoint or a hypothetical relationship may be 'limited' by several factors in the sense that the relationship may behave in a modified - but still lawful - way in certain circumstances.  Such limits do not undermine the validity of the relationship: they merely specify the ways in which its form may be expressed, or may point to factors which signify that the relationship is not as central in certain circumstances as it would be in others. Three versions of this point have been put forward in this context:

<u>The attitudes may never get discussed</u>  Although attitude similarity influences attraction, it may be the case that those attitudes that are important for an individual may never get an airing in a particular relationship and thus he may never find out that the Other person is similar to himself. Whilst possible, this does not undermine the significance of the attitude-attraction relationship. A particular pan of water may never get heated, but that is not to say that it would not boil at $100^{\circ}$C if it were. The important point to be extracted here, however, is the implication that in 'real life' individuals may attend to things other than attitude similarity in determining their attraction to a stranger. Clearly they do (see Chapters 3 and 4) but the important question is whether their treatment of these other cues is guided by the same (or similar) principles as their treatment of attitude similarity. Individuals can be classically conditioned to the positive affect from a variety of cues; they can draw inferences to personality on the basis of attitudes or other cues and the same principles may be involved whether attitudes are discussed or not. When the attitudes <u>are</u> discussed then the inferences may simply be safer and more significant influences on attraction.

<u>The percentage of reinforcement may be higher in the laboratory</u>  In any laboratory study of the reinforcement properties of attitude similarity the percentage reinforcements are strongly manipulated: in real life they may not be so strong or obvious. In the laboratory two different strangers may be as much as 80% or as little as 20% similar to the subject and the difference is obvious: in real life they may not be so markedly similar/dissimilar or so notably discrepant from each other (e.g. 41% and 45%: could subjects detect the difference?). Truly, in 'real life' the subjects are likely to encounter harder discrimination tasks than they are given in the laboratory and it may be that the relationship between attitude similarity and attraction would be weakened. However, since this hypothesis has not yet been tested, it remains

equally possible that attitude similarity is invested with even <u>greater</u> significance in 'real life', since it is clear evidence about a person's personality. Indeed, Duck and Richards (1976) established that attitude similarity discriminated between friends and non-friends in established non-student populations in a natural field study. Once again, therefore, this present objection on the limits of the attitude-attraction relationship may have been overstated: the most it can establish is that attitudes play a less central role in determining attraction when other factors are also present. This is ultimately an empirical question which could be illuminated either by complex multifactorial laboratory experiments manipulating attitude similarity along with many other factors or (less satisfactorily) by 'real life' correlational studies.


<u>'Stranger' techniques accelerate and truncate real life processes</u> Although studies of attraction involving attitude manipulations are intended to be studies reflecting what occurs in meetings with strangers, this appearance may be deceptive. It has been claimed above that attitudes do not come to a central position in acquaintance until <u>after</u> initial processes of encounter (cf. Berger and Calabrese's suggestions on entry and personal phases of acquaintance, Chapter 2). Indeed, Newcomb (1961) found that pre-acquaintance attitude similarity predicted the friendship choices made after four months of acquaintance but not initial choice activity. In a more intensive situation Griffitt and Veitch (1974) studied the ability of pre-acquaintance attitude-similarity levels to predict the attraction responses of individuals confined in a fall-out shelter. However, the first occasion of measurement of liking/disliking was after the end of the first day of this intensive interaction, so the analogue with the Bogus Stranger studies is not exact. All other attempts by Byrne and co-workers to apply his methods to real life attraction (e.g. the Byrne, Ervin and Lamberth, 1970 study of computer dating) have involved subjects being given far longer to acquaint in the real life analogue than they get in the laboratory. The argument here is therefore that the stranger techniques actually 'rush' subjects through processes that take longer in real life and thus that Byrne's work on strangers, whilst <u>appearing</u> to reflect initial response to others is actually <u>tapping later</u> processes (perhaps ones that typically occur only hours later, depending on the intensity of the interaction - but

later than 'initial responses' all the same). This of course does not undermine the findings of these studies nor their theoretical importance; it merely suggests that examination of the place of the attitude-similarity effects in developing <u>acquaintance</u> may show their relevance to be later rather than earlier.

Since these considerations are relevant only to the basic approach entailed in the <u>methods</u> of Byrne's work, they do not amount to systematic consideration of the significance of the <u>theoretical</u> aspects of the paradigm: they represent a much lower-level consideration of possible criticisms. Predictably, Byrne's work has also been examined from several different theoretical levels (Clore and Byrne, 1974). In considering these next it should be clear that other things than attitudes could be identified as reinforcers (and this would support rather than undermine Byrne's views). For the present theoretical schema adopted here, we need establish only the place of attitudes in the hypothetical sequence of reinforcement variables in order to draw conclusions about the value of a reinforcement model in the explanation of developing <u>acquaintance</u> - which, to reiterate the point, is something that may be more our present concern than it is Byrne's.

Evaluation

There are many ways in which the opponents of a theoretical viewpoint and an associated experimental paradigm can attempt to prove it valueless. It can be valueless because it is wrong, quite simply wrong; valueless because it is inappropriate; valueless because it is artificial; valueless because it is unrepresentative of the phenomenon it attempts to explain; valueless because its operational form does not relate to its theoretical form (i.e. it does not adequately practise what it preaches); or valueless because it is right but obvious. Byrne's position has been variously, frequently and vigorously declared valueless in all of these ways. At present, however, it must be admitted that the majority of evidence is on Byrne's side. This section concerns itself with the more limited issue of the strength of Byrne's position by looking at some of the evidence for and against it; whilst the final section examines some broader issues including the paradigm's ability to account for acquaintance rather than simply attraction in first encounters. It should be borne in mind that there are several levels at which empirical findings apply to a theoretical formulation (Clore and Byrne, 1974) and only some of them are related to the truth or falsity of the theoretical propositions - as opposed to the value of the methods that are used to test them.

In the light of the findings presented in the previous section it would clearly be absurd to argue that Byrne is wrong, without qualification. His model has been shown consistently to provide predictive accounts of attraction behaviour in the setting in which it is studied; where other investigators have appeared to produce conflicting results it can often be shown that they have taken an unnecessarily and unjustifiably restrictive view of his theoretical stance (Taylor, 1970; Senn, 1971; Duck, 1971) limiting it to a similarity-attraction hypothesis - which it is not - instead of a classical conditioning model in which similarity of attitudes is cast as a reinforcing agent under certain conditions. Given the empirical law of attraction derived by Byrne and Nelson (1965) it has proved possible to indicate circumstances in which similarity of attitudes is <u>un</u>attractive (McCarthy and Duck, 1976); and, indeed, Byrne and Lamberth (1971) have been able to predict precisely the amount of adjustment in an attitude's valence which is necessary to convert unattractive similarity into attractive similarity (i.e. they have shown the precise arithmetical weighting required to reverse the attractiveness/unattractiveness of attitude similarity). The facility with which the theory predicts precisely and accurately the empirical relationship between relevant variables must count strongly in its favour and clearly refutes the argument that the position is wrong, pure and simple.

Some other misgivings have centred on the more qualified argument that Byrne's position is wrong in the sense that it is artificial and that, whatever might appear to happen in the laboratory in the hypothetical stranger paradigm, real-life just is not like that (Kaplan and Anderson, 1973). This persistent argument has been partially refuted by Byrne, Ervin and Lamberth (1970) who demonstrated that initial attitude similarity does effectively predict dating behaviour up to several months after the original pairing of the partners. The refutation is only partial because this work tells us that the experimental study of attitude similarity does correctly identify a feature relevant in real-life acquainting but it does not tell us the relative importance of attitude similarity in real-life activity or the extent to which it acts as a 'starter'. In other words, whilst similarity of attitudes may cause two people to be attracted after relatively brief encounters, it is not argued by Byrne to be the sole cause (or even the most important cause) of the development of an acquaintance into something deeper than initial attraction (see section above). With this reservation (which after all does not attack the value of the paradigm when it comes to attraction), it is clear that the paradigm cannot be condemned as inappropriate or artificial in any simple and obvious sense.

Perhaps a more serious issue is the question of the appropriateness and representativeness of the attitude measures and manipulations used. In the hypothetical stranger paradigm subjects are presented with data on the attitudes of Others and they express their attraction ratings of the Others on the basis of such information. This method therefore not only claims that people react to others' attitudes (which Byrne shows they do), but also makes the fairly substantial assumption that they respond to attitude scales in the same way as they would respond to attitudes presented by other means in real-life. Yet it is fairly clear that in real-life situations we do not gain the same _kind_ of access to other people's attitudes - they don't hand us a paper and pencil report of their attitudes in normal circumstances: the question is whether this difference matters psychologically. There are several distinct but related ways in which the hypothetical stranger paradigm could be declared artificial once this point is made. _First_, it could be claimed that we in fact respond to attitude scales in very different ways from those characterising our responses to real people. _Secondly_, and alternatively, it could be claimed that whilst everyone responds to attitude scales and real-life attitude information in comparable ways (i.e. that if the first objection above may be met) in real-life people have differential abilities in speed and accuracy of perception and identification of others' attitudes and when presented with attitude scales directly these deficiencies are obscured. This would mean that the attitude paradigm would mask variations in ability at the attitude assessment task in real-life and could therefore have led to a false evaluation of the importance of attitudes in acquaintance or attraction. _Thirdly_, it could be claimed that attitude presentation omits much contextual information which is generally present in real-life (e.g. in real-life an attitude may be evaluated not only for its similarity to one's own but also in terms of its source. The same attitude uttered by blacks and whites may have different valences - Byrne and Wong, 1962; the same attitudes from tall and short people may be evaluated differently - Bleda, 1972; the same attitude espoused by someone who looks attractive may be rated differently from its espousal by someone who is ugly - cf. Dion, 1972).

These three objections have been variously investigated. Banikiotes, Russell and Linden (1972) attempted to examine the question of whether reactions to information provided in the hypothetical stranger paradigm adequately reflected reactions to real-life material. They found some support for Byrne in that attraction in experimental and real-life conditions was predictable from knowledge of how two individuals had filled up an attitude survey. The laboratory-based hypothetical stranger manipulations were found to be more powerful in showing this effect than were real-life comparisons, but the effect was nevertheless present in both cases. The latter discrepancy can be explained in terms of topic importance which was found to have a greater effect on attraction in real-life than in the laboratory. So the proportion of agreements between two subjects may be a salient factor in the laboratory attraction settings, but in real-life the effect is much modified by specific attitudes and their importance. On the other hand, the representativeness of the hypothetical stranger methods when it comes to personality characteristics (as opposed to attitudes) was neither clearly supported in this study nor clearly undermined. On balance therefore these results show that hypothetical stranger methods might need to be viewed with some caution in certain circumstances but certainly they do not give grounds for rejecting the approach out of hand.

The second issue above (whether differential real-life perceptual accuracy is obscured in the hypothetical stranger paradigm) has not been directly studied. It is clear that people manifest different levels of ability at judging other people (Cook, 1977), but whether this suggests marked differences in attitude perception is an open empirical question. Such evidence as there is (e.g. Duck, 1973a) suggests that people tend to overestimate the existence of attitude similarity between themselves and their friends and underestimate it between themselves and non-friends. Clearly if there exist such differences and inaccuracies then the importance of attitudes in the acquaintanceships of people who are poorer at attitude recognition is likely to be overemphasised by the Bogus Stranger paradigm. This is especially so in the light of the previously-noted evidence from Banikiotes, Russell and Linden (1972) which showed that, in real-life, topic importance may be a central determinant of attraction responses. The strength with which some attitudes are held may be one factor that is less clear (and therefore perceived with much more variable accuracy) in real-life than is the case in the laboratory studies using a hypothetical stranger paradigm.

On the third question above (context) there are two points to be made. On the one hand 'context' may affect the attractiveness of similarity: thus Taylor and Mettee (1971) showed that attitude similarity to an obnoxious Other was less attractive than similarity to a pleasant Other. Moreover, Mascaro and Graves (1973) found that the influence of similarity to one stranger depended on the level of similarity previously experienced in respect of another stranger. Thus 50% similarity was attractive if the subject had previously been 10% similar to another stranger, but it was unattractive when the previous stranger had been 90% similar to the subject. However this kind of finding can be integrated into Byrne's reinforcement paradigm once it is clear that his is not simply a similarity-attraction paradigm but a reinforcement - or <u>relative</u> reinforcement one (Byrne and Lamberth, 1971). On the other hand, context could affect the use made of similarity or indeed the perception of whether similarity exists at all. It is clearly established that when an Other is first met (especially if he is judged as attractive) then people have a propensity to assume that he is similar to themselves attitudinally (Newcomb, 1961). Conversely, if someone is perceived as unattractive he is perceived as dissimilar from themselves (Bleda, 1974). This might indicate that attractiveness is sometimes assessed before similarity is even considered - and certainly before attitudes come into it. If so, then the search for attitude similarity is less likely to be entered upon in real-life when one decides someone is unattractive and it is likely to become relevant only after some initial level of attractiveness has been established. Therefore, by presenting subjects with attitudes alone, the hypothetical stranger paradigm may be collapsing and focussing the acquaintance (and attraction) process unduly and giving greater weight to one feature than it deserves (cf. Byrne, 1971). But this objection claims that attitude similarity may never be a relevant feature only of some relationships, may be the basis of discriminative choices only in some acquaintances or some attractions. It does not mean that, if our interest is in explaining acquaintance, we should reject the study of the attitude-attraction relationship; merely that we should determine what is its place in the acquaintance process.

In summarising the foregoing paragraphs therefore one can conclude that the position on the question of the representativeness of the hypothetical stranger paradigm remains open. It is not clear either that the Byrne approach is unreservedly representative of attraction in acquaintance or that it is not, as measured by the studies seeking to examine the relevance and applications of attitude scale measures.

However a related problem surrounds the issue of whether attitude similarity and attractiveness manipulated in other modalities would yield the same kind of results as are obtained when using attitude scales. There are several examples of studies where different modalities have been employed to effect the attitude similarity manipulation (Byrne and Lamberth, 1971, p.70). For example, one can ask whether attitude manipulations presented orally rather than by paper-and-pencil sheets are perceptible by subjects and if so whether they are effective in the same ways. McWhirter and Jecker (1967) tested both a hypothetical stranger paradigm and a real stranger interaction (i.e. where the subject met an unknown confederate). In this latter condition both 'subjects' (i.e. real subject and confederate) completed attitude scales and then read out their responses. By having the confederate respond second it was possible to have him agree with the subject a fixed percentage of times and thus to effect the manipulation of attitude similarity levels and subject's perception of them without simply presenting him with someone else's attitude scale to read. Findings (although largely aimed at a different question from that considered here) were comparable in the two kinds of presentation of attitude similarity-dissimilarity. Similar findings are reported by Griffitt and Jackson (1973) who used videotaped presentations to effect the manipulation. It is therefore plausible to maintain that the hypothetical stranger paradigm and attitude similarity manipulations in different modalities are not inappropriate or misrepresentative of what they seek to examine.

A further possible objection outlined at the beginning of this section was that the operational form of the paradigm does not adequately represent the theoretical form. Aronson and Worchel (1966) argued that Byrne's paradigm did not adequately exclude the possibility that attitude similarity leads a subject to expect that another person will evaluate him positively, will like him, rather than leading the subject to feel that his attitudes have received consensual validation. In other words the paradigm does not tie down its theoretical variables in a precisely satisfactory operational manner. In a test of this critique, Aronson and Worchel manipulated similarity levels and liking levels by having a similar or dissimilar (confederate) partner state that he liked or disliked the subject. In their study the only significant effect was attributable to the liking variable rather than to the similarity level. Byrne and Griffitt (1966a), in taking issue with this analysis, claimed that Aronson and Worchel had altered the usual range of attitude similarity-dissimilarity presented in the Byrne paradigm and therefore decreased the attitude similarity-dissimilarity variance. They therefore extended the somewhat restricted range of attitude similarity-dissimilarity in the Aronson and Worchel experiment and - sure enough - found significant effects of both similarity and liking. Insko, et al. (1973) presented data in support of a complex model which integrates these two positions and suggests that similarity causes liking; liking causes implied evaluation (i.e. some cognitive judgemental process); and implied evaluation results in further liking. Thus rather than being competing explanations for the attraction process the two possibilities combine in a causal chain, similarity coming first. Indeed Ajzen (1974; 1977) has argued that the attractiveness of attitude similarity is due to beliefs that individuals form about the attributes of similar strangers. He suggests that it is the attractiveness of the attributes rather than the attractiveness of the similarity which accounts for liking levels. Presumably Byrne could counter this by arguing that beliefs about someone's attributes could themselves form the basis for beliefs about similarity (i.e. X is similar in attitudes; therefore I believe him to have personality Attribute A; so have I; therefore we are similar in personality).

Finally, one earlier possible objection was that the Byrne paradigm was right but obvious, and therefore valueless. It must be clear by now that much of what Byrne says is not obvious (witness the extent to which his position has sometimes been misrepresented) especially his later and more developed position.

But even if it were obvious, the advantages of his formulation over the 'obviousness' of commonsense is exactly that argued in the Introduction here: that it ties down the obvious more precisely and imports a methodology which has led to the creation of a paradigm where the Study of Acquaintance can be detailed and unhurried so that particular aspects of it become known more elaborately. This provides a basis for further systematic advances in our understanding of the processes involved (Kuhn, 1970). Indeed the elaboration of the relationship between this particular theory and other findings in the area has led to substantial advances.

One finding which has promoted considerable clarification is one by Novak and Lerner (1968) which, at first sight, appears to conflict with Byrne's proposals. These authors conducted a study where subjects found themselves to be attitudinally similar/dissimilar to a person who was described as either mentally disturbed or not. The interest of the experiment centres on the issue of whether subjects preferred strangers who were attitudinally similar even if they were disturbed. They did not. Bleda (1974) failed to replicate these findings but the information given to subjects in the two experiments was not necessarily equivalent (Ajzen, 1977): Novak and Lerner attempted to create the impression that information about the stranger's emotional adjustment was provided inadvertently, whereas Bleda does not report that he did this. Ajzen interprets this difference to imply that subjects could have formed different beliefs about the stranger and in the absence of measurements of such beliefs the difference in findings can only be suggested to derive from this possibility. However the important points for Byrne are: that the rewardingness of attitude similarity is a function not just of the level or proportion of similarity but the source from which it emerges; and that reinforcement not similarity is the key to Byrne's position so that there could be circumstances where attitude dissimilarity is more rewarding than similarity.

Taking these two points separately, it has been argued by Murstein (1971b) that the strangers used in Byrne's work could have a certain novelty value and so the way in which people respond to them is unrepresentative of the acquaintance process as a whole, particularly deeper acquaintance. The points made earlier concerning the accelerated nature of Byrne's studies are relevant here as are those on Byrne's focus of interest, which is not acquaintance but attraction. However, Byrne could answer the 'novelty' point in a number of ways. First, 'novelty' is used in this sense with overtones of interestingness - which could be equivalent to reward. It would be consistent with Byrne's views to say that as the rewardingness of novelty decreased, so too would the attractiveness of the novel person. Second, he could argue that acquaintance (as opposed to attraction) proceeds by stages where different cues are important at different times. A given individual could therefore have a certain novelty value at each stage since new information is being provided at each point where a different aspect of the other person is probed. Furthermore, the motive to be effective (see above) could have both a general and a specific form (one may desire to be effective in several aspects of life both generally and in particular areas). It is therefore plausible that individuals would tend to satisfy a global effectance motive in different ways in different circumstances. It would then follow that different stages of acquaintance could present different effectance challenges to individuals and that different forms of reinforcement or different classically learned associations may be appropriate for each. Thus the reinforcing effects of attitude similarity may be supplanted as acquaintance proceeds (and as established levels of similarity are taken for granted and adapted to) without the principles of a classical conditioning approach being violated. McCarthy and Duck (1976) present evidence that dissimilarity is attractive at those stages of acquaintance following initial encounter and they explain this as due to a search for stimulation during a temporary weakening of attitude similarity-attraction effects as new areas of social comparability and similarity between individuals are sought.

So although one must be cautious about whether the antecedents of attraction in 'first encounters' are ultimately determinants of established relationships, a classical conditioning view of the process of acquaintance is not impossible. Its ability to account for acquaintance, however, will depend upon its ability to identify the learned associations of stimuli and reward which apply to the different levels, kinds and stages of acquaintance - once these too are identified. It is the generalised nature of reward which is significant in the development of acquaintance and the meaning of various cues (e.g. attitude similarity) to subjects which can be used as a basis for discovering the function served by a particular cue and the needs that it satisfies. In the present view, individuals have two global requirements in acquaintance: support from the other person (by means of consensual validation in the service of need for effectance); information about the other person by means of which to establish the value of the support provided - e.g. to ensure that the other is not mad - and through which to establish more closely the degree of similarity/support that the other provides. As it happens, these two needs are, but need not be, related and are in some experiments so closely related as to be capable of confusion. It is this which has occasionally provoked researchers into conflict concerning the reinforcement and informational components of attractive stimuli.

## The Information-Affect Debate

Over the last decade or so there have developed two major approaches to study of the attractiveness of stimuli: the work by Byrne discussed in this chapter at length; and the work of Anderson and his co-workers on processes of information integration (cf. Chapter 2). As noted earlier in the book (pp. 58-9) one method focuses upon attitudes and one upon personality traits; one concentrates upon the reinforcement properties of stimuli and one upon their information properties. It has recently been argued (Kaplan and Anderson, 1973) that these two approaches are not so much complementary as divergent explanations for attraction. Particularly these authors claimed that the information integration model was both qualitatively and quantitatively superior to the reinforcement model since 'information' can be a concept extending beyond the attitudinal stimuli to which they wanted to restrict Byrne's model. Equally, they claim, the mathematical basis for the information model (see Chapter 2, p. 58) allows considerable quantitative precision about the influence of combinations of informational items. Given that Anderson (1968) has established the value of individual trait items, the combinations of them, and hence their combined influence on attraction ratings, can be predicted relatively easily.

Against this view, Byrne et al. (1973 a,b) have argued that the two approaches are not necessarily inconsistent or divergent, nor does it make sense to argue that one is right and one is wrong. Rather, each has features that represent strengths relative to the other. However, a more recent development of this argument (Clore and Byrne, 1974) has claimed that information - particularly the evaluatively loaded information that is used in work on attraction - can be reinforcing through an association with positive or negative affect. Indeed, these authors argue that information is useful to people only as a function of its ability to discriminate between events and that the tendency to make evaluative discriminations 'is a legacy from (Man's) evolutionary past' (Clore and Byrne, 1974, p. 144). In other words, interpersonal evaluative discriminations might serve a similar function to those discriminations invoked in judgements of sweetness/sourness or approachableness/avoidance and may similarly be associated with positive or negative affect (i.e. feelings of pleasure or pain). In other words again, interpersonal evaluations can be seen to depend on reinforcement, since reinforcing events become associated with affect and stimuli associated with the reinforcement develop the same capacity for evoking affect so that positively evaluated stimuli are liked and negative ones disliked. In short, the reinforcement model explains how information comes to be attractive or unattractive, positively or negatively-evaluated, liked or disliked rather than simply stating that it does. Byrne, Rasche and Kelley (1974) further argue that personal evaluations and attitudinal agreement/disagreement contain both informational and affective components. If someone says he likes you that both indicates a state of affairs (information) and is probably pleasurable (affect). Byrne, Rasche and Kelley (1974) showed that attraction towards strangers was influenced by both information and affect.

Taking an entirely contrary view, Ajzen (1974; 1977) argues that similarity of attitudes is attractive not because it is reinforcing but because it leads subjects to form positive beliefs about the other characteristics possessed by the stranger (see Chapter 2, p.58). In other words, attitude similarity provokes subjects to assume that the other person has a desirable personality and the other person is liked for this reason, not for his similarity. However, it is not entirely clear whether the other person's personality appears not only desirable but also similar to one's own. Duck (1975a) has argued that similarity of attitudes with a stranger leads subjects to assume that he will be similar in personality, too, and this is reinforcing for the same reasons as those offered by Byrne to explain the effects of attitude similarity. Thus although Ajzen may correctly have identified a process occurring in evaluation it is an empirical question whether there may not be an additional process involved where the person assesses the similarity of the other person's implied personality as well as its desirability.

One point in this debate is worth noting. When Byrne talks about similarity this is really attitudinal similarity, i.e. agreement; when Anderson talks about similarity it is similarity of traits not agreement about attitudes. Two people can be similar but may not agree (two leftwing, tall, handsome, dark, students of equal intelligence, both extrovert, reliable, and witty ... may nonetheless take opposite views on a given issue). Equally, two individuals may not be similar but may agree. Thus 'agreement' and 'similarity' can be logically distinct firstly in ways not recognised by the two sides in this debate and secondly in a manner that is crucially relevant to the debate. However, it may be that human subjects are not always logical and the very confusion evident in the literature may be a precise analogue of the confusion that subjects have on this point. Perhaps when two people see that they agree they will assume that they are similar in some ways not yet observed; when two people see that they are similar in some respects they may assume that they will agree on specific attitudinal items. In other words 'agreement' and 'similarity' may not be logically the same but are psychologically related from the subjects' viewpoint during acquaintance.

Related to this proposal is the point that information about people can be obtained at many levels (Duck, 1976b; Duck and Craig, 1977), ranging from physical description through attitudes to personality traits. In their various ways, and at varying levels of certainty, these different levels of information inform about personality. They are not competing but complementary sources for deductions about the other person; similarly attitudinal information and personality information can be seen as different levels of information about the person's cognition in ways that render them complementary rather than mutually antagonistic elements in an acquaintance process.

It is clear, then, that the information-affect debate is capable of resolution in a number of ways. It could be argued that one component (information) operates in the service of the other (affect); or that there are two parallel processes (affective responses to information; affective responses to constructive uses made of information); or that information and affect are equally important but different components of attraction responses; or that 'information' is a term susceptible of multiple levels of analysis, and therefore that some types are more and some less relevant to the processes of attraction and acquaintance. (Byrne, in press, has made similar points in relation to sexual behaviour).

A further possibility is suggested by the emphases of the present book: that subjects respond to information in the context of developing acquaintance (as opposed to static choice behaviour in attraction) in terms of the rewards and affect it produces during the forward-looking strategic search by individuals to discover more about their partner's personality. In other words information is attractive as a function of the amount of personality similarity it implies; the probability (confidence) with which this implication may be held, taking account of the type of information whence it derives; and the affect produced by the result of this equation (affect that will depend on the strength of the subject's need for similarity or support as a whole, or in particular respects and the subjective importance of this need). At different points of acquaintance different types of evidence could be used to make guesses or gather indirect information about personality - but most important is direct information about personality whenever it is available and when it is of the right or appropriate type (Duck 1973c). This, therefore, is the subject of the next chapter.

# CHAPTER SIX

## PERSONALITY AND ACQUAINTANCE

As suggested by the comments made throughout the earlier part of this book, personality is hypothesised here to have a central, if varied, role as a determinant of acquaintance behaviour. However, the discussion so far has centred mainly upon the impressions of or inferences about an individual's personality which are made by his partner in an acquaintance. This chapter concerns more explicitly the likely influences of a person's 'true' personality (rather than the influences of his partner's beliefs about it). Unfortunately this problem is really a collection of problems - all clouded by the irritating ingenuity of research psychologists. They have offered many views about the nature of personality and it is rare to find any two researchers using the same view or investigating the same <u>kinds</u> of thing under the heading of 'personality'. For example, some workers (e.g. Winch, 1958) examine 'needs', such as nurturance or succorance (i.e. needs to help, protect and look after someone or the need to receive such help, protection and care); other investigators (e.g. Palmer and Byrne, 1970) examine the effects of personality traits (such as Dominance-Submission defined from responses to an adjective checklist), whilst yet others have explored mood and temperament (e.g. Hoffman and Maier, 1966). Equally, there are those researchers who restrict themselves to the study of specific test dimensions which are known to be good predictors of specific behaviour (e.g. Byrne, Griffitt and Stefaniak, 1967, using the Repression-Sensitisation scale) whilst others employ tests that indicate general attitudes or dispositions rather than specific behaviour (e.g. Hogan and Mankin, 1970, using the California Psychological Inventory). This ingenuity creates many methodological disputes about who is using the right tools. However, the aim of this chapter is to argue that such disputes contribute little to clarification of the important issues whilst they are regarded as separable from real or important conceptual (substantive) disputes. In other words, it will be argued here that each methodology conceals the investigator's belief about how personality influences acquaintance and so each methodology is really a theoretical statement rather than a simple practical one. The differing views can then be partly reconciled once the complementary rather than opponent nature of these theoretical explanations is recognised.

From the outset, therefore, it is important to remember (as indicated in previous chapters) that 'personality' has several non-exclusive influences on attraction, liking and acquaintance. That is to say, it influences acquaintance in several different ways, has several complementary places in relationship development and promotes liking (and continued liking) by several different processes - whether the person's personality is considered on its own or in relation to the partner's also. For one thing, a person's personality determines his selective responses to other people (cf. discussions in Chapter 3, pp. 77-87 on effects of chronic anxiety on liking for similarity; on Authoritarianism as an influence on liking for power figures; and - on the other side of selective activity - the discussions on the different general attractiveness of different personality 'types', like Extroverts). For another thing, personality exerts an influence over the processing of information (as already noted in Chapter 3, pp. 82-87) and hence over both the impressions formed about other people and the evaluation of their attractiveness. Thirdly, the amount of information disclosed to another person about one's own personality is both an indicator of the progress of an acquaintance and also something which influences its direction. Fourthly, the two personalities of the parties involved in an acquaintance may have a logical relationship to one another (e.g. they may be similar in some way; or opposite in some way; or they may complement each other in certain respects). This relationship of the personalities (as opposed to the individual characteristics of one of the personalities) may act as an influence upon the liking of the partners for each other. Fifthly, and implicit in the above analysis, different aspects of personality may be relevant to acquaintance at different times, such that two individuals may be attracted to the other's personality so far as they know it, but may subsequently discover information that they dislike. Therefore, depending on the point of relationship examined, the type of personality test employed, and the kind of analysis used, 'personality' may be declared to 'cause' acquaintance by one investigator and to 'cause' breakdown of relationship by another - using the same pair of people as subjects.

In view of these facts, it is not surprising that the literature on personality and acquaintance is, as shall be seen, equivocal, neither showing that personality causes acquaintance nor that it can be ruled out as a cause; neither showing that similarity causes acquaintance nor that complementarity or oppositeness does (Duck, 1977b). In part this is due to the fact that the several levels of relationship between personality and acquaintance have often been confounded or lumped together or inadequately distinguished as noted earlier. Since several of the places of a single personality's effect on acquaintance have been considered in various guises already (Chapters 3-5), this chapter concentrates on what happens when the two acquainters' personalities become more revealed to one another (i.e. it concentrates on the place and significance of Self-Disclosure - that is, the amounts, depths and breadths of personality intimately revealed to the other person); and on the various forms of relationship between two personalities that may be so disclosed and may exert influence on acquaintance. It should be noted that the extent to which someone is prepared to disclose himself to you can be attractive or unattractive (see below); and that relationships between personalities can be attractive or unattractive (ditto). Here, then, we are considering two further ways in which personality affects acquaintance.

### Disclosure of Self

Self-Disclosure is defined by Jourard (1971) as 'a mutual unfolding of people to one another ... highly dependent on favourable outcomes such as liking and reciprocity'. People do not disclose themselves indiscriminately but do so when a liking relationship is developed. As a relationship proceeds, greater information about personality at greater depths of intimacy is revealed by the partners involved and this process depends on and can be an indicator of liking. Equally, the implication of Jourard's suggestion is that individuals are under some pressure to reciprocate the disclosure provided by the Other in most circumstances. Several questions then arise: Does this happen? What is reciprocated in interactions; is it similar content, or information of equal intimacy? How do individuals agree on the level of intimate disclosure that is appropriate to their encounter? Is self disclosure attractive? If so why, and what is learned about the other person in the course of seeing him self disclose? Is Self-Disclosure essential to acquaintance?

Jourard's original contention was that a self-disclosing individual would be construed as having a healthy personality: he would not be seen as neurotic, defensive or 'closed'. Thus a discloser would be attractive and individuals would wish to reciprocate disclosure in order to demonstrate their own psychological health. Alternatively it could be claimed that self-disclosure is attractive because the receipt of intimate information from another person is rewarding for another reason: it implies that the other person likes and trusts oneself since he is making himself vulnerable and thus gives one power over him (Tedeschi, 1974; Kelvin, 1977; Chapter 4). Initially, then, there are good, if different, reasons for assuming that intimate disclosers will appear to be more attractive than non-disclosers - as a general rule. However, Derlega, Harris and Chaikin (1973) found that this depended on what was disclosed. They employed confederates to reveal conventional or deviant (e.g. homosexual) information and found that conventional high disclosers were liked more than deviant high disclosers. Equally, Cozby (1973) reports that high disclosers are liked less than moderate disclosers and it seems likely that in initial encounters high disclosers would be seen as lacking in discretion or trustworthiness. However, it is found that subjects are more willing in initial encounters to disclose to Others whom they like (Worthy, Gary and Kahn, 1969) and that they are more willing to do so in highly intimate areas than in non-intimate ones (Altman and Taylor, 1973). Indeed, Rubin (1970) suggests a distinction between 'liking' and 'loving' relationships, with self-disclosure being more positively related to love than liking. It is plausible, however, that in developing acquaintance, rather than initial encounters, importance attaches more to the content actually disclosed rather than to absolute level of disclosure manifested by one or other partner.

Davis (1976) considered the ways in which individuals negotiated the level of intimacy that was appropriate and comfortable in an acquaintance exercise. By having like-sex strangers disclose alternately in an interaction, it was possible to establish the degree to which intimacy increased over time and to see which partner was primarily responsible for the increases in intimacy that occurred. It was found that intimacy increased in a linear fashion as encounters progressed; that partners matched both their rates of increase in intimacy and their average intimacy level; and that one partner tended to assume major responsibility for prescribing the level of intimacy and the other person largely reciprocated - to some extent being encouraged to get more intimate by the level and nature of the information disclosed by the 'leader'.

Whilst studies of reciprocity in strangers are the norm in this area of enquiry, the findings of Derlega, Wilson and Chaikin (1976) were that reciprocity of Self-Disclosure in a single laboratory encounter was more likely between dyads composed of strangers than close friends - and these differences are highly significant for the conceptualisation of the role of disclosure reciprocity in developing acquaintance. Strangers tended to vary the intimacy level of disclosures as a direct function of their partner's disclosing input, whilst friends' intimacy of disclosure was independent of the intimacy of disclosure input by the partner. This highlights two things: first, the fact that strangers' self-disclosing and friends' self-disclosing may differ in important ways yet unexplored (so that, as Derlega et al. argue, future studies should focus more attention on disclosure patterns in already established relationships); second, that other things than pure reciprocity have to be 'managed' in the context of developing relationships rather than single encounters. One thing which is presumably important in this way is the timing and pacing of disclosure of different types of content. Just as immediate disclosing of highly intimate information is suspect for various reasons (see above), so it seems probable that inappropriately large jumps in level of intimacy of disclosure would also be aversive in the development of acquaintance (Murstein, 1977). It will be recalled from earlier chapters that the finding of Jones and Gordon (1972) was that the timing of disclosure of positive and negative facts about oneself was crucial to their interpretation by the recipient: disclosure of positive facts too early was aversive. The use of self-disclosure as an ingratiation tactic is therefore more complex than appears on the surface. Indeed, Frankel and Morris (1976) have shown that favourable information about a courtroom defendant actually does him harm (i.e. he gets harsher penalties from role-playing jurors) if he reveals the information himself rather than having it disclosed by other (presumably impartial) agents. Self-disclosure may thus be seen as an aspect of self-presentation (cf. Chapters 3 and 4) which could be associated with attributional processes (i.e. the person receiving self-disclosure can make inferences about what is disclosed, why it is disclosed and how it is done). Hence self-disclosure acts as a provider of structure in interactions. As noted above, early or too high self-disclosure produces negative responses, presumably because it is not seen as due to the Other's reaction to self alone but as a personal trait of the Other. However, Jones and Archer (1976) found that personalistic self-disclosers (i.e. disclosers who revealed to the subject but not to other people) were liked more than non-disclosers but not necessarily more than non-personalistic disclosers (i.e. those who revealed to others as well as to the subject).

Other aspects of self-disclosure than simple intimacy level and timing or personalism of disclosure are relevant to acquaintance if one assumes that attributional processes are a basis for liking other persons. The actual content of disclosures could clearly be an important factor since it provides a basis for assessing how similar the other person is to oneself in attitudes, experience and personality. Daher and Banikiotes (1976) found that similarity of disclosed content was significantly related to interpersonal attraction but found only partial support for the hypothesis that a similar level of self-disclosure was related to attraction. Also, Knecht, Lippman and Swap (1973) found that subjects were more willing to disclose to a bogus stranger from whom they had received attitude-congruent messages, especially in highly intimate areas. It seems plausible that the reverse is also likely to be true: that similar content revealed during self-disclosure leads individuals to assume similarity of other personality characteristics. Certainly, at the very least, the greater the amount of information revealed in self-disclosure by the Other person the better the basis for a subject to erect a model of that person's personality and to draw conclusions about similarity levels between his own and the stranger's personality. It is less likely therefore that reciprocity of actual content alone would be found in studies of self-disclosure (Ehrlich and Graeven, 1971). It is more likely that in developing acquaintance, the content, intimacy level and timing of disclosure combine with the extent to which the Other reciprocates one's own disclosure to provide one with a clearer picture of his personality (structure and content) and that liking and continued acquaintance are related to the beliefs about personality thus generated.

Such possibilities are considered by Altman (1974) who, as indicated earlier, has developed a model of relationship growth that leans heavily on the concepts of Self-Disclosure. Altman's term for the wider process (which includes Self-Disclosure) is 'Social Penetration' and this term is preferred since it includes things over and above self-disclosure as discussed above. For example, it concerns increasing intimacy revealed by means of nonverbal cues or by the nature of the situation surrounding the relationship growth or by the other aspects of interaction such as personal space usage - all of which, as we have seen earlier in this book, are indicators and antecedents of increasing intimacy in relationships. Altman's model also includes various subjective processes of attribution and evaluation about the Other person that change as the relationship develops. However, the role of self-disclosure is given considerable emphasis and is described in terms of an 'onion skin' model: that is, the personality is seen as composed of many layers, rather like an onion, and social penetration describes the process by which individuals 'proceed systematically ... from superficial non-intimate areas to increasingly intimate, deeper layers of the personalities of the actors' (Altman, 1974, p.125). Such progress depends on expectations about the likely or actual profit resulting from allowing progress to occur. This model is particularly useful in that it stresses a _breadth_ and a _depth_ dimension to increasing disclosure, and hence that individuals can find out increasing amounts about one another in two dimensions. At the extremes, one could build up a broad picture of one layer of someone else's personality without getting deeper into his structure (a broad, flat wedge into the onion, as it were); or could penetrate very deeply and narrowly (a thin wedge into the onion). Furthermore, in emphasising the expectancies and attributions that are a corporate part of social penetration, Altman's suggestion provides an interesting means of linking up the work on self-disclosure as an influence on acquaintance with attribution work and with the main body of work that concerns the influence of the (perceived) relationship between two personalities as an influence on liking. Presumably, as self-disclosure proceeds, the two acquaintance partners are better able to draw inferences about the likely relationship between the discloser's personality and their own.

**Pairs of Personalities in Acquaintance**

The relationship between the actors' personalities may not be relevant to some acquaintances (i.e. those which never proceed far enough for it to be assessed) but in those cases where it does become relevant to the level of liking or to the development of the acquaintance, the interesting psychological questions centre upon the nature of the relationship between the personalities. Do similar personalities create liking or do opposite ones? Alas, there is little uniformity in the research on these questions, as we shall see in the next section, and different workers adopt very different approaches, so that comparisons between studies are difficult and the extraction of a coherent picture therefore almost impossible. Byrne, Griffitt and Stefaniak (1967, p.83) have noted that 'One reason for empirical inconsistency is the peculiar penchant of personality and social psychologists for methodological creativity such that almost every investigation represents an exploration in procedural novelty'. Whilst this is undoubtedly an excellent encapsulation of a problem, it should not obscure the fact that serious, substantive theoretical issues lie behind these methodological differences (Levy, pers. comm.). The tools, experimental designs and methods that an investigator selects in order to study the personality-acquaintance relationship will reflect, perhaps unwittingly, his theoretical beliefs about the nature of acquaintance and the nature of personality as well as his beliefs about what individuals actually do in acquaintance.

**Substantive or methodological issues?** For one thing the investigator must decide upon the aspects of acquaintance that are best suited to study the possible personality-acquaintance links and this is not simply a matter of expediency. What is true of dating may not be true of same-sex friendship, so that the relationship between the actors' personalities may be relevant to one and not to the other. Unfortunately, different investigators have often sought to test essentially the same proposition (whether personality relates to acquaintance) on essentially different types of acquaintance without always pointing out that this may matter theoretically in the interpretation of the results. To list only a few of the many possible examples, the personality-acquaintance relationship has been studied with respect to <u>fictitious strangers</u> (Byrne, Griffitt and Stefaniak, 1967; Byrne and Griffitt, 1969); <u>marital choice</u> (Murstein, 1973); <u>discussion groups</u> (Hoffman and Maier, 1966); <u>same sex friendships</u> (Duck and Spencer, 1972); <u>courtship couples</u> (Day, 1961); <u>best friends</u> (Izard, 1960a) - even in relation to selection of <u>least and most preferred partners</u> in a problem solving team (Rychlak, 1965). Small wonder that the results are as confusing and contradictory as the list is mind-boggling. Perhaps one reason why the results are inconsistent is that investigators have not considered the relative depth of intimacy in the different studies and the extent to which different depths of intimacy may be accounted for by different psychological antecedents.

The same goes for measures of personality, where the investigator's choice of measure may have important implications for the interpretation of results. The range of conceptualisations of personality is bewildering. Is 'personality' a person's needs or moods or temperament or values or beliefs or traits or habitual thought processes or total cognition? Is it reflected by his sign of the zodiac, his test scores, his behaviour, his bodily build or his balance between Yin and Yang? Again, different investigators have taken different views about personality - again without much apparent concern that the differences may matter in some way that affects the nature of the hypothesis about personality and acquaintance. Most work reported below looks at personality in terms of 'needs' or 'values' (e.g. Need for Abasement, for Nurturance, for Achievement); but some personality measures reflect common beliefs that people have personality <u>traits</u> and the tests thus assess things like Introversion-Extroversion

(Hendrick and Brown, 1971) or Dominance-Submission (Palmer and Byrne, 1970). Again there is a serious substantive issue lying beneath this apparently methodological point and the choice about how to measure personality does reflect a hypothesis about how subjects assess one another's personality in acquaintance. Do they try to classify one another as Extrovert or Introvert? Do they work out who shall be dominant and who submissive? How accurately does the personality measure (paper and pencil) reflect the actual behaviours that occur in interaction (i.e. does a high score on the dominance scale really mean the person is dominant in interaction or merely that he would like to be)? Or perhaps people don't have much awareness of personality as it relates to real life acquaintances.

Thirdly: how shall similarity be assessed? At first sight it seems that there is no problem - certainly there seems to be no theoretical problem: either two personalities are similar or they are not and it doesn't matter how you assess this. Unfortunately this is shortsighted, and once again it is true that differences in investigators' methods reflect differences in their theoretical beliefs about personality and acquaintance. Essentially there are two modes of assessment: one based on the raw data provided by the personality test (e.g. the actual answers to the test questions); the other based on some processing of these answers (e.g. translating them into dimensions like Extroversion-Introversion, or adding up all the 'Yes' answers and all the 'No' and all the '?' answers to produce three totals). The point here is not to ask which of them is right but to suggest again that an investigator's choice of method will reflect his belief about the psychological processes occurring in acquaintance. For example, if I believe that individuals must be aware of similarity before it can influence their acquaintance behaviour, then I must assess similarity in a way that subjects themselves could probably use in real life. So I might choose to measure similarity by comparing both subjects' specific answers to specific questions ('Did they both answer "Yes" to Question 5?'). If I believe that individuals simply work out whether they are similar in terms of overall Extroversion-Introversion level, and that is what influences their acquainting, then I would probably measure similarity in terms of their two total scores on Introversion-Extroversion ('Irrespective of how they both answered each specific question, did each person score the same total of "Yes" answers?'). If I thought that subjects' perceptions about similarity were largely irrelevant or not influential and it just happens that 'true' similarity was what counted, then I may assess similarity by processing the raw data in a way that, I felt, accurately reflected Nature's measure of 'true similarity' (e.g. I may take the logarithm of the square of the difference between their total scores divided by 7). Each of these methods may be a fair, valid and acceptable method for assessing similarity but (need it be stressed again?) the choice of method reflects the investigator's theoretical belief about acquaintance - not just his methodological preference.

These three examples are intended to show what I mean by 'Substantive or methodological issues?' in this section. With those points in mind we can examine the research that has been done on the relationship between two acquainting personalities.

## Relationships Between Personalities

As will be clear from the earlier parts of this chapter, there are many ways of conceiving personality and many ways of conceiving the relationship between two personalities as a function of the parts chosen for analysis and the method of comparing them. Thus work under this heading has examined relationships between individuals' self-concepts (e.g. Griffitt, 1969); between the Actual Self of one and the Ideal Self of the other (e.g. Griffitt, 1966); between one's own and the other person's beliefs about one's Self (Backman and Secord, 1962); between the individuals' levels of Extroversion-Introversion (Hendrick and Brown, 1971); and between the individuals' needs (Seyfried, 1977) as well as several other aspects of personality previously noted.

Although these researchers consider different aspects of personality the primary focus for much of the research on personality and acquaintance over the last 25 years concerns the debate about whether similarity or complementarity of personality promotes acquaintance (Tharp, 1963; Levinger, 1964; Seyfried, 1977). If this debate is yet resolving itself, then it is because similarity and complementarity between two personalities are 1. not the only kinds of relationship that are possible between them (e.g. they could be opposite rather than complementary; structurally similar rather than similar in content; or unrelated altogether); 2. not mutually exclusive when one is dealing with such a global entity as personality, so that similarity and complementarity and oppositeness and unrelatedness can all be simultaneously true of the same pair of personalities depending on the aspects examined and the definitions chosen (Seyfried, 1977). However, the components of this debate can be instructive when examined on their own, before being taken together in this way.

Similarity

In taking issue with traditional assumptions, Wright (1965) argued that rather than being initially neutral towards every stranger that he meets, every individual is either attracted towards or ambivalent about others, and that those who are ambivalent may be cautious or defensive and therefore not particularly attractive even to someone similar to themselves. This suggestion, which argues that personality similarity may not be relevant at all in some relationships has most often been highly commended and then roundly ignored. However, it is important to note that even where similarity of personality is considered influential, this is not to say that it is the only factor in acquaintance nor that it will be relevant on all occasions. Indeed, Wright (1968) proceeded to argue that an individual made the initial decision whether to associate with someone on the basis of whether he felt comfortable with them - before personality similarity came into it.

Most work, however, has examined the success or failure of personality similarity (somehow defined and operationalised) as a predictor or correlate of expressed liking or choice, and several forms of such similarity have been considered. A great deal of work has examined the extent to which an individual chooses friends who are similar to his Actual Self or Ideal Self (i.e. the Self as he thinks he is or the Self as he would like to be - e.g. Beier, Rossi and Garfield, 1961; Griffitt, 1966; Murstein, 1971b). Whilst Beier, et al. and Murstein found that best friends tended to be similar to subjects' Ideal Self, Griffitt did not. This discrepancy is explained by Murstein (1971b) as due to the different stages of relationship examined in these studies - but the methods were also very different.

Griffitt presented subjects with direct access to the necessary information in the laboratory on self-rating profiles, whilst the other two studies examined subjects' impressions acquired in long-established real-life relationships through process of judgement, reassessment and reconsideration over time which (most important) lacked the specious appearance of 'accuracy' and objectivity created by any data presented on printed profiles in a scientific laboratory. It is not adequate to conclude merely that different points of the relationship were examined, since this is only superficially true. The Griffitt method, by providing 'accurate' information immediately to subjects, may either represent abnormal processes of information gathering or else may have accelerated the acquaintance process by casting subjects headlong into a point of knowledge about the other person which would usually be achieved in real life with considerable effort and time. However it may prove to be wise to consider the Actual Self/Ideal Self discrepancy within subjects before looking at the Actual Self/Ideal Self similarity levels between subjects. The static, chronic characteristics of the chooser are relevant before one considers the way in which chooser and chosen interact and interweave their personality characteristics. Similarly, the level of Self Esteem (the worth or value in which the Self is held by the Self) and Self Acceptance (a measurement of, and coming to terms with, the Self's position vis à vis 'objective' but internalised standards) may relate to differences in tolerance for dissimilarity, just as level of security does (Goldstein and Rosenfeld, 1969). Different levels of self esteem may lead to temporary fluctuations in willingness to expose oneself to dissimilar others, whilst Low Levels of Self Acceptance may have more chronic influences upon the sociometric activity manifested by 'the chooser'. Those with Low Self Esteem might be predicted to find similar others attractive since the Others naturally suggest that the Self Esteem level is misplaced - Others at least have the same inabilities; however those with Low Self Acceptance, having already decided that the characteristics they possess are objectively unacceptable, are likely to derogate and dislike similar Others, whose existence merely multiplies the frequency of objectively unacceptable properties.

Whilst the work on Self is considerable, a great amount has also been done on similarity of personality profiles. For example, Izard (1960a, b; 1963) examined similarity on the

Edwards Personal Preference Schedule (EPPS) and its relation to development of friendship in a population of acquaintances. He showed that actual similarity was an antecendent of unilateral choices (i.e. nominations of someone as the most likeable person) and also that mutual friends had similar personality profiles. He also showed that mutual friends had significantly more correlations when consideration was paid to some of the separate personality characteristics making up the personality profile. Against this, Day (1961), also using the EPPS, was unable to detect an influence of similarity of personality upon selection of either courtship partners or same-sex friends.

Evidence against the effects of personality-similarity on interpersonal attraction is provided by Hoffman (1958) and Hoffman and Maier (1966) both of which studies made up groups of students matched on certain personality dimensions (using the Guilford-Zimmerman Temperament Survey). After periods of discussion that varied in the two studies, liking for group members was assessed and found to be unrelated to the degree of similarity existing between the group members on the initial matching.

Before one even considers the <u>relative importance</u> of similarity and complementarity, then, it is clear that the literature on similarity of personality is ambivalent. Some studies are for it, and some against. In a recent attempt to explain these discrepancies, Duck (1977b) has argued, as he has above in this chapter, that the key to the problem is to be found in the different levels and lengths of relationship that are examined by different investigators. Thus some workers may have been using on discussion groups of unacquainted persons those measures that are best suited to be used on groups who have known each other for some time. If personality is gradually unfolded bit by bit (cf. earlier section on Self-Disclosure) and if this process means anything, then the aspects of personality that are relevant to the personality similarity-acquaintance relationship are likely to be different at different times in acquaintance development.

Complementarity

Most work on complementarity derives from Winch's (1958)

work and concerns complementarity of needs which can occur in one of two ways (Winch, Ktsanes and Ktsanes, 1954): <u>Type I Complementarity</u> exists where two needs of different type exist but are of the same intensity (thus a highly succorant person and a highly nurturant person are complementary in this way since one likes to be looked after and the other likes to do the looking after); <u>Type II Complementarity</u> exists where two people have different degrees of the same need (thus a highly dominant person is complementary in this way to someone who is extremely low in dominance needs and is controllable). Before one can compare the relative roles of complementarity against similarity, of course, the internal coherence of the viewpoint and the evidence for it must be considered on its own as was done above in relation to similarity. When this is done in the context of the above observations, however, it is clear that there will be an immediate problem in specifying in advance those needs where complementarity is predicted to be attractive and those where it is not. What general and generalisable principle leads to the pairing of Nurturance with Succorance in this theory and is anything else complementary to Nurturance? Is low Achievement complementary to high need for Achievement? How different must Dominance needs be before they are counted as complementary? It must be admitted that some of these questions are asked more often than they are answered, and that the answers, when given, have tended to be post hoc empirical ones rather than hypothetical derivations.

Apart from the original research by Winch and his co-workers (Winch, 1955a, b; Winch, Ktsanes and Ktsanes, 1954, 1955) most work on complementarity has implicitly or explicitly set out to compare complementarity against similarity but there is some work on complementarity alone. The original research appears to support the complementarity hypothesis with respect to married couples if one does not press the questions above too vigorously. Working with married couples, Winch and co-workers hypothesised that 344 interspousal correlations involving two different needs (Type I Complementarity) would be positive whilst 44 involving the same needs would be negative (Type II Complementarity) and found that a significant number of these correlations were in the direction predicted by the complementary needs hypothesis. However, Tharp (1963) argued that these predicted intercorrelations were not independent of one another and thus the likelihood of getting many significant correlations as a result of chance alone is considerably - and artifactually - increased. More recently, however, and using all male subjects (who were counsellors at three camps), Wagner (1975) provided some support for the complementarity hypothesis by showing that counsellors who liked one another were complementary on the need pairs of nurturance-succorance, aggression-abasement, responsibility-nurturance, exhibition-deference and dominance-autonomy in most of the populations studied.

Most work, however, contrasts similarity with complementarity as a major aim, and explicitly. Thus Day (1961) looked for homogamy (i.e. similarity) or complementarity in courtship couples and their respective same-sex friends, and failed to find a systematic influence of either variable, although the specific needs and need combinations that were significantly related to selection of a courtship partner were found to be considerably different from those relevant to same-sex friendships. If independently confirmed, this finding would naturally cast doubt on the generality of the influence of particular needs on relationships of different types. Reilly, Commins and Stefic (1960), examining friendship choices only, found that friends did not see themselves as more consistently complementary than similar - but neither were they definitely similar in friendship needs! If anything, friends in this study tended to be similar in values rather than needs, a point that will be revisited below. Rychlak (1965), however, found no evidence for a need similarity hypothesis but found data consistent with a need compatibility or incompatibility thesis. Palmer and Byrne (1970) contrasted similarity and complementarity in relation to Dominance-Submission and found that more dominant individuals were preferred by all subjects but that there was some evidence for the similarity hypothesis. Equally, Seyfried and Hendrick (1973) contrasted complementarity and similarity with respect to Nurturance-Succorance and found a similar pattern: general positivity towards a nurturant stranger but a strong preference for a stranger with similar rather than complementary needs.

One or two observations are in order concerning this literature (Marlowe and Gergen, 1969; a good review is given by Seyfried, 1977). First, the basic principle of Winch's view is that need gratification is reinforcing and it is unfortunate that this has often been obscured by concentration on only one method of need gratification (i.e. discovery of a complementary-dissimilar Other). In certain cases similar behaviour can gratify a given need (e.g. two people who are both high on need for affiliation could gratify one another by both engaging in affiliative behaviour). Second, the behaviours (or other aspects of a person) that are relevant to the complementarity hypothesis are not always the same as those relevant in 'the similarity hypothesis' with which it is often contrasted: needs in the one case, specific trait dimensions or attitudes in the other. The two theories need not therefore in every case be competing for the same ground, although there will be cases where they do compete directly. Third, Winch's research was concerned primarily with courtship and marriage and it may be more suited to that relationship than to any other kinds of relationships. Fourth, it may be that interactions are sequential and selective as argued earlier, such that the antecedents of initial attraction are related to but not necessarily the same as those promoting later intimacy. Thus, as argued by Seyfried (1977), it could be that both similarity and complementarity are influential in relationship development - a point previously missed because studies contrasting the two theories have typically not been longitudinal in design. Kerckhoff and Davis (1962), for example, found that similarity of values predicted early choices amongst a pool of subjects but that need complementarity eventually took over as the causal force behind subsequent liking. This interesting finding was not replicated by Levinger, Senn and Jorgensen (1970), however, and its status thus remains in doubt.

Whilst this debate between similarity and complementarity has done much during the past few years to clarify certain issues and to improve the quality and precision of research, it could well be concluded that such debates are useful only as guides to research at the early stages of development in an area (Palmer and Byrne, 1970). Certainly, it is wise to remind oneself that similarity and complementarity are only opponent explanations: 1. for the influence of personality on liking; 2. if all other possible relationships between a pair of personalities are legitimately ruled out as uninteresting or irrelevant; 3. if the two explanations are not themselves complementary or supportive of one another in explaining relationship development in respect of some aspects of relationships at particular points in their development (see above paragraph); 4. in respect of some levels of analysis of personality; 5. in relation to some measures of 'similarity'; 6. if Type II complementarity is explicitly defined; 7. where relevant needs are precisely defined, clearly different and non-overlapping, and not found together in the same individual.

## Conclusions

The area of personality and acquaintance is not the best example of rigorous scientific scrutiny: rarely in the field of human experiment has so much been done by so many to so little effect. The complexity of the relationship between personality and acquaintance has led to much confusion and little clarity, but several independent workers have begun to focus on the line of enquiry that is most likely to be productive: namely, the clear need to introduce the clarification of terms and the essentially theoretical issues that lie behind them. When this is done it is likely that further progress can be made by bringing the notion of relationship development into the argument, by defining the quality of interaction that indicates this development and by reaching a better understanding of the psychological bases for the changes in intimacy level that are observed.

At present the terms of the personality-acquaintance equation are so poorly-defined and differently conceptualised and so global in nature as to be tested in controlled circumstances only with great difficulty and uncertainty. It is also true that many different studies are compared when they are not comparable, since they use different types of acquaintance and different measures of personality and similarity. It is also probably true that these problems and differences have diverted reviewers from the answer to the question: that different parts and aspects of personality are relevant to developing acquaintance at different points at different levels and in different ways (Duck, 1977b). Since personality has many different measurable qualities and since each has its own well established research tradition it is unlikely to be true that one measure of personality, and one alone, holds the key to the personality-acquaintance riddle. Far more likely is the possibility that the different aspects of personality are complementary causes - relevant to given points of acquaintance (e.g. attraction, liking, friendship). The most salient is that which is available to real-life acquainting individuals at the time: for example, assessments of an individual's Introversion-Extroversion are easier and available sooner than are assessments of an individual's placement on several dimensions like Femininity, Psychological Mindedness and Sense of Well Being as measured on the CPI. It is likely, therefore, that the former of these measures is relevant earlier than the latter - and indeed we find, consistent with this proposition that Hendrick and Brown (1971) used Extroversion-Introversion successfully in a Bogus Stranger (Attraction setting), whilst one finding of Duck (1973c) was that similarity on the CPI predicted sociometric choices by individuals in a face-to-face discussion group. This argument can, however, be extended. Since both personality and acquaintance have several facets it may be possible to arrange the facets of each in some conceptual order and to detect parallels between these orders. In other words, just as attraction precedes dating precedes courtship precedes marital choice (and attraction precedes non-intimate friendship precedes deep friendship etc.) so too broad, gross facets of personality may precede more differentiated facets may precede very fine detail as antecedents of developing liking. To rephrase this point again, progress in clarifying the personality-acquaintance relationship is likely to be made by overturning the previous absolutist, stimulus bound view that it is merely a question of finding the right measure of personality or the right traits within personality that cause acquaintance - and that would be that. A relativist view seems preferable: namely a view that sees the task as that of identifying the aspects of personality that are relevant at the different points of acquaintance development. 'The right measure of personality at the right time' should be substituted for 'the right measure of personality' above. Thus Duck (1973c) showed that two personality tests (CPI and Reptest) were each able to predict liking and choice in only one of two cases: the CPI (but not the Reptest) in newly acquainted populations and the Reptest (but not the CPI) in well established friendship groups. Equally, Duck and Craig (in prep) have shown that three measures of personality used in the acquaintance literature are differently appropriate and useful measures to employ as predictors of liking at different points in the longitudinal development of relationships.

On a related point, whilst Byrne, Griffitt and Stefaniak (1967) were indubitably correct in focussing on personality measures with a good test-behaviour relationship in the study of responses to strangers' personality, it is arguable whether this can be extended to other kinds of social relationship. As acquaintance proceeds, it could be claimed, prediction of very narrowly limited aspects of behaviour becomes less important than a wider and more intimate picture of the other's personality, since greater knowledge of the other person is predicated not upon specific (but limited) predictive power but rather on a general model of the other person in many different situations. The theoretical explanation of different findings noted above is related to the methodological issues, therefore, since the global aspects of personality, the influence of multiple aspects of personality and the general nature of assumptions about other people's traits are likely to be most important in precisely those situations where similarity cannot be experimentally manipulated in a satisfactory or credible manner (namely, established, non-stranger populations). Of course, in these cases it follows that precise controls (and hence 'good' scientific deduction) are less easy to establish. Wright (1965) has noted the inadequacy of looking at the personality characteristics of established groups of friends, since one cannot by this means discover whether friendship causes observed similarity or similarity is what caused the friendship. Despite the lack of economy of time and the vast efforts needed to complete them, it seems likely that longitudinal studies of friendship (as it develops in the field) will be the only satisfactory way to solve these conceptual problems.

One further point could be made. Byrne, Griffitt and Stefaniak (1967) argue that behavioural similarity in terms of test performance, attitudes, values, judgements, and so on, is attractive and can be used as a measure of personality-relevant activity. On the other hand, Lott and Lott (1974, p. 182) claim that, 'Personality traits . . . are relatively unambiguous and not generally classifiable as reflections of how we view the world'. Contrarily, Duck and Spencer (1972) have argued that some measures of personality are comparable to attitudinal measures and that behaviour represents an individual's way of acting out his attitudes or beliefs about the world. If this view of personality is preferred to that of Lott and Lott, then 'personality' becomes something that is as much in need of testing as are attitudes (cf. Chapter 5) and could be compared to the personality (view of the world) of other people, just as attitudes are (Byrne, 1971). The same or similar justifications for the influence of personality similarity could then be advanced as are offered for attitude similarity (Duck and Spencer, 1972; Duck, 1973b).

Thus the relation between personality and acquaintance would, with all the complications noted above be this: another person's personality is attractive as a function of what is known about it, the confidence one attaches to what one knows about it and the level of support (usually, but as in the case of attitudes, not exclusively provided by similarity) offered by it for one's own personality. As the relationship proceeds, more information is revealed about each person to his partner in the acquaintance and so, presumably, both his knowledge and confidence about it increase and he is better able to assess the support that the other person's personality provides for his own as a function of this complex and multifaceted process.

# CHAPTER SEVEN

# DEVELOPMENT AND BREAKDOWN OF RELATIONSHIPS

Given the general orientation to relationship development outlined and discussed in the previous few chapters, what can be said of the growth of love? And if the processing and exchange of information about other people's personality is the cornerstone of acquaintance, what can be said of children's friendships (since children lack an adult framework for interpreting other people's personality)? Last, and probably most important, does a model of relationship development offer any insight into the question of why relationships fail to develop or falter in their progress, or, once formed, totter or collapse?

## The Growth of Love

Some of the earliest scratchings on the walls of caves appear to indicate that interest in the question of the nature of love has been a primary concern for theorists and actual performers for some time. An interesting addition to speculations of this type has been provided by Berscheid and Walster (1974) during the course of an essay on love which considers more issues than space permits us here. These authors are concerned with passionate love (comprising romantic attraction and sexual attraction) and offer a suggestion based on the work of Schachter (1964). This latter author proposed, on the basis of several experiments, that individuals applied emotional labels to themselves when they were physiologically aroused (without necessarily knowing why) and when it seemed appropriate, in the circumstances, to interpret this arousal in emotional terms. For example, Schachter and Singer (1962) had injected subjects with epinephrine (which induces the classic symptons of arousal, such as increased heart rate and breathing rate) and informed half of the subjects about the likely effects of the drug. The other half were left unenlightened and then had to wait in the company of others (confederates) who behaved either euphorically or aggressively. During the course of measurement, subjects were asked how euphoric or angry they felt. Sure enough, when physiologically aroused, subjects 'explained' their arousal in terms appropriate to the circumstances, taking their cue from the confederates' responses. This two-component theory (arousal plus appropriate cognition) was applied by Walster and Berscheid (1971) to 'love'. Essentially the proposal is that, when experiencing the physiological arousal often associated with intense liking, the individual looks for an appropriate label. Searching through his past history, cultural agreements about labelling of emotions, evidence about how others behave, and encouraged by memories of popular songs, literature and the silver screen he finds the appropriate label to be: 'love'.

Whilst work on this proposal is still at a fairly rudimentary stage (Berscheid and Walster, 1974) other work on the development of liking and loving has been conducted by Rubin (1974) based primarily on self report rather than on the physiological states giving rise to such reports. As a first step, Rubin constructed measures of liking and loving in an attempt to examine more adequately the nature of these two responses (rather than simply their antecedents). A collection of items where individuals were described and rated in affective terms (e.g. 'How much do you trust ___?', 'How much does ___ get on your nerves?') were considered by a panel of judges and rated for the extent to which they would inform about a subject's liking or love for the person concerned. These items were then sorted into two scales: a Liking scale and a Loving scale. The validity of the scales was then established in terms of their ability to discriminate between pairs of people who were involved in personal relationships with one another at different levels, and to assess the relative amounts of liking and loving that are involved in relationships of different strengths and potential. Whilst again, due to its relative recency of appearance, the work is still at a fairly rudimentary stage (Rubin, 1974, p. 400), there does appear to be a satisfactory amount of predictive accuracy from the scales and they appear to relate reasonably well to other indices of liking and loving such as Gazing and Eye Contact (cf. Chapter 4).

More extensive work on the antecedents of growth of those relationships where love is presumably a component (as opposed to work on the nature of the response) has been carried out by Murstein (1971a; 1976; 1977). The Stimulus-Value-Role (SVR) model of courtship development proposed by Murstein postulates that the development of courtship is characterised by a change in the focus of concern by participants. At initial stages of partner-selection, individuals respond to the physical or stimulus properties of one another, such that there is, among other things, a significant relationship between the level of physical attractiveness of the two partners (Murstein, 1971a). A second stage (and there is no suggestion that these stages are of equal duration, mutually exclusive or non-overlapping; Murstein, 1977) is characterised by value compatibility: that is, the partners begin to assess the degree to which their values are similar in valence and intensity. This is done through the normal processes of conversation and verbal interaction. In support of this proposal Murstein (1976) has presented a number of pieces of work, among which is evidence that individuals considering marriage show a significant tendency towards similarity in respect of their hierarchy of values concerning several items (but particularly concerning marriage). At the third (role) stage, Murstein postulates that individuals become concerned to establish 'role fit', that is: to function in characteristically expected ways (roles) that are compatible both with one another and with each person's beliefs about what adequate role performance is like. Thus 'a wife's role as defined by her husband consists of his perception of the behaviour that is expected of a wife' (Murstein, 1977, p. 121) and one aspect of role fit here (from the husband's point of view) would mean that the wife acted in the way that the husband perceived a wife should act. The other aspect of role fit (again, from the husband's point of view) would concern the extent to which his view of a husband's role and his view of a wife's role were compatible. Both partners would be attracted to a relationship where they achieved a satisfactory degree of 'role fit'.

Clearly this theory is concerned with a complex longitudinal development in relationships and is particularly addressed to courtship progress. It is concerned with the stages through which relationships pass and the cues which are preponderantly important at each stage. It is one such theory among several (cf. Chapter 2) but is unique in the extent of its empirical support (Murstein, 1971a; 1976) since most other stage theories have been proposed relatively recently and have not been as thoroughly investigated empirically. The emphasis on courtship development (where the empirical work has largely been concentrated) does not necessarily restrict the utility of the model as a general perspective upon acquaintance (Murstein, 1977). Certainly it is likely that a Stimulus stage at least characterises the earliest points of most relationships in one way or another and there is evidence that even young children use this information as the basis of their early friendship choices (Duck and Gaebler, 1976). However, pending further empirical evidence that SVR theory is suitable as a general theory of acquaintance, one must bear in mind that courtship is virtually unique among relationships, since progress is towards a relationship where only a single partner is 'permitted' and one where social and religious recognition is often formalised. The nature of the 'marketing' of the relationship to other people is thus one of its main distinctive features and success in the later stages of courtship presumably requires skilful handling of many more elements to the relationship than those present in most other forms of acquaintance (e.g. the sexual aspects and the social conventions). Role behaviour may well be emphasised in this type of relationship more explicitly than in other ones.

Courtship failure likewise probably arises from more sources than those leading to failure of other relationships (see below) and success at acquaintance does not inevitably entail success in courtship, notwithstanding the early learning that presumably takes place in childhood and adolescence concerning love, courtship and marriage. Indeed, Strauss (1946) has argued that adult love choices are linked closely with childhood affectional experiences. Actual management of such relationships is likely to be encountered first in adolescence, but learning about the theory, as it were, can begin earlier and may be influenced by a child's relationship to its parents as well as to its peers. The next section therefore looks at children's development of friendship concepts.

# Learning to Like: Friendship in Childhood and Adolescence

Many theorists have advocated the view that an adult's capacities for liking, loving and acquainting are 'fixed' during the experiences of childhood (e.g. Bowlby, 1969). More interest derives in this context, however, from consideration of how children's thought processes develop from infancy to adulthood and how this influences their attitudes to friendship or acquaintance or liking or attraction. Do children form attachments on the same basis as adults? How is their concept of 'friendship' developed? How influential are adults on children's choices?

Lickona (1974, p. 33) has argued that both 'liking and loving ... have their roots in the organisation of thought' (as is argued here) and this leads to the prediction that as thought develops during ontogenesis from childhood to adulthood, so too will there be developments both in the person's conception of the nature of interpersonal relationships and in the basis of the very relationships themselves. Lickona suggests that the conception and nature of interpersonal relationships could usefully be compared with Kohlberg's (1971) six-stage model of development of moral reasoning in children. In this model, the first stages concern the assessments of the morality of actions that are based simply on the rewardingness of the consequences, whilst later stages are increasingly concerned with assessment in terms of consequences for the feelings of others or satisfaction that one has lived up to one's own principles. In terms of the silver screen, most Western villains operate at Stage 1 or Stage 2 whilst John Wayne and Gary Cooper act out their lives with moral dilemmas at Stage 6. It is Kohlberg's main contention that children progress through the stages sequentially, beginning with the stage where they evaluate wrongness in terms only of the extent of the damage caused (6 dinner plates broken is worse than 3) rather than the underlying motive (6 broken trying to help Mother wash-up is 'better' than 3 broken through careless play). Lickona (1974) argues that the development of understanding of moral concepts is a useful background for studying growth in understanding of relationships, since both processes seem to involve a growing ability to grasp the reasoning of other people - particularly an increasing insight into the causes of human action in terms of internal motivational states that can be assessed for their attractiveness and desirability.

This latter aspect of explanation (psychological causality) is developed into a sequential theory by Loevinger and Wessler (1970) who examined ego development - rather than development of comprehension of only moral concepts - and hence dealt with understanding of others' motives, actions, attributes and reasons at various levels. Level 1 describes the growth from infant presocial functioning to a dawning awareness of others as primarily social objects. At Level 2, psychological functioning is explained largely in concrete terms and character is seen in terms of opportunistic hedonism (e.g. 'Men are lucky because they are cute', 'If I can't get what I want, I run away'). The more advanced levels involve increasing degrees of awareness of others' autonomy, the fact that they have personal value systems and reasons or pressures for doing things, or needs for self-fulfilment.

Both views suggest that children of different ages (who are therefore ex hypothesi probably at different stages) will respond in acquaintance to different aspects of other people, will expect different things of relationships and will make personal evaluations of others as a function of different beliefs about their behaviour, its appropriateness and its causality. Regrettably, these suggestions have been late arrivals in the literature on interpersonal attraction and detailed systematic study of their implications is lacking. However, there are studies which, although conducted in different frameworks, cast light on the fertility of a stage-and-sequence model in respect of children's friendships. Campbell and Yarrow (1961), in a study of preadolescent children, showed that more effective children (who showed leadership or successful functioning in a group) differed significantly from ineffective ones in terms of the quality of their perceptions about other children. In short, they were more detailed and accurate in their assessments of others' qualities, both behavioural, reputational and cognitive. A further finding was that children who were more accepted (and liked) by peers showed greater freedom of action and had better reputations (often formed at initial meeting and resistant to change in the light of subsequent behaviour!). An early study by Potashin (1946) examined the influence of traditional factors like intelligence and age on mutual choice as well as analysing dynamic processes of sociometric development and change as a function of such factors. It was suggested that personality development was influenced by sociometric factors and vice versa, with a particularly interesting possibility being that friendship in childhood was some sort of training ground for interactional techniques. This suggestion - echoed below in a study on adolescents - raises interesting possibilities concerning the value of further research aimed at assessing the usefulness of direct teaching about social relationships as part of school curricula.

However, other factors also influence children's friendship choices. Austin and Thompson (1948) found that propinquity and similarity of interests or tastes were factors in acquaintance of importance second only to liking for the personality characteristics of the selected friend. (The children in this study were 6th grade, i.e. about $10\frac{1}{2}$ years old, and it is not quite clear what features of general 'personality characteristics' are relevant, since this was a self report study where subjects responded by writing down their reasons for having friends of certain types and those responses were classified by <u>content of answer</u> into categories chosen by the experimenter, which were then analysed for frequency of occurrence.) Seagoe (1933) equally showed the importance of propinquity (defined as distance between the parental homes of associates) whilst Byrne (1961b) noted the influence of proximity in the classroom itself and the opportunities that it provided for interaction during school hours. On a behavioural level, Smith, Chapman and Foot (1976) report differences in the amounts of laughter and mirthful behaviour as a function of sex and the intimacy level in a children's friendship pair. Boys used laughter as a tension releaser in situations that were too intimate for comfort, whilst girls laughed more when the situation was insufficiently intimate. The authors suggest that mirthful behaviour serves, in children, to signal the appropriate level of intimacy for an interaction and hence influences childhood friendship.

Whilst such factors are undoubtedly relevant to childhood friendship just as, mutatis mutandis, they are for adults, greater interest attaches to the discovery of the ways in which children conceive of 'friendship' and the expectancies that they have about it. La Gaipa and Bigelow (1972) examined changes in friendship expectations of children in grades 1 to 8 (i.e. between about $5\frac{1}{2}$ and 13 years of age). The study was concerned with the attitudes or beliefs that the child had developed concerning the important characteristics of a 'best friend', and the authors anticipated the theoretical work of Lickona in relating the development of friendship concepts to development of moral and cognitive concepts. The study examined the relative salience of several factors at different ages derived from content analysis of children's descriptions of their expectations about a best friend as opposed to other acquaintances. Whilst results showed that children did not move through these stages at the same rate (and thus that the correspondence of friendship concepts to age was poor) results did suggest that the factors relevant to friendship followed a sequence where an instrumental orientation (where the friend is someone who satisfies one's own needs) is replaced by a stage where an evaluative dimension appears (friends' character, achievement and social responsibility become important). Later (around 6th grade: age $10\frac{1}{2}$) Loyalty, Commitment and Acceptance became important, with a desire for Genuineness (and, in females, Intimacy of Communication) appearing around 8th grade (13 years). La Gaipa and Bigelow (1972) considered that one implication of the findings was that children who are 'behind' their peers in terms of concepts about friendship are likely to experience problems in peer interaction: 'A child in the sixth grade that views a friend as one who gives him things (Instrumental) rather than in terms of Loyalty and Commitment is perhaps more likely to be rejected' (La Gaipa and Bigelow, 1972, p. 6). Once again, then, there are results to suggest parallels between cognitive and interpersonal development - which also tend to support the view that childhood may be the training ground for interaction (and beliefs about one's social attractiveness). For in all stage theories (especially those using the term 'development') there is the implication that 'completeness' is achieved only by those who reach the 'final' stage, and the inherent value judgements implicit in stage theories suggest a qualitative deficiency in those who fail (note the word) to reach later parts of the process, or do so more slowly than others. One implication of all this is that individuals may become 'fixed' at a certain stage of development of concepts about friendship such that their adult relationships may be paralysed or constrained by their inability to proceed beyond childish conceptions.

There is thus considerable evidence not only that the basis of children's friendships is different from that in adults but also that the basis alters with age during childhood itself. However, the factors involved are obviously exceedingly complex and it is too early to say how precisely children's friendship is related to cognitive development. However there is likely to be some relationship, for the reason observed by Levinger and Snoek (1972) that the ability to interpret cues (which, of course, changes and develops as children mature) is necessary to assess how much people have enjoyed an interaction and why. A further problem that is instanced by the evidence considered above is the issue of the aspect of children's friendships that is influenced by such processes. Does the influence fall on the mechanisms or processes that children employ to select their friends? If so, the processes clearly interact with lots of other factors in children just as with adults (cf. Chapters 3 and 4). Or does the developmental process influence children's concepts of what friends should provide? Or else their concept of what friendship is? Or what 'a friend' does or how he behaves? Furthermore, there are several neglected factors in research on children's friendship. For one thing, children's liking for other children is likely to be qualitatively different from their liking for adults, but the basis for these possible differences is not clear. Adults' perception of children's sociometry appears to be moderately accurate (Duck and Gaebler, 1976) but adults attribute the origin of the friendship choices to markedly different factors from those that the children themselves report as the basis for their choices. La Gaipa (personal communication) also considers that the influence of parental attitudes and pressures on children's choices is a neglected area of research.

A further point is also relevant. So far we have considered how some aspect of children's friendship ('development of relationships') may be influenced by their moral or psychological development. Another version of this ontogenetic point can be made in connection with the other sense of 'development of relationships' (i.e. the ways in which acquaintance develops from first encounter to firm friendship). Levinger and Snoek (1972) have observed that a person's needs may change with time - and this applies both to child development and acquaintance. Perhaps the progress occurring in adult relationships reflects to a degree, the nature of development inherent in children's friendship concepts (i.e. that ontogenetic development is a process that parallels the microcosmic progress of acquaintance in adults). This speculation has not yet received much attention in children, but there has been a study on adolescents that suggests its plausibility. Hypothesising that growth of personality occurred in adolescents - and thus that the similarity of personality relevant to friendship choice would equally grow and change during adolescence - Duck (1975b) found that early adolescent relationships were based on similarity of Factual description (and also in girls only, similarity of Physical description). Mid-adolescent girls formed friendships on the basis of similarity of Psychological descriptions (whilst for boys the relevant personality similarity was centred on description of Interaction Behaviour) and indeed at late adolescence girls' friendships followed an almost adult pattern, being based partly on similarity of Psychological descriptions of other people and partly on similarity of Physical descriptions. This suggests that adolescents gradually develop a relationship style that comes to reflect the adult pattern - a pattern that has to be <u>learned</u> and tried out. This gives another meaning to the phrase 'relationship development'.

Since childhood and adolescence may be a testing ground for relational techniques one may suppose that some people will, by circumstances, leave the testing ground in a better condition for acquainting than others. 'Development of relationships' clearly presupposes change in some aspect of the relationship, whether change in intimacy level, in permitted or expected behaviour, or (as argued in this book) in the kinds and types of information that have salience and significance - or a combination of them all. If this latter view is correct (not necessarily uniquely correct, but if it identifies one important factor) then the 'goodness' of - and satisfactory progress in - a relationship will depend on the skills and abilities of the two partners to adapt, to sequence their behaviour and information-transmission appropriately, and to respond to one another in ways defined as appropriate on the basis of available information and present intimacy level. This suggests (as it did in Chapter 4) a certain kind of skill in the two partners and this prompts the prediction that there are probably individual differences in level of such ability.

### Relationship Failure and Breakdown

Many stage theories are based on the study of successful courtship couples or other successful relationships but many people are not so fortunate or skilful as to maintain and develop proper personal relationships. Clearly, though, a mature understanding of the stages in successfully progressing relationships may help to identify reasons for the failure to progress in unsuccessful relationships. Stage theories (cf. Chapter 2) may thus offer the best basis for explaining breakdown and failure in relationship - certainly they offer the best basis for a parsimonious explanation (i.e. explanation of successful and unsuccessful relationships in terms of the same set of principles). There are, however, two kinds of 'failure' in this respect: one observed in those individuals who completely fail to initiate or maintain relationships as a general rule; the other observed in 'natural' breakdown of relationship or the lapse of relationships between habitually successful acquainters.

## 'Abnormal' Relationships and Relaters

There is a paucity of research on relaters who are abnormal in some way and one interesting hypothesis that deserves more attention than it has so far received is the possibility of a complex relationship between abnormal symptoms and interpersonal failures (which causes which?). However there has been some work directly addressed to friendship in neurotics, schizophrenics, the depressed patient and alcoholics - as well as some work that involves interpersonal attraction in such populations during studies on other issues.

La Gaipa (1977b) reports studies conducted on the friendship concepts of some patients with personality disorders (e.g. passive-aggressives or alcoholics), others who were schizophrenic and some who were neurotic. In comparison with 'normal' samples, several differences of emphasis and of kind appear in the aspects of friendship and friendship behaviour that the 'abnormal' groups rate as most salient. For example, male neurotics tended to overemphasise disclosure of intimate material whilst females de-emphasised it (relative to the normal sample) and it was noted that neurotics tended to resemble the opposite sex normal group in their friendship beliefs. La Gaipa offers the suggestion that role-confusion about appropriate friendship responses may be partly responsible for the observed neurotic symptoms. Other findings, however, suggested that, taken as a whole, psychiatric groups differed from normals in the emphasis they placed on strength of character and the lack of interest they took in similarity. Overall, La Gaipa (1977b) identifies several possible differences in the cognitive structuring of attitudes to, and beliefs about, friendship in abnormal populations.

In other work on neurotics, Murstein (1973) set out to test the hypothesis that neurotics, having a much reduced reward power relative to other interactors, would tend to settle for other neurotics as marriage partners. This would, of course, be due not so much to a liking for other neurotics as to an inability to attract non-neurotic partners (whose reward power would be higher) in the absence of other mitigating reward powers (such as beauty or wealth or reputation). It was found that neurotics' perceptions of each other were, however, considerably less congruent that non-neurotics' perceptions of non-neurotics in a courtship pair. This again suggests that ability to perceive either the partner or the role of 'courtship partner' (or 'friend') may be a characteristic of neurotic or 'abnormal' populations.

Similarly, Duck (1976a) has argued that many 'abnormal' patients have encoding or decoding problems (see Chapters 3 and 4) in relationships involving relatively intimate interaction and thus lack the necessary skills to steer or conduct relationships to an appropriate depth. This may be one component in their withdrawal from social interaction: through lack of appropriate management, maintenance and information-transmission skills (e.g. failures to Self-Disclose appropriately; failures to pace relationship development adequately) mentally-disturbed individuals, or those with personality disorders may fail to set up those very personal relationships which might have helped them to remain stable.

Breakdown, Break Up and Lapse

Relationships may disintegrate either through breakdown (i.e. the parties come to dislike each other or to desire a _less_ intimate relationship) or through lapse (i.e. the relationship may be curtailed by incidental factors like graduations breaking up groups of student friends). Most relationships that break up do not simply regress to a former level of intimacy (e.g. when people get divorced they do not simply return to the level of intimacy that characterised courtship: the whole relationship stops) whereas one characteristic of relationships that merely lapse is that they tend to 'stick' at the level where they were before the lapse, and neither progress nor retrogress. However, work on lapsed relationships is almost non-existent and work on breakdown of relationships is confined almost exclusively to marital relationships where the breakdown is often institutionalised in the law courts. It is not clear therefore, what <u>general</u> principles apply to the breakdown of relationships and this is an area of research which could benefit from the close attention of research workers. It could, for example, be claimed that breakdown of relationships is caused by a simple decrease in rewards, or the appearance of a more attractive alternative, or an increase in costs. It is not clear, however, what would be the relevant variables here since exchange factors in more well-established relationships are less well studied than those in initial relationships.

From the viewpoint of the themes running through this book, however, failure of relationships can be postulated to be due to a faulty model of the other person's personality. In other words, failure is due to the breakdown or inadequacy of those processes hypothesised to characterise relationship development: attribution, erection of probabilistic models of the Other's personality, assessment of that model against one's own personality for similarity. To recapitulate: on the basis of what I observe about you I form expectancies and estimates about your personality; from time to time I observe new relevant information and may need to re-evaluate my model of your personality. Perforce, therefore, my estimate of our similarity will be affected by the relationship between this new model of your personality and my own personality as I see it. If my original model overestimated the amount of similarity that existed, and if the subsequent model is more accurate and shows us to be less similar than expected then I would be inclined (according to the principles outlined in the hypothesis running through this book) to find you less likable. Relationship breakdown occurs when each subsequent piece of evidence ratifies and confirms the second (discordant) model of your personality and thus emphasises its lack of sufficient similarity to my personality.

Equally, if the thesis proposed in this book is correct, then there is a further good reason for taking the view that relationship breakdown is caused by the same processes as lead to the setting up of relationships. Individuals' personalities are conceived to be dynamically changing, multifaceted things and so two previously similar personalities may change and develop in ways that render them less similar than they were before. In just as natural ways as two personalities can grow more similar, so can they grow less similar. Since similarity or support for one's personality is the taproot of acquaintance, the affective bonds would naturally be likely to weaken when such growth apart occurred. When the differences become significant enough to undermine the basis of the relationship, as outlined above, then, too, 'natural wastage' of the relationship could occur. Indeed, 'natural wastage' is perhaps a less perjorative term than 'relationship failure' to describe breakdown in relationships and is a term that emphasises its links with the natural development of acquaintance and hence its explanation in the most parsimonious way using the same set of principles. Far better, I would suggest, to adopt such a view than to follow the stigmatising approach to relationship breakdown that is summarised in Darwin's assertion that the duration of a man's friendships is the best measure of his worth.

Indirect evidence for this approach is provided by the work of Duck and Allison (in prep.) who studied a student friendship group at the point where they were forced to move out of their Hall of Residence into smaller living units and so had to select from their groups of friends a set of three or four others with whom to live more closely. The members of the population were significantly more similar in personality than a set of randomly chosen subjects - as would be consistent with work on personality and friendship (see Chapter 6). However, groups who chose to live with one another were significantly more similar on specific deeper aspects of personality than those who chose not to live with one another and those chosen as flatmates by no one were overall least similar of all. This tentative and tangential evidence is at least indicative of suport for the proposal running through this book.


## Epilogue

This book, has, of course, not been primarily and obviously concerned with relationship failure, breakdown and collapse but with the successful setting up of acquaintance and its development from initial encounter to firm friendship. However, this latter section is a timely reminder that the inability to form relationships, the collapse of relationships, and the lapsing of relationships are all human problems of considerable personal significance. The ill effects of such events may perhaps be counteracted by some of the principles considered during the course of this book. Relationship development involves skills that revolve around the handling of complex cognitive activity, the processing of complex types and layers of information and the transmission and reception of detail about personality. In cases where relationships are deficient or decaying it may be that such skills are lacking also and that relational ability may be repaired by some form of 'training' or conscious attention to the development of such acquaintance skills. This is ultimately an empirical question that would repay the considerable research effort that it implies. For if one thing has become clear from the present view of the literature it is that psychology's function as a helping science is well served by an expansion of research activity into development of acquaintance. One much needed area of expansion lies in the <u>longitudinal</u> study of developing relationships, for only then shall we begin to achieve a fuller understanding of the psychological functions of friendship and the fundamental significance of its contribution to psychological health.

# REFERENCES

Adams, J.S. (1965), 'Inequity in social exchange', in Berkowitz, L. (ed.), Advances in Experimental Social Psychology, London and New York: Academic Press; vol. 2.

Adler, A. (1926), The neurotic constitution, New York: Dodd, Mead.

Ajzen, I. (1974), 'Effects of information on interpersonal attraction: Similarity versus affective value', J. Pers. Soc. Psych. (29) pp. 374-80.

Ajzen, I. (1977), 'Information processing approaches to interpersonal attraction', in Duck, S.W. (ed.), Theory and practice in interpersonal attraction, London: Academic Press.

Allgeier, A.R. and Byrne, D. (1973), 'Attraction towards the opposite sex as a determinant of physical proximity', J. Soc. Psych. (90) pp. 213-20.

Altman, I. (1974), 'The communication of interpersonal attitudes: an ecological approach', in Huston, E.L. (ed.), Foundations of interpersonal attraction, New York: Academic Press.

Altman, I. (1975), The environment and social behaviour, Monterey, Calif.: Brooks/Cole.

Altman, I. and Taylor, D.A. (1973), Social penetration: The development of interpersonal behaviour, New York: Holt, Rinehart and Winston.

Anderson, A.B. (1975), 'Combined effects of interpersonal attraction and goal path clarity on the cohesiveness of task-oriented groups', J. Pers. Soc. Psych. (31) pp. 68-76.

Anderson, N.H. (1968), 'Likeableness ratings of 555 personality-trait words', J. Pers. Soc. Psych. (9) pp. 272-9.

Anderson, N.H. (1970), 'Functional measurement and psychophysical judgement', Psych. Rev. (77) pp. 153-70.

Anthony, S. (1974), 'Immediacy and non-immediacy: Factors in communicating interpersonal attraction', J. Soc. Psych. (93)

pp. 141-3.

Argyle, M. (1967), The psychology of interpersonal behaviour, Harmondsworth: Penguin.

Argyle, M. (1969), Social Interaction, London: Social Science Paperbacks.

Argyle, M. (1975), Bodily communication, London: Methuen.

Argyle, M., Alkema, F. and Gilmour, R. (1972), 'The communication of friendly and hostile attitudes by verbal and nonverbal signals', Eur. J. Soc. Psych (1) pp. 385-402.

Argyle, M. and Dean, J. (1965), 'Eye-contact, distance and affiliation', Sociometry (28) pp. 289-304.

Argyle, M. and Kendon, A. (1967), 'The experimental analysis of social performance' in Berkowitz, L. (ed.), Advances in Experimental Social Psychology, New York and London: Academic Press, vol. 3.

Argyle, M. and McHenry, R. (1971), 'Do spectacles really affect judgements of intelligence?' Brit. J. Soc. Clin. Psychol. (10) pp. 27-9.

Argyle, M., Salter, V., Nicholson, H., Williams, M. and Burgess, P. (1970), 'The communication of inferior and superior attitudes by verbal and nonverbal means', Brit. J. Soc. Clin. Psychol. (9) pp. 221-31.

Aronson, E. and Carlsmith, J.M. (1968), 'Experimentation in social psychology' in Lindzey, G. and Aronson, E. (eds), The handbook of social psychology, New York: Academic Press, vol. 4.

Aronson, E. and Cope, V. (1968), 'My enemy's enemy is my friend', J. Pers. Soc. Psych. (8) pp. 8-12.

Aronson, E. and Linder, D. (1965), 'Gain and loss of esteem as determinants of interpersonal attractiveness', J. Exp. Soc. Psych. (1) pp. 156-71.

Aronson, E. and Worchel, P. (1966), 'Similarity versus liking as determinants of interpersonal attractiveness', Psychon. Sci. (5) pp. 157-8.

Austin, M.C. and Thompson, G.G. (1948), 'Children's friendships: a study of the bases on which children select and reject their best friends', J. Educ. Psych. (39) pp. 101-16.

Backman, C. and Secord, P.F. (1959), 'The effects of perceived liking on interpersonal attraction', Hum. Relat. (12) pp. 379-84.

Backman, C. and Secord, P.F. (1962), 'Liking, selective interaction and misperception in congruent interpersonal relations', Sociometry (25) pp. 321-35.

Banikiotes, P.G., Russell, J.M. and Linden, J.D. (1972), 'Interpersonal attraction in real and simulated interactions', J. Pers. Soc. Psych. (23) pp. 1-7.

Batchelor, T.R. and Tesser, A. (1971), 'Attitude base as a moderator of the attitude similarity-attraction relationship', J. Pers. Soc. Psych. (19) pp. 229-36.

Baugher, D.M. and Gormly, J. (1975), 'Effects of personal competence on the significance of interpersonal agreement and disagreement: Physiological activation and social evaluations', J. Res. in Pers. (9) pp. 356-65.

Beier, E.G., Rossi, A.M. and Garfield, R.L. (1961), 'Similarity plus dissimilarity of personality: Basis for friendship?', Psych. Rep. (8) pp. 3-8.

Berger, C. (1975), 'Proactive and retroactive attribution processes in interpersonal communication', Hum. Comm. Res. (2) pp. 33-50.

Berger, C. and Calabrese, R.J. (1975), 'Some explorations in initial interaction and beyond: Toward a developmental theory of interpersonal communication', Hum. Comm. Res. (1) pp. 99-112.

Berscheid, E., Boye, D. and Darley, J.M. (1968), 'Effects of forced association upon voluntary choice to associate', J. Pers. Soc. Psych. (8) pp. 13-19.

Berscheid, E. and Walster, E.H.(1969), Interpersonal attraction, Reading, Mass.: Addison-Wesley.

Berscheid, E. and Walster, E.H. (1974), 'A little bit about love' in Huston, E.L. (ed.), Foundations of interpersonal attraction, New York: Academic Press.

Blau, P.M. (1964), Exchange and power in social life, New York: Wiley.

Bleda, P.R. (1972), 'Perception of height as a linear function of attitude similarity', Psychon. Sci. (27) pp. 197-8.

Bleda, P.R. (1974), 'Towards a clarification of the role of cognitive and affective processes in the similarity-attraction relationship', J. Pers. Soc. Psych. (29) pp. 368-73.

Blumberg, H.H. (1969), 'On being liked more than you like', J. Pers. Soc. Psych. (11) pp. 121-8.

Bogardus, E.S. (1925), 'Measuring social distance', J. Appl. Sociol. (9) pp. 299-308.

Bowlby, J. (1969), Attachment and loss: Volume 1: Attachment, Harmondsworth: Penguin.

Brickman, P., Meyer, P. and Fredd, S. (1975), 'Effects of varying exposure to another person with familiar or unfamiliar thought processes', J. Exp. Soc. Psych. (11) pp. 261-70.

Brickman, P. and Seligman, C. (1974), 'Effects of public and private expectancies on attributions of competence and interpersonal attraction', J. Pers. (42) pp. 558-69.

Bugenthal, D.E., Kaswan, J.W. and Love, L.R. (1970), 'Perception of contradictory meanings conveyed by verbal and nonverbal channels', J. Pers. Soc. Psych. (16) pp. 647-55.

Byrne, D. (1961a), 'Interpersonal attraction and attitude similarity', J. Abn. Soc. Psych. (62) pp. 713-15.

Byrne, D. (1961b), 'The influence of propinquity and opportunity for interaction on classroom relationships', Hum. Relat. (14) pp. 63-9.

Byrne, D. (1969), 'Attitudes and attraction' in Berkowitz, L. (ed.), Advances in experimental social psychology, New York: Academic Press, vol. 4.

Byrne, D. (1971), The attraction paradigm, New York: Academic Press.

Byrne, D. (in press), 'Social psychology and the study of sexual behaviour', Pers & Soc. Psych. Bull. (in press).

Byrne, D., Baskett, G.D. and Hodges, L. (1971), 'Behavioral indicators of interpersonal attraction', J. Appl. Soc. Psych. (1) pp. 137-49.

Byrne, D. and Cherry, F. (in press), 'A plumber's friend in need is a plumber's friend indeed', J. Res. in Pers.

Byrne, D. and Clore, G.L. (1967), 'Effectance arousal and attraction', J. Pers. Soc. Psych. Monog. (6: Whole No: 638).

Byrne, D., Clore, G.L., Griffitt, W., Lamberth, J. and Mitchell, H.E. (1973a), 'When research paradigms converge: Confrontation or integration?' J. Pers. Soc. Psych. (28) pp. 313-20.

Byrne, D., Clore, G.L., Griffitt, W., Lamberth, J. and Mitchell, H.E. (1973b), 'One more time', J. Pers. Soc. Psych. (28) pp. 323-4.

Byrne, D., Clore, G.L. and Worchel, P. (1966), 'Effect of economic similarity-dissimilarity on interpersonal attraction, J. Pers. Soc. Psych. (4) pp. 220-4.

Byrne, D., Ervin, C.R. and Lamberth, J. (1970), 'Continuity between the experimental study of attraction and real life computer dating', J. Pers. Soc. Psych. (16) pp. 157-65.

Byrne, D., Gouax, C., Griffith, W., Lamberth, J., Murakawa, M., Prasad, M., Prasad, A. and Ramirez, M. III (1971), 'The ubiquitous relationship: Attitude similarity and attraction. A cross cultural study', Hum. Relat. (24) pp. 201-7.

Byrne, D. and Griffitt, W. (1966a), 'Similarity versus liking: A clarification', Psychon. Sci. (6) pp. 295-6.

Byrne, D. and Griffitt, W. (1966b), 'A developmental investigation of the law of attraction', J. Pers. Soc. Psych. (4) pp. 699-702.

Byrne, D. and Griffitt, W.(1969), 'Similarity and awareness of similarity of personality characteristics as determinants of attraction', J. Exp. Res. in Pers. (3) pp. 179-86.

Byrne, D. and Griffitt, W. (1973), 'Interpersonal attraction', Ann. Rev. Psych. (24) pp. 317-36.

Byrne, D., Griffitt, W. and Golightly, C. (1966), 'Prestige as a factor in determining the effect of attitute similarity-dissimilarity on attraction', J. Pers. (34) pp. 434-44.

Byrne, D., Griffitt, W., Hudgins, W. and Reeves, K. (1969), 'Attitude similarity-dissimilarity and attraction: Generality beyond the college sophomore', J. Soc. Psych. (79) pp. 155-61.

Byrne, D., Griffitt, W. and Stefaniak, D. (1967), 'Attraction and similarity of personality characteristics', J. Pers. Soc. Psych. (5) pp. 82-90.

Byrne, D. and Lamberth, J. (1971), 'Cognitive and reinforcement theories as complementary approaches to the study of attraction' in Murstein, B.I. (ed.), Theories of attraction and love, New York: Springer.

Byrne, D., McDonald, R.D. and Mikawa, J. (1963), 'Approach and avoidance affiliation motives', J. Pers. (31) pp. 21-37.

Byrne, D. and Nelson, D. (1965), 'Attraction as a linear function of proportion of positive reinforcements', J. Pers. Soc. Psych. (1) pp. 659-63.

Byrne, D., Nelson, D. and Reeves, K. (1966), 'Effects of consensual validation and invalidation on attraction as a function of verifiability', J. Exp. Soc. Psych. (2) pp. 98-107.

Byrne, D., Rasche, L. and Kelley, K. (1974), 'When "I like you" indicates disagreement: An experimental differentiation of information and affect', J. Res. in Pers. (8) pp. 207-17.

Byrne, D. and Rhamey, R. (1965), 'Magnitude of positive and

negative reinforcements as a determinant of attraction', J. Pers. Soc. Psych. (2) pp. 884-9.

Byrne, D. and Wong, T.J. (1962), 'Racial prejudice, interpersonal attraction and assumed dissimilarity of attitudes', J. Abn. Soc. Psych. (65) pp. 246-52.

Campbell, J.D. and Yarrow, M.R. (1961), 'Perceptual and behavioural correlates of social effectiveness', Sociometry (24) pp. 1-20.

Cavior, N., Miller, K. and Cohen, S.H. (1975), 'Physical attractiveness, attitude similarity and length of acquaintance as contributors to interpersonal attraction among adolescents', Soc. Beh. & Pers. (3) pp. 133-41.

Chapman, R.N. (1928), 'The quantitative analysis of environmental factors', Ecology (9) pp. 111-22.

Cherry, F., Byrne, D. and Mitchell, H.E. (1976), 'Clogs in the bogus pipeline: Demand characteristics and social desirability', J. Res. in Pers. (10) pp. 69-75.

Clore, G.L. (1977), 'Reinforcement and affect in attraction' in Duck, S.W. (ed.), Theory and practice in interpersonal attraction, London:Academic Press.

Clore, G.L. and Byrne, D. (1974), 'A reinforcement-affect model of attraction' in Huston, E.L. (ed.), Foundations of interpersonal attraction, New York: Academic Press.

Clore, G.L. and Gormly, J.B. (1974), 'Knowing, feeling and liking: A psychophysiological study of attraction', J. Res. in Pers. (8) pp. 218-30.

Clore, G.L., Wiggins, N.H. and Itkin, S. (1975), 'Gain and loss in attraction: Attribution from nonverbal behavior', J. Pers. Soc. Psych. (31) pp. 706-12.

Cook, M. (1977), 'The social skill model and interpersonal attraction' in Duck, S.W. (ed.), Theory and practice in interpersonal attraction, London: Academic Press.

Cooper, J. and Jones, E.E. (1969), 'Opinion divergence as a

strategy to avoid being miscast', J. Pers. Soc. Psych. (13) pp. 23-30.

Cozby, P.C. (1973), 'Self-disclosure: A literature review', Psych. Bull. (79) pp. 73-91.

Craig, R.G. and Duck, S.W. (1977), 'Similarity, interpersonal attitudes and attraction: the evaluative-descriptive distinction', Brit. J. Soc. Clin. Psych. (16) pp. 15-21.

Crockett, W.H. (1965), 'Cognitive complexity and impression formation ' in Maher, B.A. (ed.), Progress in experimental personality research, New York, Academic Press, vol. 2.

Curran, J.P. (1973), 'Correlates of physical attractiveness and interpersonal attraction in the dating situation', Soc. Beh. & Pers. (1) pp. 153-8.

Curry, T.J. and Emerson, R.M. (1970), 'Balance theory: A theory of interpersonal attraction?', Sociometry (33) pp. 216-38.

Daher, D.M. and Banikiotes, P.G. (1976), 'Interpersonal attraction and rewarding aspects of disclosure content and level', J. Pers. Soc. Psych. (33) pp. 492-6.

Davis, J.D. (1976), 'Self-disclosure in an acquaintance exercise: Responsibility for level of intimacy', J. Pers. Soc. Psych. (33) pp. 787-92.

Day, B.R. (1961), 'A comparison of personality needs of courtship couples and same-sex friends', Sociol. & Soc. Res. (45) pp. 435-40.

DeCharms, R., Carpenter, V. and Kuperman, A. (1965), 'The origin-pawn variable in person perception', Sociometry (28) pp. 241-58.

Derlega, V.J., Harris, M.S. and Chaikin, A.L. (1973), 'Self-disclosure reciprocity, liking and the deviant', J. Exp. Soc. Psych. (9) pp. 277-84.

Derlega, V.J., Wilson, M. and Chaikin, A.L. (1976), 'Friendship and disclosure reciprocity', J. Pers. Soc. Psych. (34) pp. 578-

Dion, K.K. (1972), 'Physical attractiveness and evaluations of children's transgressions', J. Pers. Soc. Psych. (24) pp. 207-13.

Dion, K.K. (1974), 'Children's physical attractiveness and sex as determinants of adult punitiveness', Dev. Psych. (10) pp. 772-8.

Dion, K.K. and Berscheid, E. (1974), 'Physical attractiveness and peer perception among children', Sociometry (37) pp. 1-12.

Dion, K.K., Berscheid, E. and Walster, E.H. (1972), 'What is beautiful is good', J. Pers. Soc. Psych. (24) pp. 285-90.

Dittes, J.E. (1959), 'Attractiveness of a group as a function of self esteem and acceptance by the group', J. Abn. Soc. Psych. (59) pp. 77-82.

Duck, S.W. (1971), 'Personal constructs and friendship formation', Unpub. PhD thesis: University of Sheffield, England.

Duck, S.W. (1973a), 'Similarity and perceived similarity of personal constructs as influences on friendship choice', Brit. J. Soc. Clin. Psych. (12) pp. 1-6.

Duck, S.W. (1973b), Personal relationships and personal constructs: A study of friendship formation, London: Wiley.

Duck, S.W. (1973c), 'Personality similarity and friendship formation: Similarity of what, when?', J. Pers. (41) pp. 543-58.

Duck, S.W. (1975a), 'Attitude similarity and interpersonal attraction: Right answers and wrong reasons', Brit. J. Soc. Clin. Psych. (14) pp. 311-12.

Duck, S.W. (1975b), 'Personality similarity and friendship choices by adolescents', Eur. J. Soc. Psych. (5) pp. 70-83.

Duck, S.W. (1976a), 'Some applications of friendship research to psychiatry', IRCS: Forum (4) pp. 490-2.

Duck, S.W. (1976b), 'Interpersonal communication in developing acquaintance' in Miller, G. (ed.), Explorations in interpersonal communication, New York: Sage.

Duck, S.W. (1977a), 'Inquiry, hypothesis and the quest for validation: Personal construct systems in the development of acquaintance' in Duck, S.W. (ed.), Theory and practice in interpersonal attraction, London: Academic Press.

Duck, S.W. (1977b), 'Personality similarity and friendship formation' in Mikula, G. and Stroebe, W. (eds), Freundschaft und Ehe: Psychologische Grundlagen zwischenmenschlicher Beziehungen, Huber Verlag: Bern.

Duck, S.W. (1977c), 'Tell me where is fancy bred: Some thoughts on the study of interpersonal attraction' in Duck, S.W. (ed.), Theory and practice in interpersonal attraction, London: Academic Press.

Duck, S.W. and Allison, D. (in prep.), 'I like you but I can't live with you: When friends must part', Unpub. manuscript.

Duck, S.W. and Craig, R.G. (1975), 'Effects of type of information upon interpersonal attraction', Soc. Beh. & Pers. (3) pp. 157-64.

Duck, S.W. and Craig, R.G. (1977), 'The relative attractiveness of different types of information about another person', Brit. J. Soc. Clin. Psych. (16).

Duck, S.W. and Craig, R.G. (in prep.), 'Personality similarity and the longitudinal development of friendship: An experimental study', Unpub. manuscript.

Duck, S.W. and Gaebler, H.C. (1976), 'Physical attractiveness and ratings of popularity by children and teachers', IRCS: Res. on Psych. & Psychiat. (4) p. 143.

Duck, S.W. and Richards, D.M. (1976), 'Attitude similarity and attraction in real life contexts', IRCS: Res. on Psych. & Psychiat. (4) p. 43.

Duck, S.W. and Spencer, C.P. (1972), 'Personal constructs and friendship formation', J. Pers. Soc. Psych. (23) p. 40-5.

Dutton, D.G. (1973), 'Attribution of cause for opinion change and liking for audience members', J. Pers. Soc. Psych. (26) pp. 208-16.

Ehrlich, H.J. and Graeven, D.B. (1971), 'Reciprocal self-disclosure in a dyad', J. Exp. Soc. Psych. (7) pp. 389-400.

Ehrlich, H.J. and Lipsey, C. (1969), 'Affective style as a variable in person perception', J. Pers. (37) pp. 522-40.

Eiser, J.R. (1976), 'Attribution processes in social behaviour', Address to conference of the Social Section of the British Psychological Society, September 1976.

Festinger, L. (1954), 'A theory of social comparison processes', Hum. Relat. (7) pp. 117-40.

Festinger, L., Schachter, S. and Back, K. (1950), Social pressures in informal groups, New York: Harper.

Fiedler, F.E. (1953), 'The psychological distance dimension in interpersonal relations', J. Pers. (22) pp. 142-50.

Foa, U.G. and Foa, E.B. (1971), 'Resource exchange: Toward a structural theory of interpersonal relations' in Siegman, A.W. and Pope, B. (eds), Studies in dyadic communication, New York: Pergamon Press.

Frankel, A. and Morris, W.N. (1976), 'Testifying in one's own defense: The ingratiator's dilemma', J. Pers. Soc. Psych. (34) pp. 475-85.

Freedman, N., Blass, T. and Rifkin, A. (1973), 'Body movements and the verbal encoding of aggressive affect', J. Pers. Soc. Psych. (26) pp. 72-85.

Freud, S. (1914), 'On Narcissism' in Jones, E. (ed.), The collected papers of Sigmund Freud, New York: Basic Books (1959).

Fromm, E. (1939), 'Selfishness and self love', Psychiatry (2) pp. 507-23.

Gaes, G.G., Quigley-Fernandez, B. and Tedeschi, J.T. (1977), 'Unclogging the bogus pipeline: A critical reanalysis of the

Cherry, Byrne and Mitchell study', J. Res. in Pers. (11).

Geen, R.G. and Stonner, D. (1974), 'Similarity, conditioned affect and interpersonal attraction', J. Psych. (87) pp. 111-18.

Geller, D.M., Goodstein, L., Silver, M. and Sternberg, W.C. (1974), 'On being ignored: The effects of violation of implicit rules of social interaction', Sociom. (37) pp. 541-56.

Goethals, G.R. and Nelson, R.E. (1973), 'Similarity in the influence process: The belief-value distinction', J. Pers. Soc. Psych. (25) pp. 117-22.

Goffman, E. (1964), Stigma: Notes on the management of spoiled identity, Englewood Cliffs, NJ: Prentice Hall.

Goffman, E. (1971), Relations in public, London: Allen Lane.

Goldman, J.A. and Olczak, P.V. (1976), 'Psychosocial maturity and interpersonal attraction', J. Res. in Pers. (10) pp. 146-54.

Goldstein, J.W. and Rosenfeld, H.M. (1969), 'Insecurity and preference for persons similar to oneself', J. Pers. (37) pp. 253-68.

Golightly, C. and Byrne, D. (1964), 'Attitude statements as positive and negative reinforcements', Science (146) pp. 798-9.

Golightly, C., Huffman, D. and Byrne, D. (1972), 'Liking and loaning', J. Appl. Psych. (56) pp. 521-3.

Gormly, J., Gormly, A. and Johnson, C. (1972), 'Consistency of socio-behavioural responses in interpersonal disagreement', J. Pers. Soc. Psych. (24) pp. 221-4.

Griffitt, W. (1966), 'Interpersonal attraction as a function of self-concept and personality similarity-dissimilarity', J. Pers. Soc. Psych. (4) pp. 581-4.

Griffitt, W. (1969), 'Personality similarity and self-concept as determinants of interpersonal attraction', J. Soc. Psych. (78) pp. 137-46.

Griffitt, W. (1974), 'Attitude similarity and attraction' in

Huston, E.L. (ed.), Foundations of interpersonal attraction, New York: Academic Press.

Griffitt, W. and Guay, P. (1969), ' "Object" evaluation and conditioned affect', J. Exp. Res. in Pers. (4) pp. 1-8.

Griffitt, W. and Jackson, T. (1973), 'Simulated jury decisions: The influence of jury-defendant attitude similarity-dissimilarity', Soc. Beh. & Pers. (1) pp. 1-7.

Griffitt, W., Nelson, J. and Littlepage, G. (1972), 'Old age and responses to agreement-disagreement', J. Gerontol. (27) pp. 269-74.

Griffitt, W. and Veitch, R. (1971), 'Hot and crowded: Influences of population density and temperature on interpersonal behaviour', J. Pers. Soc. Psych. (17) pp. 92-8.

Griffitt, W. and Veitch, R. (1974), 'Pre-acquaintance attitude similarity and attraction revisited: Ten days in a fall-out shelter', Sociometry (37) pp. 163-73.

Gullahorn, J.T. (1952), 'Distance and friendship as factors in the gross interaction matrix', Sociometry (15) pp. 123-34.

Guthrie, E.R. (1938), The psychology of human conflict, Harper: New York.

Hall, E.T. (1963), 'The anthropology of manners', Sci. Amer. (192) pp. 84-90.

Hardy, K.R. (1957), 'Determinants of conformity and attitude change', J. Abn. Soc. Psych. (54) pp. 289-94.

Harlow, H.F. and Harlow, M.K. (1965), 'The affectional systems' in Schrier, A.M. et al. (eds), Behaviour of nonhuman primates, New York: Academic Press.

Harré, R. (ed.) (1976), Life sentences: Aspects of the social role of language, London: Wiley.

Harré, R. (1977), 'Friendship as an accomplishment: An ethogenic approach to social relationships' in Duck, S.W. (ed.), Theory and practice in interpersonal attraction, London:

Academic Press.

Harré, R. and DeWaele, J.P. (1976), 'The ritual for incorporation of a stranger' in Harré, R. (ed.), Life sentences: Aspects of the social role of language, London: Wiley.

Harvey, J.H. and Kelley, D.R. (1973), 'Effects of attitude similarity and success-failure on attitudes towards other persons', J. Soc. Psych. (90) pp. 105-14.

Heider, F. (1958), The psychology of interpersonal relations, New York: Wiley.

Hendrick, C. and Brown, S.R. (1971), 'Introversion, extroversion and interpersonal attraction', J. Pers. Soc. Psych. (20) pp. 31-6.

Hess, E.H. (1965), 'Attitude and pupil size', Sci. Amer. (212) pp. 46-54.

Hoffman, L.R. (1958), 'Similarity of personality: A basis for interpersonal attraction?', Sociometry (21) pp. 300-8.

Hoffman, L.R. and Maier, N.R.F. (1966), 'An experimental re-examination of the similarity-attraction hypothesis', J. Pers. Soc. Psych. (3) pp. 145-52.

Hogan, R. and Mankin, D. (1970), 'Determinants of interpersonal attraction: A clarification', Psych. Rep. (26) pp. 235-8.

Hollander, E.P. and Julian, J. (1969), 'Contemporary trends in the analysis of leadership processes', Psych. Bull. (71) pp. 387-97.

Holmes, D.S. and Jackson, T.H. (1975), 'Influences of locus of control on interpersonal attraction and affective reactions in situations involving reward and punishment', J. Pers. Soc. Psych. (31) pp. 132-7.

Homans, G.C. (1961), Social behaviour: Its elementary forms, New York: Harcourt Brace.

Homans, G.C. (1971), 'Attraction and power' in Murstein, B.I. (ed.), Theories of attraction and love, New York: Springer.

Horney, K. (1939), New ways in psychoanalysis, New York: Norton.

Huesman, L.R. and Levinger, G. (1976), 'Incremental exchange theory: A formal model for progression in dyadic social interaction' in Berkowitz, L. and Walster, E.H. (eds), Advances in experimental social psychology, New York: Academic Press, vol. 9.

Huston, E.L. (1974), 'A perspective on interpersonal attraction' in Huston, E.L. (ed.), Foundations of interpersonal attraction, New York: Academic Press.

Insko, C.A., Thompson, V.D., Stroebe, W., Shaud, K.F., Pinner, B.E. and Layton, B.D. (1973), 'Implied evaluation and the similarity-attraction effect', J. Pers. Soc. Psych. (25) pp. 297-308.

Izard, C.E. (1960a), 'Personality similarity, positive affect and interpersonal attraction', J. Abn. Soc. Psych. (61) pp. 484-5.

Izard, C.E. (1960b), 'Personality similarity and friendship', J. Abn. Soc. Psych. (61) pp. 47-51.

Izard, C.E. (1963), 'Personality similarity and friendship: A follow-up study', J. Abn. Soc. Psych. (66) pp. 598-600.

Johnson, C.D., Gormly, J. and Gormly, A. (1973), 'Disagreement and self-esteem: Support for the competence reinforcement model of attraction', J. Res. in Pers. (7) pp. 165-72.

Johnson, M.J. and Tesser, A. (1972), 'Some interactive effects of evaluative similarity, structural similarity and type of interpersonal situation on interpersonal attraction', J. Exp. Res. in Pers. (6) pp. 154-61.

Johnston, S. and Centres, R. (1973), 'Cognitive systemization and interpersonal attraction', J. Soc. Psych. (90) pp. 95-104.

Jones, E.E. and Archer, R.L. (1976), 'Are there special effects of personalistic self disclosure?', J. Exp. Soc. Psych. (12) pp. 180-93.

Jones, E.E. and Davis, K.E. (1965), 'From acts to dispositions:

The attribution process in person perception' in Berkowitz, L. (ed.), *Advances in experimental social psychology*, New York: Academic Press, vol. 2.

Jones, E.E. and Gordon, E.M. (1972), 'Timing of self disclosure and its effects on personal attraction', *J. Pers. Soc. Psych.* (24) pp. 358-65.

Jones, E.E. and Nisbett, R.R. (1971), *The actor and the observer: Divergent perceptions of the causes of behaviour*, New York: General Learning Press.

Jones, E.E. and Sigall, H. (1971), 'The bogus pipeline: A new paradigm for measuring affect and attitude', *Psych. Bull.* (76) pp. 349-64.

Jones, E.E., Stires, L.K., Shaver, K.G. and Harris, V.A. (1968), 'Evaluation of an ingratiator by target persons and bystanders', *J. Pers.* (36) pp. 349-85.

Jones, E.E. and Wein, G.A. (1972), 'Attitude similarity, expectancy violation and attraction', *J. Exp. Soc. Psych.* (8) pp. 222-35.

Jones, S.C. and Panitch, D. (1971), 'The self-fulfilling prophecy and interpersonal attraction', *J. Exp. Soc. Psych.* (7) pp. 356-66.

Jones, S.C. and Regan, D.T. (1974), 'Ability evaluation through social comparison', *J. Exp. Soc. Psych.* (10) pp. 133-46.

Jourard, S.M. (1971), *Self disclosure*, New York: Wiley.

Kaplan, K.J., Firestone, I.J., Degnore, R. and Moore, M. (1974), 'Gradients of attraction as a function of disclosure probe intimacy and setting formality: On distinguishing attitude oscillation from attitude change - study one', *J. Pers. Soc. Psych.* (30) pp. 638-46.

Kaplan, M.F. (1973), 'Stimulus inconsistency and response dispositions in forming judgements of other persons', *J. Pers. Soc. Psych.* (25) pp. 58-64.

Kaplan, M.F. and Anderson, N.H. (1973), 'Information integration theory and reinforcement theory as approaches to interpersonal attraction', J. Pers. Soc. Psych. (28) pp. 301-12.

Katz, D. (1960), 'The functional approach to the study of attitudes', Pub. Opin. Q. (24) pp. 163-204.

Kelley, H.H. (1950), 'The warm-cold variable in first impression of persons', J. Pers. (18) pp. 431-9.

Kelley, H.H. (1967), 'Attribution theory in social psychology' in Levine, D. (ed.), Nebraska symposium on motivation, Lincoln, Neb.: Univ. of Nebraska Press.

Kelly, G.A. (1955), The psychology of personal constructs, New York: Norton.

Kelvin, R.P. (1970), The bases of social behaviour, London: Holt, Rinehart and Winston.

Kelvin, R.P. (1977), 'Predictability, power and vulnerability in interpersonal attraction' in Duck, S.W. (ed.), Theory and practice in interpersonal attraction, London: Academic Press.

Kerckhoff, A.C. (1964), 'Patterns of homogamy and the field of eligibles', Soc. Forces (42) pp. 289-97.

Kerckhoff, A.C. (1974), 'The social context of interpersonal attraction' in Huston, E.L. (ed.), Foundations of interpersonal attraction, New York: Academic Press.

Kerckhoff, A.C. and Davis, K.E. (1962), 'Value consensus and need complementarity in mate selection', Amer. Sociol. Rev. (27) pp. 295-303.

Kian, M., Rosen, S. and Tesser, A. (1973), 'Reinforcement effects of attitude similarity and source evaluation on discrimination learning', J. Pers. Soc. Psych. (27) pp. 366-71.

Kleck, R., Ono, H. and Hastorf, A.H. (1966), 'The effects of physical deviance upon face-to-face interaction', Hum. Relat. (19) pp. 425-36.

Kleck, R. and Rubinstein, C. (1975), 'Physical attractiveness, perceived attitude similarity and interpersonal attraction in the opposite sex encounter', J. Pers. Soc. Psych. (31) pp. 107-15.

Kleinke, C.L., Meeker, F.B. and Fong, C.L. (1974), 'Effects of gaze, touch and use of name on evaluation of "engaged" couples', J. Res. in Pers. (7) pp. 368-73.

Kleinke, C.L., Staneski, R.A. and Berger, D.E. (1975), 'Evaluation of an interviewer as a function of interviewer gaze, reinforcement of subject gaze and interviewer attractiveness', J. Pers. Soc. Psych. (31) pp. 115-22.

Kleinke, C.L., Staneski, R.A. and Pipp, S.L. (1975), 'Effects of gaze, distance and attractiveness on males' first impressions of females', Rep. Res. in Soc. Psych. (6) pp. 7-12.

Knecht, L., Lipman, D. and Swap, W. (1973), 'Similarity, attraction and self disclosure', Proc. 81st Ann. Conv. A.P.A. Montreal, Canada (8) pp. 205-6.

Koenig, F. (1971), 'Positive affective stimulus value and accuracy of role perception' Brit. J. Soc. Clin. Psych. (10) pp. 385-6.

Kohlberg, L. (1971), 'From is to ought: How to commit the naturalistic fallacy and get away with it in the study of moral development' in Mischel, T. (ed.), Cognitive development and epistemology, New York: Academic Press.

Krebs, D. and Adinolfi, A.A. (1975), 'Physical attractiveness, social relations and personality style', J. Pers. Soc. Psych. (31) pp. 245-53.

Kuhn, T.S. (1970), The structure of scientific revolutions, (2nd ed.), Chicago: University of Chicago Press.

La Gaipa, J.J. (1977a), 'Interpersonal attraction and social exchange' in Duck, S.W. (ed.), Theory and practice in interpersonal attraction, London: Academic Press.

La Gaipa, J.J. (1977b), 'Testing a multidimensional approach to friendship' in Duck, S.W. (ed.), Theory and practice in interpersonal attraction, London: Academic Press.

La Gaipa, J.J. and Bigelow, B. (1972), 'The development of friendship expectations', Paper read at the meeting of the Canadian Psychological Association, Montreal.

Latta, R.M. (1976), 'There's method in our madness: Interpersonal attraction as a multi-dimensional construct', J. Res. in Pers. (10) pp. 76-82.

Layton, B.D. and Insko, C.A. (1974), 'Anticipated interaction and the similarity attraction effect', Sociometry (37) pp. 149-62.

Lemmert, E.M. (1962), 'Paranoia and the dynamics of exclusion', Sociometry (25) pp. 2-20.

Leonard, R.L. (1976), 'Cognitive complexity and the similarity attraction paradigm', J. Res. in Pers. (10) pp. 83-8.

Lerner, M.J., Dillehay, R.C. and Sherer, W.C. (1967), 'Similarity and attraction in social contexts', J. Pers. Soc. Psych. (5) pp. 481-6.

Levinger, G. (1964), 'Note on need complementarity in marriage', Psych. Bull. (51) pp. 153-7.

Levinger, G. (1972), 'Little sand box and big quarry: Comments on Byrne's paradigmatic spade for research on interpersonal attraction', Rep. Res. in Soc. Psych. (3) pp. 3-19.

Levinger, G. (1974), 'A three level approach to attraction: Towards an understanding of pair relatedness' in Huston, E.L. (ed.), Foundations of interpersonal attraction, New York: Academic Press.

Levinger, G., Senn, D.J. and Jorgensen, B.W. (1970), 'Progress towards permanence in courtship: A test of the Kerckhoff-Davis hypothesis', Sociometry (33) pp. 427-43.

Levinger, G. and Snoek, J.D. (1972), Attraction in relationship: A new look at interpersonal attraction, Morristown, NJ: General Learning Press.

Lewis, R.A. (1972), 'A developmental framework for the analysis of premarital dyadic formation', Family Process (11) pp. 17-48.

Lewis, R.A. (1973), 'A longitudinal test of a developmental framework for premarital dyadic formation', J. Marr. Fam. (35) pp. 16-25.

Libby, W.L. and Yaklevich, D. (1973), 'Personality determinants of eye contact and direction of gaze aversion', J. Pers. Soc. Psych. (27) pp. 197-206.

Libet, J.M. and Lewinsohn, P.M. (1973), 'Concept of social skill with special reference to the behaviour of depressed persons', J. Consult. Clin. Psych. (40) pp. 304-12.

Lickona, T. (1974), 'A cognitive-developmental approach to interpersonal attraction' in Huston, E.L. (ed.), Foundations of interpersonal attraction, New York: Academic Press.

Likert, R. (1932), 'A technique for the measurement of attitudes', Arch. Psych. (140) pp. 44-53.

Lindzey, G. and Byrne, D. (1968), 'Measurement of social choice and interpersonal attractiveness', in Lindzey, G. and Aronson, E. (eds), Handbook of social psychology, Reading, Mass.: Addison-Wesley.

Loevinger, J. and Wessler, R. (1970), Measuring ego development 1: Construction and use of a sentence completion test, San Francisco: Jossey-Bass.

Lombardo, J.P., Weiss, R.F. and Buchanan, W. (1972), 'Reinforcing and attracting functions of yielding', J. Pers. Soc. Psych. (21) pp. 359-68.

Lott, A.J. and Lott, B.E. (1974), 'Reward in the formation of positive interpersonal attitudes' in Huston, E.L. (ed.), Foundations of interpersonal attraction, New York: Academic Press.

Lott, B.E. and Lott, A.J. (1960), 'The formation of positive attitudes towards group members', J. Abn. Soc. Psych. (61) pp. 297-300.

McCarthy, B. (1976), 'Agreement and friendship: affective and cognitive responses to attitudinal similarity-dissimilarity among same-sex friends', Unpub. PhD thesis, University of Lancaster, England.

McCarthy, B. and Duck, S.W. (1976), 'Friendship duration and responses to attitudinal agreement-disagreement', Brit. J. Soc. Clin. Psych. (15) pp. 377-86.

McCarthy, B. and Duck, S.W. (in prep.), 'When "I disagree" means "I will like you": attributions of causality in acquaintance', Unpub. manuscript.

McLaughlin, B. (1971), 'Effects of similarity and likeableness on attraction and recall', J. Pers. Soc. Psych. (20) pp. 65-9.

McPherson, F.M., Buckley, F. and Draffan, J. (1971), ' "Psychological" constructs, thought-process disorder and flattening of affect', Brit. J. Soc. Clin. Psych. (10) pp. 267-70.

McWhirter, F. and Jecker, J. (1967), 'Attitude similarity and inferred attraction', Psychon. Sci. (7) pp. 225-6.

Marlowe, D. and Gergen, K. (1969), 'Personality and social interaction' in Lindzey, G. and Aronson, E. (eds.), The handbook of social psychology, Reading, Mass.: Addison-Wesley, vol. 3.

Mascaro, G.F. and Graves, W. (1973), 'Contrast effects of background factors in the similarity-attraction relationship', J. Pers. Soc. Psych. (25) pp. 346-50.

Maslow, A. (1953), 'Love in healthy people' in Montagu, A. (ed.), The meaning of love, New York: The Julian Press.

Mehrabian, A. (1968), 'The effect of context on judgements of speaker attitudes', J. Pers. (36) pp. 21-32.

Mehrabian, A. (1970), 'When are feelings communicated inconsistently?', J. Exp. Res. in Pers. (4) pp. 198-212.

Mehrabian, A. and Ksionzky, S. (1974), A theory of affiliation, Lexington, Mass.: Lexington Books.

Mehrabian, A. and Williams, M. (1969), 'Nonverbal concomitants of perceived and intended persuasiveness', J. Pers. Soc.

Psych. (13) pp. 37-58.

Mettee, D.R., Taylor, S.E. and Friedman, H. (1973), 'Affect conversion and the gain-loss liking effect', Sociometry (36) pp. 494-513.

Miller, C.E. and Norman, R.M.G. (1976), 'Balance, agreement and attraction in hypothetical social situations', J. Exp. Soc. Psych. (12) pp. 109-19.

Miller, G. (ed.) (1976), Explorations in interpersonal communication, New York: Sage.

Miller, N., Campbell, D.T., Twedt, H. and O'Connell, E.J. (1966), 'Similarity, contrast and complementarity in friendship choice', J. Pers. Soc. Psych. (3) pp. 3-12.

Mitchell, H.E. and Byrne, D. (1973), 'The defendant's dilemma: Effects of jurors' attitudes and authoritarianism on judicial decisions', J. Pers. Soc. Psych. (25) pp. 123-29.

Moreno, J.L. (1934), Who shall survive?, Washington: Nervous and Mental Disease Publishing Co.

Morton, T.L., Alexander, J.F. and Altman, I. (1976), 'Communication and relationship definition' in Miller, G.R. (ed.), Explorations in interpersonal communication, New York: Sage.

Murstein, B.I. (1971a), 'A theory of marital choice and its applicability to marriage adjustment' in Murstein, B.I. (ed.), Theories of attraction and love, New York: Springer.

Murstein, B.I. (1971b), 'Critique of models of dyadic attraction' in Murstein, B.I. (ed.), Theories of attraction and love, New York: Springer.

Murstein, B.I. (1973), 'Perceived congruence among premarital couples as a function of neuroticism', J. Abn. Psych. (82) pp. 22-6.

Murstein, B.I. (1976), Who will marry whom? Theories and research in marital choice, New York: Springer.

Murstein, B.I. (1977), 'The Stimulus-Value-Role (SVR) theory of dyadic relationships' in Duck, S.W. (ed.), Theory and practice in interpersonal attraction, London: Academic Press.

Newcomb, T.M. (1961), The acquaintance process, New York: Holt, Rinehart and Winston.

Newcomb, T.M. (1971), 'Dyadic balance as a source of clues about interpersonal attraction' in Murstein, B.I. (ed.), Theories of attraction and love, New York, Springer.

Norman, R. (1976), 'When what is said is important: A comparison of expert and attractive sources', J. Exp. Soc. Psych. (12) pp. 294-300.

Novak, D.W. and Lerner, M.J. (1968), 'Rejection as a consequence of perceived similarity', J. Pers. Soc. Psych. (9) pp. 147-52.

Nowicki, S., Jr and Blumberg, N. (1975), 'The role of locus of control of reinforcement in interpersonal attraction', J. Res. in Pers. (9) pp. 48-56.

Nowicki, S., Nelson, D.A. and Ettinger, R.F. (1974), 'The role of need for social approval in initial attraction', J. Soc. Psych. (94) pp. 149-51.

Palmer, J. and Altrocchi, J. (1967), 'Attribution of hostile intent as unconscious', J. Pers. (35) pp. 164-76.

Palmer, J. and Byrne, D. (1970), 'Attraction toward dominant and submissive strangers: Similarity versus complementarity', J. Exp. Res. in Pers. (4) pp. 108-15.

Perrin, F.A.C. (1921), 'Physical attractiveness and repulsiveness', J. Exp. Psych. (4) pp. 203-17.

Posavac, E.J. and McKillip, J. (1973), 'Effects of similarity and endorsement frequency on attraction and expected agreement', J. Exp. Res. in Pers. (6) pp. 357-62.

Posavac, E.J. and Pasko, S.J. (1974), 'Attraction, personality similarity and popularity of the personality of a stimulus person', J. Soc. Psych. (92) pp. 269-76.

Potashin, R. (1946), 'Sociometric study of children's friendship', Sociometry (9) pp. 48-70.

Procter, C.H. and Loomis, C.P. (1951), 'Analysis of sociometric data' in Jahoda, M., Deutsch, M. and Cook, S.W. (eds), Research methods in social relations, New York: Dryden.

Regan, D.T., Straus, E. and Fazio, R. (1974), 'Liking and the attribution process', J. Exp. Soc. Psych. (10) pp. 385-97.

Reilly, M.St.A., Commins, W.D. and Stefic, E.C. (1960), 'The complementarity of personality needs in friendship choice', J. Abn. Soc. Psych. (61) pp. 292-4.

Richardson, H.M. (1939), 'Studies of mental resemblance between husbands and wives and between friends', Psych. Bull. (36) pp. 104-20.

Ring, K. (1964), 'Some determinants of interpersonal attraction in hierarchical relationships: A motivational analysis', J. Pers. (32) pp. 651-65.

Robbins, G.E. (1975), 'Dogmatism and information gathering in personality impression formation', J. Res. in Pers. (9) pp. 74-84.

Rogers, C.R. (1951), Client-centred therapy, Boston: Houghton Miflin.

Roloff, M.E. (1976), 'Communication strategies, relationships and relational changes' in Miller, G.R. (ed.), Explorations in interpersonal communication, New York: Sage.

Rosenberg, M.J. (1965), 'When dissonance fails: On eliminating evaluation apprehension from attitude measurement', J. Pers. Soc. Psych. (1) pp. 28-42.

Rubin, Z. (1970), 'Measurement of romantic love', J. Pers. Soc. Psych. (16) pp. 265-73.

Rubin, Z. (1974), 'From liking to loving: Patterns of attraction in dating relationships' in Huston, E.L. (ed.), Foundations of interpersonal attraction, New York: Academic Press.

Rychlak, P. (1965), 'The similarity, compatibility or incompatibility of needs in interpersonal selection, J. Pers. Soc. Psych. (2) pp. 334-40.

Sachs, D.H. (1975), 'Belief similarity and attitude similarity as determinants of interpersonal attraction', J. Res. in Pers. (9) pp. 57-65.

Saegert, S., Swap, W. and Zajonc, R.B. (1973), 'Exposure, context and interpersonal attraction', J. Pers. Soc. Psych. (25) pp. 234-42.

Santee, R.T. (1976), 'The effect on attraction of attitude similarity as information about interpersonal reinforcement contingencies', Sociometry (39) pp. 153-6.

Schachter, S. (1959), The psychology of affiliation, Stanford, Calif.: Stanford University Press.

Schachter, S. (1964), 'The interaction of cognitive and physiological determinants of emotional state' in Berkowitz, L. (ed.), Advances in experimental social psychology, New York: Academic Press.

Schachter, S. and Singer, J.F. (1962), 'Cognitive, social and physiological determinants of emotional state', Psych. Rev. (69) pp. 379-99.

Scherwitz, L. and Helmreich, R. (1973), 'Interactive effects of eye contact and verbal content on interpersonal attraction in dyads', J. Pers. Soc. Psych. (25) pp. 6-14.

Schiffenbauer, A. and Schiavo, R.S. (1976), 'Physical distance and attraction: An intensification effect', J. Exp. Soc. Psych. (12) pp. 274-82.

Schwartz, S.H. and Tessler, R.C. (1972), 'A test of a model for reducing measured attitude-behaviour discrepancies', J. Pers. Soc. Psych. (24) pp. 225-36.

Scott, W.C. (1973), 'Linear relationship between interpersonal attraction and similarity: An analysis of the "unique stranger" technique', J. Soc. Psych. (91) pp. 117-26.

Seagoe, M.V. (1933), 'Factors influencing selection of associates', J. Educ. Res. (27) pp. 32-40.

Secord, P.F. and Backman, C. (1961), 'Personality theory and the problem of stability and change in individual behaviour: An interpersonal approach', Psych. Rev. (63) pp. 21-32.

Senn, D. (1971), 'Attraction as a function of similarity-dissimilarity in task performance', J. Pers. Soc. Psych. (18) pp. 120-3.

Seyfried, B.A. (1977), 'Complementarity in interpersonal attraction' in Duck, S.W. (ed.), Theory and practice in interpersonal attraction, London: Academic Press.

Seyfried, B.A. and Hendrick, C. (1973), 'Need similarity and complementarity in interpersonal attraction', Sociometry (36) pp. 207-20.

Shotland, R.L. and Straw, M.K. (1976), 'Bystander response to an assault: When a man attacks a woman', J. Pers. Soc. Psych. (34) pp. 990-9.

Simons, H., Berkowitz, N. and Moyer, R. (1970), 'Similarity, credibility and attitude change: A review and a theory', Psych. Bull. (73) pp. 1-16.

Smith, A.J. (1957), 'Similarity of values and its relation to acceptance and the projection of similarity', J. Psych. (43) pp. 251-60.

Smith, J., Chapman, A. and Foot, H. (1976), 'Friendship and sex as variables in children's social interaction', Paper presented to the annual conference of the BPS Social Section at University of York, September 1976.

Snoek, J.D. (1962), 'Some effects of rejection upon attraction to a group', J. Abn. Soc. Psych. (64) pp. 175-82.

Stalling, R.S. (1970), 'Personality similarity and evaluative meaning as conditioners of attraction', J. Pers. Soc. Psych. (14) pp. 77-82.

Stang, D.J. (1973), 'Effect of interaction rate on ratings of leadership and liking', J. Pers. Soc. Psych. (27) pp. 405-8.

Stapleton, R.E., Nacci, P. and Tedeschi, J.T. (1973), 'Interpersonal attraction and the reciprocation of benefits', J. Pers. Soc. Psych. (28) pp. 199-205.

Stephan, C. (1973), 'Attribution of intention and perception of attitude as a function of liking and similarity', Sociometry (36) pp. 463-75.

Strauss, A. (1946), 'The influence of parent-images upon marital choice', Amer. Sociol. Rev. (11) pp. 554-9.

Stroebe, W. (1977), 'Self esteem and interpersonal attraction' in Duck, S.W. (ed.), Theory and practice in interpersonal attraction, London: Academic Press.

Stroebe, W., Eagly, A.H. and Stroebe, M.S. (1977), 'Friendly or just polite? The effects of self esteem on attributions', Eur. J. Soc. Psych. (7).

Stroebe, W., Insko, C.A., Thompson, V.D. and Layton, B.D. (1971), 'The effects of physical attractiveness, attitude similarity and sex on various aspects of interpersonal attraction', J. Pers. Soc. Psych. (18) pp. 79-91.

Sutherland, A.E. and Insko, C.A. (1973), 'Attraction and interestingness of anticipated interaction', J. Pers. (41) pp. 234-44.

Tagiuri, R. and Kogan, N. (1960), 'Personal preference and the attribution of influence in small groups', J. Pers. (28) pp. 257-65.

Taylor, H.F. (1970), Balance in small groups, New York: Von Nostrand, Rheinhold.

Taylor, S.E. and Mettee, D. (1971), 'When similarity breeds contempt', J. Pers. Soc. Psych. (20) pp. 75-81.

Tedeschi, J.T. (1974), 'Attribution, liking and power' in Huston, E.L. (ed.), Foundations of interpersonal attraction, New York: Academic Press.

Tesch, F.E., Huston, E.L. and Indenbaum, E.A. (1973), 'Attitude similarity, attraction and physical proximity in a dynamic space', J. Appl. Soc. Psych. (3) pp. 63-72.

Tesser, A. (1971), 'Evaluative and structural similarity of attitudes as determinants of interpersonal attraction', J. Pers. Soc. Psych. (18) pp. 92-6.

Tesser, A. (1972), 'Attitude similarity adnd intercorrelation as determinants of interpersonal attraction', J. Exp. Res. in Pers. (6) pp. 142-53.

Tharp, R.G. (1963), 'Psychological patterning in marriage', Psych. Bull. (60) pp. 97-117.

Thibaut, J.W. and Kelley, H.H. (1959), The social psychology of groups, New York: Wiley.

Thomas, W.F. and Young, P.T. (1938), 'Liking and disliking persons', J. Soc. Psych. (9) pp. 169-87.

Tiger, L. and Fox, R. (1972), The imperial animal, London: Secker and Warburg.

Tognoli, J. and Keisner, R. (1972), 'Gain and loss of esteem as determinants of interpersonal attraction', J. Pers. Soc. Psych. (23) pp. 201-4.

Touhey, J.C. (1974), 'Situated identity, attitude similarity and interpersonal attraction', Sociometry (37) pp. 363-74.

Touhey, J.C. (1975), 'Interpersonal congruency, attitude similarity and interpersonal attraction', J. Res. in Pers. (9) pp. 66-74.

Wagner, R.V. (1975), 'Complementary needs, role expectations, interpersonal attraction and the stability of working relationships', J. Pers. Soc. Psych. (32) pp. 116-24.

Walster, E.H. (1970), 'The effects of self esteem on liking for dates of various social desirabilities', J. Exp. Soc. Psych. (6) pp. 248-53.

Walster, E.H. and Berscheid, E. (1971), 'Adrenaline makes the heart grow fonder', Psych. Today (5) pp. 46-72.

Walster, E.H., Walster, G.W., Piliavin, J. and Schmidt, L. (1973), ' "Playing hard to get": Understanding an elusive phenomenon', J. Pers. Soc. Psych. (26) pp. 113-21.

Warr, P.B. (1965), 'Proximity as a determinant of positive and negative sociometric choice', Brit. J. Soc. Clin. Psych. (4) pp. 104-9.

Werner, C. and Latané, B. (1974), 'Interaction motivates attraction: Rats are fond of fondling', J. Pers. Soc. Psych. (29) pp. 328-34.

Wheaton, B. (1974), 'Interpersonal conflict and cohesiveness in dyadic relationships', Sociometry (37) pp. 328-48.

Wheeler, L. (1974), 'Social comparison and selective affiliation' in Huston, E.L. (ed.), Foundations of interpersonal attraction, New York: Academic Press.

Willerman, B. and Swanson, L. (1952), 'An ecological determinant of differential amounts of sociometric choices within college sororities', Sociometry (15) pp. 326-9.

Winch, R.F. (1955a), 'The theory of complementary needs in mate selection: A test of one kind of complementariness', Amer. Sociol. Rev. (20) pp. 52-6.

Winch, R.F. (1955b), 'The theory of complementary needs in mate selection: Final results on the test of the general hypothesis', Amer. Sociol. Rev. (20) pp. 552-5.

Winch, R.F. (1958), Mate selection: A study in complementary needs, New York: Harper and Row.

Winch, R.F., Ktsanes, T. and Ktsanes, V. (1954), 'The theory of complementary needs in mate selection: An analytic and descriptive study', Amer. Sociol. Rev. (19) pp. 241-9.

Winch, R.F., Ktsanes, T. and Ktsanes, V. (1955), 'Empirical elaborations of the theory of complementary needs in mate selection', J. Abn. Soc. Psych. (51) pp. 509-13.

Winslow, C.N. (1937), 'A study of the extent of agreement between friends' opinions and their ability to estimate the opinions of each other', J. Soc. Psych. (8) pp. 433-42.

Worthy, M., Gary, A.L. and Kahn, G.M. (1969), 'Self disclosure as an exchange process', J. Pers. Soc. Psych. (13) pp. 59-63.

Wright, P.H. (1965), 'Personality and interpersonal attraction: Basic assumptions', J. Indiv. Psych. (27) pp. 127-36.

Wright, P.H. (1968), 'Need similarity, need complementarity and the place of personality in interpersonal attraction, J. Exp. Res. in Pers. (3) pp. 126-35.

Wright, P.H. and Crawford, A.C. (1971), 'Agreement and friendship: A close look and some second thoughts', Rep. Res. in Soc. Psych. (2) pp. 52-69.

Wynne-Edwards, V.C. (1962), Animal dispersion in relation to social behaviour, Edinburgh and London: Oliver and Boyd.

Zaidel, S.F. and Mehrabian, A. (1969), 'The ability to communicate and infer positive and negative attitudes facially and vocally', J. Exp. Res. in Pers. (3) pp. 233-41.

# NAME AND FIRST AUTHOR INDEX

Adams, J.S. 51
Adler, A. 81
Ajzen, I. 58-9, 157, 158, 166ff
Allgeier, A.R. 24
Altman, I. 31, 66ff, 167, 170-1
Anderson, A.B. 108
Anderson, N.H. 58, 160
Anthony, S. 91
Argyle, M. 11, 30, 106, 120, 121, 122, 124, 125, 126, 133
Aronson, E. 29, 40, 113-14, 131, 157
Austin, M.C. 191

Backman, C. 55, 56, 85, 174
Banikiotes, P.G. 154, 155
Batchelor, T.R. 138-9
Baugher, D.M. 117
Beier, E.G. 175
Berger, C. 68, 71, 150
Berscheid, E. 21, 33, 88, 95, 103, 185, 186
Blau, P.M. 51
Bleda, P.R. 154, 155, 158
Blumberg, H.H. 54
Bogardus, E.S. 34
Bowlby, J. 189
Brickman, P. 88, 130
Bugenthal, D.E. 125
Byrne, D. 17, 21, 23, 24, 28, 30, 32, 34, 35, 41, 48, 49, 78, 95, 97, 112, 114, 123, 124, 141-8, 150-63, 165, 171, 172, 182, 183, 191

Campbell, J.D. 190
Cavior, N. 100
Chapman, R.N. 4
Cherry, F. 35
Clore, G.L. 30, 48, 49, 114, 118, 145, 151, 161

Cook, M. 11, 30, 121, 154
Cooper, J. 101, 141
Cozby, P.C. 115, 167
Craig, R.G. 84, 138
Crockett, W.H. 5
Curran, J.P. 100
Curry, T.J. 54

Daher, D.M. 169
Davis, J.D. 116, 168
Day, B.R. 172, 177, 179
DeCharms, R. 112
Derlega, V.J. 167, 168
Dion, K.K. 8, 99, 154
Dittes, J.E. 80
Duck, S.W. 19, 39, 57, 70-2, 85, 100, 139, 150, 152, 154, 161, 162, 163, 166, 172, 177, 181, 182, 183, 184, 188, 193, 194, 196, 198
Dutton, D.G. 60

Efran, M.G. 123
Ehrlich, H.J. 81, 170
Eiser, J.R. 61

Festinger, L. 56ff, 94, 95
Fiedler, F.E. 84
Foa, U.G. 52
Frankel, A. 169
Freedman, N. 131
Freud, S. 47
Fromm, E. 81

Gaebler, H.C. 186, 188, 193
Gaes, G.G. 35
Geen, R.G. 50
Geller, D.M. 127
Goethals, G.R. 138
Goffman, E. 92, 101
Goldman, J.A. 84
Goldstein, J.W. 78, 176

Golightly, C. 146
Gormly, J. 128
Griffitt, W. 4, 50, 142, 148, 150, 156, 174, 175-6
Gullahorn, J.T. 93
Guthrie, E.R. 79

Hall, E.T. 76
Hardy, K.R. 77
Harlow, H.F. 46
Harré, R. 15, 17, 92, 96, 97, 121
Harvey, J.H. 108
Heider, F. 2, 53, 60
Hendrick, C. 89, 173, 174, 182
Hess, E.H. 30
Hoffman, L.R. 164, 172, 177
Hogan, R. 165
Hollander, E.P. 111
Holmes, D.S. 82
Homans, G.C. 51, 111
Horney, K. 81
Huesman, L.R. 52
Huston, E.L. 32, 65

Insko, C.A. 115, 157
Izard, C.E. 172, 176

Johnson, C.D. 117
Johnson, M.J. 140
Johnston, S. 84
Jones, E.E. 34, 61, 62, 114, 116, 117, 132, 141, 169
Jones, S.C. 57, 106
Jourard, S.M. 117, 166-7

Kaplan, K.J. 116
Kaplan, M.F. 83, 152, 160
Katz, D. 138
Kelley, H.H. 61, 97
Kelly, G.A. 70
Kelvin, R.P. 21, 110, 121, 167
Kerckhoff, A.C. 6, 64, 69, 87, 94, 180
Kian, M. 146
Kleck, R. 100, 101
Kleinke, C.L. 40, 119, 121
Knecht, L. 169
Koenig, F. 86
Kohlberg, L. 189
Krebs, D. 100
Kuhn, T.S. 158

La Gaipa, J.J. 30, 51, 52, 109, 191-2, 193, 195-6
Latané, B. 4
Latta, R.M. 23, 123
Layton, B.D. 95
Lemmert, E.M. 5, 101
Leonard, R.L. 84
Lerner, M.J. 95
Levinger, G. 27, 65, 66, 69, 96, 147, 174, 180, 193
Levy, P. 171
Lewis, R.A. 69-70
Libby, W.L. 127
Libet, J.M. 134
Lickona, T. 189
Likert, R. 33
Lindzey, G. 26, 32, 33
Loevinger, J. 190
Lombardo, J.P. 146
Lott, A.J. 183
Lott, B.E. 50

McCarthy, B. 20, 27, 63, 72, 139, 148, 152, 159
McLaughlin, B. 141
McPherson, F.M. 133
McWhirter, F. 156
Marlowe, D. 72, 179
Mascaro, G.F. 155
Maslow, A. 81
Mehrabian, A. 78, 86, 91, 123, 129
Mettee, D.R. 114
Miller, C.E. 54

Miller, G. 65
Miller, N. 97
Mitchell, H.E. 146
Moreno, J.L. 35
Morton, T.L. 27, 66, 67
Murstein, B.I. 70, 94, 115, 158, 169, 172, 175, 185ff, 196

Newcomb, T.M. 19, 55, 141, 150, 155
Norman, R. 130
Novak, D.W. 158
Nowicki, S. 78, 89

Palmer, J. 130, 164, 173, 179, 180
Pavlov, I. 48-9
Perrin, F.A.C. 90, 98ff
Posavac, E.J. 89, 141
Potashin, R. 190
Procter, C.H. 26

Regan, D.T. 60, 109
Reilly, M.St A. 179
Richardson, H.M. 141
Ring, K. 111
Robbins, G.E. 83
Rogers, C.R. 81
Roloff, M.E. 65
Rosenberg, M.J. 32
Rubin, Z. 167, 186-7
Rychlak, P. 172, 179

Sachs, D.H. 137
Saegert, S. 93
Santee, R.T. 47, 140
Schachter, S. 1, 4, 78, 185-6
Scherwitz, L. 124
Schiffenbauer, A. 123
Schwartz, S.H. 22, 24
Scott, W.C. 131
Seagoe, M.V. 95, 191
Secord, P.F. 55

Senn, D. 107, 152
Seyfried, B.A. 174, 175, 179, 180
Shotland, R.L. 92
Simons, H. 23
Smith, A.J. 142
Smith, J. 191
Snoek, J.D. 80
Stalling, R.S. 141
Stang, D.J. 120
Stapleton, R.E. 109
Stephan, C. 129
Strauss, A. 188
Stroebe, W. 17, 79, 80, 81
Sutherland, A.E. 95

Tagiuri, R. 129
Taylor, H.F. 152
Taylor, S.E. 155
Tedeschi, J.T. 110, 167
Tesch, F.E. 123
Tesser, A. 140-1
Tharp, R.G. 174, 178
Thibaut, J.W. 51
Thomas, W.F. 90
Tiger, L. 45
Tognoli, J. 114
Touhey, J.C. 56, 131

Wagner, R.V. 179
Walster, E.H. 40, 80, 132, 186
Warr, P.B. 94
Werner, C. 4
Wheaton, B. 108
Wheeler, L. 57
Willerman, B. 94
Winch, R.F. 87, 164, 177-80
Winslow, C.N. 141
Worthy, M. 167
Wright, P.H. 19, 147, 175, 183
Wynne-Edwards, V.C. 45

Zaidel, S.F. 86
Zajonc, R. 93-4

## SUBJECT INDEX

Acquaintance 6, 20, 150: as a 'gut' response 9, 136-63; defined 14-15; development of see Relationships; inadequate conceptualisation of 24

Adolescents see Children's friendships

Affect 117ff, 160f, 162ff: Conversion of 114

Affiliation 4, 16, 44, 45-6

Alcoholism 67, 78, 148: and friendship 195ff

Animals' relationships 4, 45-6

Anxiety 78, see also Affiliation

Artificiality 39-42, 146-7, 152-6

Association (in classical conditioning) 49-50: Forced 95

Attitudes 20ff, 136ff: and attraction 24ff, 33, 95, 100, 136-63; Components of 21ff; Structure of 140; Testing of 56, see also Consensual validation; Types of 47, 137ff; see also Attraction as an attitude

Attraction 16, 19, 33ff, 49, 110ff: as an attitude 20ff, 24ff, 33-5; Paradigm 142ff; see also Interpersonal attraction

Attractiveness: and personality 82, 126ff; Assessments of 109, 110, 126ff, 155; Physical 8-9, 18, 80-1, 98ff, 119-20

Attribution 59ff, 103-4, 129-31, 169, 197: Proactive and retroactive 68ff, 71

Balance Theory 53ff

Behaviour 123ff: in acquaintance 22ff, 107ff, 123, 180; sequences 112-21

Beliefs 58-9, 137, 161ff

Blondes see Gentlemen

Bogus Pipeline 34-5

Bogus Stranger 136-63, 143ff, 147

Children's friendships 63, 99-100, 125, 189ff: as influence on adult choices 188

Choice: Causes of 23, 87, 175, 177, 179; Measurement 32ff; Mutual 35, 175ff, 177, 179, 190; Responsibility for 10-11; Selective 4, 44, 47-63, 175

Classical conditioning 48ff, 145

Cognition 70, 83, 88, 136-84, 192: development of see Children's friendships; see also Liking and cognition

Cognitive complexity 84

Common sense 1, 12, 113: notions about acquaintance 2ff; conflict in 12

Communication and acquaintance 66, 68

Comparison Level 51

Comparison Level for Alternatives 51

Competition 95, 107ff

Complementarity see Personality

Conflict 108

Congruency 55ff, 85

Consensual validation 57, 70, 145ff

Co-operation 107ff
Cost 51, see also Profit, Reward
Courtship 16, 178, 187ff
Culture 87ff: and relationship style 76; Cultural agreement on attractiveness 8, 87, 89-93, 107

Dating 16, 17-18, 100, 172
Decoding 86, 106, 133, 196
Dentists 2
Development of acquaintance see Relationships
Disagreement 117, 127-8
Disliking 90, 92, 94, 106, 109, 116, 123, 125, 146, 150, 196
Dissimilarity 139, 146, 159, see also Disagreement
Distance and Liking 30, 119-20, 123, see also Nonverbal indicators
Dogmatism 82

Edwards Personal Preference Schedule 177ff
Effectance 145ff, 159
Encoding 86, 106, 133, 196
Entry phase 68
EPPS see Edwards Personal Preference Schedule
Equity Theory 51
Evaluation: by others 113; Implied 114-15, 157; of Self 56-7, 79
Exit phase 68
Experimenting on acquaintance 38ff
Eye contact 30, 120, 124, 127, see also Nonverbal indicators

'Failure' in relationships 194ff
Feindschaft 15

Fictitious Stranger see Bogus Stranger
Field: Closed 94; of availables 88; of desirables 88, 89; of eligibles 87ff; Open 94
Filter theory 69ff, 71, 99
First encounters 19, 33ff, 88, 100, 159, see also Attraction
Friendliness-Hostility 124-6
Friends as influences on choice 41
Friendship 16, 191ff: Children's see Children's friendship; expectations 191ff; function of 1, 4, 10; Psychological significance of 2, 4; Study of 18ff, 179

Gain-Loss of Esteem 113ff, 118-19
Gaze 30, 119-20, 121, see also Nonverbal indicators
Gentlemen, preference of 8

Homeostasis 45
Hypothetical Stranger see Bogus Stranger

IJS see Interpersonal Judgement Scale
Immediacy 91, 92
Inconsistency 86, 124-6
Incremental Exchange Theory 52
Information 162ff: integration 58ff, 158, 160ff; Mechanistic/constructive models of 58-9, 158; Transmitting and receiving 75, 105
Ingratiation 101, 115ff, 137, 169
Interpersonal Attraction 16:

Antecedents 21; consequences of 24; indicators of 24-5, 30; Multidimensional nature of 24-5; Types of 15; defined 16

Interpersonal Judgement Scale (IJS) 34, 123, 142

Intimacy 172: Communication of 66ff; Growth of 65ff, 168; Measurement of 66; Negotiation of 116, 168

Laboratory study of acquaintance 17, 148ff

Liking 16, 85, 90, 109, 112, 123, 125, 131, 133, 150, 167, 186: and cognition 52ff, 88; and information 58ff; and reward 48ff; constraints on expressing 22; measurement of 25ff, 31ff, 186: behavioural measures 25, 29ff, 34-5, operational measures 27, paper and pencil measures 23, 25-9, 31-2, 34-5, physiological measures 30ff, see also Interpersonal Judgement Scale; Perception of 85, 133

Love 167, 185ff: anaclitic and dependent 47; at first sight 10, 83; narcissistic 47

Marital selection 16, 178
Matching 80
Mere exposure 93ff

Needs 69, 172, 177ff
Neurotics 195ff
Nonverbal indicators of liking 23, 30ff, 92ff, 118-19, 119ff, 123-8, 133, 170, see also Eye contact, Distance, Gaze, Verbal indicators

Pair relatedness 65ff
Personal constructs 70
Personal phase 68, see also Entry phase, Exit phase
Personality 70, 89, 110, 122, 126, 154, 161, 164-84, 190, 197, 198: and information processing 82ff; as an influence on interaction 75ff, 82ff, 181-4; as hypotheses 70, 183-4, see also Personal constructs; complementarity 174, 177-81; similarity 110, 163, 170, 171ff, 175ff; see also Attribution
Physical cues 75, 98, 99-102, 106, 187, see also Attractiveness
Playing hard to get 132ff
P-O-X see Balance Theory
Power 110ff
Prestige 110ff
Profit 51, 170
Proximity 94ff

Queen Victoria 115

Reinforcement 48, 51, 82, 111, 145, 159, 161, 179
Rejection 80, 94
Relationship definition 66ff
Relationship: Animal see Animal; breakdown of 10-11, 194ff; Development of 63ff, 85, 102, 122, 167, 170, 177, 181, 185-8; Functions of see Friendship; Long term 15-16; Management of 107ff, 121ff, 168; Short term 15-16; Stages in 65ff, 175-6, 190ff; Types of

9, 15, 25ff, 179
Reputation 96-7
Research: sequential nature of 39-42, 142ff
Resource theory 52
Responsibility and liking 62
Reward 48, 51, 82, 111, 145, 159
Reward Class 52
Reward Power 111
Ritual indication of liking 92ff
Roles see Stimulus-Value-Role (SVR) Theory

Schizophrenics 133, 148, 195
SE see Self Esteem
Self Acceptance 176
Self-Disclosure 27, 115ff, 132, 166-71
Self Esteem 79-82, 113, 176
Self presentation 82, 98, 169
Self validation 57, 144ff
Similarity 19, 57, 84, 85, 88, 95, 100, 114, 138, 140, 142ff, 169, 174, 175ff, 180: Assumed 85, 88, 95, 161-2, 169
Simulated Stranger see Bogus Stranger
Skill 86, 115, 120, 133ff, 188, 194, 196, 199
Social Comparison 56, 70, 144
Social penetration 170
Sociological influences on relationships 64, 76, 87ff, 93
Sociometric matrix 35, Fig. 1
Sociometric measurement 27, 33, 35-8, see also Liking, Measurement of
Stage theories 63, 69ff, 187, 192, 194ff
Standard Stranger see Bogus Stranger
Status 110ff
Stigma 101, 132
Stimulus-Value-Role (SVR) Theory 70, 187ff
Strangers 38, 100, 113, 117, 139, 142ff, 168, 175, 183, see also Attraction, Bogus Stranger, First encounters

Taboos 22, 139
Target Sociogram 35, Fig. 1
Tie signs 92

Uncertainty 68
Unconditioned response 48ff
Untie signs 92

Values 69, 70, 108, 137, 172, 187
Verbal indications of liking 23, 91ff, see also Liking, paper and pencil measures, Nonverbal indicators
Vulnerability 111

Willingness to interact 77, 103, 120, 129, 133